C000127404

OCEANA

OR

ENGLAND AND HER COLONIES

BY

JAMES ANTHONY FROUDE

'Moribus antiquis stat res Romana virisque'—*Ennius*

Hot Springs, New Zealand

NEW EDITION

LONDON
LONGMANS, GREEN, AND CO.
1886

PREFACE.

I HAVE explained so fully in this work my reasons for writing it, that a further account of those reasons would be superfluous. I might therefore, so far, let it go out into the world on its own merits, without an additional word.

Some kind of preface, however, is recommended by custom, to which it is always becoming to conform.

I avail myself therefore of the opportunity, first, to thank Lord ELPHINSTONE, who was my companion during the more interesting part of my journey, for the use which he has allowed me to make of his portfolio of sketches; and secondly, to request my Colonial readers, when they find me quoting anonymous opinions or conversations, to abstain from guesses, which will necessarily be fruitless, at the persons to whom I am referring.

The object of my voyage was not only to see the Colonies themselves, but to hear the views of all classes of people there on the subject in which I was principally interested.

Where there is obviously no objection, or where I have reason to know that the speakers themselves entertain no objection, I give the names myself. Where I do not give the names, although I introduce nothing which was not said to me by someone worth attending to, I have involved my description with details of time, place, circumstance, and initials, all or most of which are intentionally misleading.

J. A. F.

ONSLOW GARDENS: *December 5,* 1885.

CONTENTS.

CONTENTS

CHAPTER XXI.

ILLUSTRATIONS.

OCEANA.

CHAPTER I.

In the seventeenth century, when the once brilliant star of Spain was hastening to its setting, when the naval supremacy which Spain had once claimed and made her own was transferred to Great Britain and Holland, and when the superior power of Great Britain, her insular position and her larger population, had assured to her rather than to the Dutch Republic the sceptre of the sea, Sir James Harrington, in a sketch of a perfect commonwealth, half real, half ideal, which he addressed to the Protector, described the future destiny which he believed to be reserved for the Scotch, English, and Anglo-Irish nations.

'The situation of these countries, being islands (as appears by Venice how advantageous such an one is to the like government), seems to have been designed by God for a commonwealth. And yet Venice, through the straitness of the place and defect of proper arms, can be no more than a commonwealth for preservation ; whereas Oceana, reduced to a like government, is a commonwealth for increase, and upon the mightiest foundation that any has been laid from the beginning of the world to this day—

> Illam arctâ capiens Neptunus compele stringit,
> Hauc autem captus glaucis amplectitur ulnis.

The sea gives the law to the growth of Venice, but the growth of Oceana gives the law to the sea.'

In the two centuries and a half which have passed over us since these words were written, the increase of Oceana has exceeded the wildest dream of the most extravagant enthusiast. Harrington would have been himself incredulous had he been told that, within a period so brief in the life of nations, more than fifty million Anglo-Saxons would be spread over the vast continent of North America, carrying with them their religion, their laws, their language, and their manners ; that the globe would be circled with their fleets ; that in the Southern Hemisphere they would be in possession of territories larger than Europe, and more fertile than the richest parts of it ; that wherever they went they would carry with them the genius of English freedom. Yet the vision is but half accomplished. The people have gone out, they have settled, they have cultivated the land, they have multiplied, and although the population of Great Britain and Ireland is now seven-fold greater than it was in the Protectorate of Cromwell, the number of our kindred in these new countries is already double that which remains in the mother country ; but Harrington contemplated that Oceana would be a single commonwealth embraced in the arms of Neptune, and the spell which can unite all these communities into one has not yet been discovered. The element on which he calculated to ensure the combination—the popular form of government—has been itself the cause which has prevented it. One free people cannot govern another free people. The inhabitants of a province retain the instincts which they brought with them. They can ill bear that their kindred at home shall have rights and liberties from which they are excluded. The mother country struggles to retain its authority, while it is jealous of extending its privileges of citizenship. Being itself self-governed, its elected rulers consider the interests and the wishes of the electors whom they represent, and those only. The provincial, or the colonist, being unrepresented, suffers some actual injustice and imagines more. He conceives that he is deprived of his birthright. He cannot submit to an inferior position, and the alternative arises whether the mother country shall part with its empire or part with its own liberties. Free Athens established a short-lived dominion. Her subordinate states hated her and revolted from her, though the same states submitted quietly immediately after to the Macedonian despotism. Republican Rome conquered the civilised world, but kept it only by ceasing to be a republic. Venice, which Harrington quotes, reserved her constitution for herself, ruling her dependencies by deputy. They envied her liberties. They did not share in her glories or her wealth, and she ceased to be what Harrington calls her, even a commonwealth for preservation. The English in North America had little to thank us for. Many of them had fled thither to escape from religious or political tyranny. They had forgotten their resentment. They were attached to the old home by custom, by feeling, by the pride of country, which in Englishmen is a superstition. They were bitterly unwilling to leave us. But when we refused them representation in the British Legislature, when English ministers, looking only, as they were obliged to look, to the British constituencies, hampered their trade, tied them down under Navigation Laws, and finally would have laid taxes on them with or without their own assent, they were too English themselves to submit to a tyranny which England had thrown off. The principles established by the Long Parliament were stronger than national affection. The first great branch of Oceana was broken off, and became what we now see it to be —the truest, in the opinion of some, to the traditions of Harrington's commonwealth, and therefore growing or to grow into the main stem of the tree.

But the parent stock was still prolific. The American provinces were gone. New shoots sprang out again, and Oceana was reconstituted once more ; this time, in a form and in a quarter more entirely suited to our naval genius, in the great islands of the South Sea, and at the south point of Africa commanding the sea route to India. The mistakes of George the Third and Lord North were not repeated in the same form, but the spirit in which they were made reappeared, and could not fail to reappear. The Colonial Minister at home and the Colonial Office represent the British Parliament. The British Parliament represents the British constituencies, and to them and to their interests, and their opinions, the minister, whoever he be, and to whatever party he belongs, is obliged to look. The colonies having no one to speak for them, were again sacrificed so long as it was possible to sacrifice them. They were used as convict stations till they rose in wrath and refused to receive our refuse any more. Their patronage, their civil appointments, judgeships, secretaryships, &c., were given as rewards for political services at home, or at the instance of politically powerful friends. It cannot be otherwise: so long as party government continues, and Secretaries of State have the nomination to public offices, they are compelled (as a high official once put it to me) ' to blood the noses of their own hounds.' Willingly enough they surrendered most of these appointments when the colonies claimed them. It is possible that for the governorships which the Crown retains, the fittest men to occupy them are *bonâ fide* sought for ; yet it is whispered that other considerations still have weight. Nay, when one such appointment was made a few years back, we were drawn into a war in consequence, because some one was the greatest bore in the House of Commons, and there was a universal desire that he should be sent elsewhere.

More serious were the differences which rose continually between the mother country and the colonists respecting the treatment of the native population, whether in Africa, Australia, or New Zealand. The colonists being on the spot, desired, and desire, to keep the natives under control ; to form them into habits of industry, to compel them by fear to respect property and observe the laws. Naturally too, being themselves willing to cultivate the soil, they have not looked very scrupulously to the rights of savages over fertile districts of which they made no use themselves nor would allow others to use them ; and sometimes by purchase, sometimes by less respectable means, they have driven the natives off their old ground and taken possession of it themselves. The people at home in England, knowing nothing of the practical difficulties, and jealous for the reputation of their country, have obliged their ministers to step between the colonists and the natives: irritating the whites by accusations either wholly false or beyond the truth, and misleading the coloured races into acts of aggression or disobedience, in which they look for support which they have not found. Never able to persist in any single policy, and producing therefore the worst possible results, we first protect these races in an independence which they have been unable to use wisely, and are then driven ourselves into wars with them by acts which they would never have committed if the colonists and they had been left to arrange their mutual relations alone.

The situation has been extremely difficult. It cannot be wondered at, that when war followed on war in New Zealand and South Africa, and British money was spent, and British troops were employed in killing Maoris and Caffres who had done us no harm, and whose crime was believed by many of us to be no more than the possession of land which others coveted, public opinion at home grew impatient. Long bills for these wars appeared in the Budgets year after year. Political economists began to ask what was the use of colonies which contributed nothing to the Imperial exchequer, while they were a constant expense to the taxpayer. They had possessed a value once as a market for English productions, but after the establishment of free trade the world was our market. The colonies, as part of the world, would still buy of us, and would continue to do so, whether as British dependencies or as free. In case of war we should be obliged to defend them and to scatter our force in doing it. They gave us nothing. They cost us much. They were a mere ornament, a useless responsibility: we did not pause to consider whether, even if it were true that the colonies were at present a burden to us, we were entitled to cut men of our own blood and race thus adrift after having encouraged them to form settlements under our flag. Both parties in the State had been irritated in turn by their experience in Downing Street, and for once both were agreed. The troops were withdrawn from Canada, from Australia, from New Zealand. A single regiment only was to have been left at the Cape to protect our naval station. The unoccupied lands, properly the inheritance of the collective British nation—whole continents large as a second United States—were hurriedly abandoned to the local colonial governments. They were equipped with constitutions modelled after our own, which were to endure as long as the connection with the mother country was maintained ; but they were informed, more or less distinctly, that they were as birds hatched in a nest whose parents would be charged with them only till they could provide for themselves, and the sooner they were ready for complete independence, the better the mother country would be pleased.

This was the colonial policy avowed in private by responsible statesmen, and half confessed in public fifteen years ago. And thus it seemed that the second group of territorial acquisitions which English enterprise had secured was to follow the first. The American provinces had been lost by invasion of their rights. The rest were to be thrown away as valueless. The separation might be called friendly, but the tone which we assumed was as offensive to the colonists as the intended action was unwelcome, and if they were obliged to leave us it would not be as friends that we should part. The English people too had not been treated fairly. A policy so far-reaching ought to have been fully explained to them, and not ventured on without their full consent. A frank avowal of an intention to shake the colonies off would have been fatal to the ministry that made it. Ambiguous expressions were explained away when challenged. We were told that self-government had been given to the colonies only to attach them to us more completely, while measures were taken and language was used which were indisputably designed to lead to certain and early disintegration.

The intention was an open secret among all leading statesmen, if it can be called a secret at all, and in the high political circles the result was regarded as assured. 'It is no use,' said an eminent Colonial Office secretary to myself when I once remonstrated, 'to speak about it any longer. The thing is done. The great colonies are gone. It is but a question of a year or two.'

Those were the days of progress by leaps and bounds, of 'unexampled prosperity,' of the apparently boundless future which the repeal of the Corn Laws had opened upon British industry and trade. The fate of Great Britain was that it was to become the world's great workshop. Her people were to be kept at home and multiply. With cheap labour and cheap coal we could defy competition, and golden streams would flow down in ever-gathering volumes over landowners and mill-owners and shipowners. . . . The 'hands' and the 'hands'' wives and children? Oh yes, they too would do very well : wages would rise, food would be cheap, employment constant. The colonies brought us nothing. The empire brought us nothing, save expense for armaments and possibilities of foreign complications. Shorn of these wild shoots we should be like an orchard tree pruned of its luxuriance, on which the fruit would grow richer and more abundant.

It was a fine theory, especially for those fortunate ones who could afford parks and deer forests and yachts in the Solent, who would not feel in their own persons the ugly side of it. But the wealth of a nation depends in the long run upon the conditions, mental and bodily, of the people of whom it consists, and the experience of all mankind declares that a race of men sound in soul and limb can be bred and reared only in the exercise of plough and spade, in the free air and sunshine, with country enjoyments and amusements, never amidst foul drains and smoke blacks and the eternal clank of machinery. And in the England which these politicians designed for us there would be no country left save the pleasure grounds and game preserves of the rich. All else would be town. There would be no room in any other shape for the crowded workmen who were to remain as the creators of the wealth. What England would become was to be seen

already in the enormously extended suburbs of London and
our great manufacturing cities: miles upon miles of squalid
lanes, each house the duplicate of its neighbour; the dirty
street in front, the dirty yard behind, the fetid smell from the
ill-made sewers, the public house at the street corners. Here,
with no sight of a green field, with no knowledge of flowers or
:orest, the blue heavens themselves dirtied with soot—amidst
objects all mean and hideous, with no entertainment but the
music hall, no pleasure but in the drink shop—hundreds of
thousands of English children are now growing up into men
and women. And were these scenes to be indefinitely multiplied? Was this to be the real condition of an ever-increasing
portion of the English nation? And was it to be supposed
·hat a race of men could be so reared who could carry on the
great traditions of our country? I for one could not believe
it. The native vigour of our temperament might defy the
influence of such a life for a quarter or for half a century.
Experience, even natural probability, declared that the grand-
children of the occupants of these dens must be sickly, poor
and stunted wretches whom no school teaching, however
excellent, could save from physical decrepitude.

The tendency of people in the later stages of civilisation
to gather into towns is an old story. Horace had seen in
Rome what we are now witnessing in England,—the fields
deserted, the people crowding into cities. He noted the growing degeneracy. He foretold the inevitable consequences.

> Non his juventus orta parentibus
> Infecit æquor sanguine Punico,
>   Pyrrhumque et ingentem cecidit
>   Antiochum, Hannibalemque dirum ;
> Sed rusticorum mascula militum
> Proles, Sabellis docta ligonibus
>   Versare glebas, et severæ
>   Matris ad arbitrium recisos
> Portare fustes.[1]

---

[1] They did not spring from sires like these,
  The noble youth who dyed the seas
    With Carthaginian gore ;
  Who great Antiochus overcame,
    And Hannibal of yore ;

And Horace was a true prophet. The Latin peasant, the legionary of the Punic wars, had ceased to exist. He had drifted into the cities, where he could enjoy himself at the circus, and live chiefly on free rations. The virtue—*virtus*—manliness was gone out of him. Slaves tilled the old farms, Gauls and Spaniards and Thracians took his place in the army. In the Senate and in the professions the Roman was supplanted by the provincial. The corruption spread. The strength which had subdued the world melted finally away. The German and the Hun marched in over the Imperial border, and Roman civilisation was at an end.

There is not much fear in England (spite of recent strange political phenomena) that we shall see idle city mobs sustained on free grants of corn ; but a population given over to employments which must and will undermine the physical vigour of the race, generations of children growing under conditions which render health impossible, will come to the same thing. Decay is busy at the heart of them, and the fate of Rome seemed to me likely to be the fate of England if she became what the political economists desired to see her. That 'man shall not live by bread alone' is as true as ever it was ; true for week days as well as Sundays, for common sense as for theology. These islands cannot bear a larger population than they have at present without peril to soul and body. It appeared as if the genius of England, anticipating the inevitable increase, had provided beforehand for the distribution of it. English enterprise had occupied the fairest spots upon the globe where there was still soil and sunshine boundless and life-giving ; where the race might for ages renew its mighty youth, bring forth as many millions as it would, and would still have means to breed and rear them strong as the best which she had produced in her early prime. The colonists

But they of rustic warriors wight
The manly offspring learned to smite
   The soil with Sabine spade,
And faggots they had to cut to bear
Home from the forest whensoe'er
   An austere mother bade.—Martix's *Horace*, Od.3 iii. 6.

might be paying us no revenue, but they were opening up the
face of the earth. By-and-by, like the spreading branches of
a forest tree, they would return the sap which they were
gathering into the heart. England could pour out among
them, in return, year after year, those poor children of hers
now choking in fetid alleys, and, relieved of the strain, breathe
again fresh air into her own smoke-encrusted lungs. With
her colonies part of herself, she would be, as Harrington
had foreshadowed, a commonwealth resting on the mightiest
foundations which the world had ever seen. Queen among
the nations, from without invulnerable, and at peace and at
health within,—this was the alternative future lying before
Oceana : in every way more desirable than the economic.
Unlike other good things it was easy of attainment; we had
but to stretch our hand out to secure it; yet we sat still
doing nothing as if enchanted, while the Sibyl was tearing out
page on page from the Book of Destiny.

Impossible ! the politicians said : yet it was not impossible
for the United States to refuse to be divided. The United
States tore their veins open and spilt their blood in torrents
that they might remain one people. There was no need for
any blood to be shed to keep us one people, yet we talked
placidly of impossibilities. The United States, it was said,
were parts of a single continent. No ocean ran between south
and north, or east and west. Our colonies were dispersed
over the globe. What Nature had divided, man could not
bind together ; without continuity of soil there could be no
single empire. Excuses are not wanting when the will is
wanting. The ocean which divides, combines also; and had
the problem been theirs and not ours, the Americans would
perhaps have found that the sea is the easiest of highways,
which telegraph wires underlie and steamers traverse with the
ease and certainty of railway cars. 'Impossibility' is a word
of politicians who are without the wish or without the capacity
to comprehend new conditions. An 'empire' of Oceana there
cannot be. The English race do not like to be parts of an
empire. But a 'commonwealth' of Oceana held together by
common blood, common interest, and a common pride in the

great position which unity can secure—such a commonwealth as this may grow of itself if politicians can be induced to leave it alone.

As the colonies have been hitherto dealt with—made use of in the interests of the mother country as long as they would submit, and then called valueless, and advised to take themselves away—they are in no mood for a union which may bring them again under the authority of Downing Street. But affronts have not estranged them. They have been in no haste to meet the offer of independence. They claim still their share in the inheritance of the nation from which they have sprung. British they are and British they wish to remain, and impossible as it is to weld together two pieces of steel while below the welding temperature, let the desire for a union of equality rise in England and rise in the colonies to sufficient heat, the impossibility will become a possibility, and of political possibilities the easiest.

Our people stream away from us. Out of the hundreds of thousands of English, Scots, and Irish who annually leave our shores, eighty per cent. have gone hitherto to the United States, and only the remaining fraction to the countries over which our own flag is flying. I once asked the greatest, or at least the most famous, of modern English statesmen whether, in the event of a great naval war, we might not look for help to the 60,000 Canadian seamen and fishermen. ' The Canadian seamen,' he said, ' belong to Canada, not to us;' and then going to the distribution of our emigrants, he insisted that there was not a single point in which an Englishman settling in Canada or Australia was of more advantage to us than as a citizen of the American Union. The use of him was as a purchaser of English manufactures—that was all. Sir Arthur Helps told me a story singularly illustrative of the importance which the British official mind has hitherto allowed to the distant scions of Oceana. A Government had gone out ; Lord Palmerston was forming a new ministry, and in a preliminary council was arranging the composition of it. He had filled up the other places. He was at a loss for a Colonial Secretary. This name and that was suggested, and thrown aside. At last he said, 'I suppose I must take the thing myself. Come upstairs with me, Helps, when the council is over. We will look at the maps and you shall show me where these places are.'

The temper represented in this cool indifference is passing away. The returns of trade show in the first place that commerce follows the flag. Our colonists take three times as much of our productions in proportion to their numbers as foreigners take. The difference increases rather than diminishes, and the Australian, as a mere consumer, *is* more valuable to us than the American. What more he may be, his voluntary presence at Suakin has indicated for him to all the world. But more than this. It has become doubtful even to the political economist whether England can trust entirely to free trade and competition to keep the place which she has hitherto held. Other nations press us with their rivalries. Expenses increase, manufactures languish or cease to profit. Revenue, once so expansive, becomes stationary. 'Business' may, probably will, blaze up again, but the growth of it can no longer be regarded as constant, while population increases and hungry stomachs multiply, requiring the three meals a day whatever the condition of the markets. Hence those among us who have disbelieved all along that a great nation can venture its whole fortunes safely on the power of underselling its neighbours in calicoes and iron-work no longer address a public opinion entirely cold. It begins to be admitted that were Canada and South Africa and Australia and New Zealand members of one body with us, with a free flow of our population into them, we might sit secure against shifts and changes. In the multiplying number of our own fellow-citizens animated by a common spirit, we should have purchasers for our goods from whom we should fear no rivalry; we should turn in upon them the tide of our emigrants which now flows away, while the emigrants themselves would thrive under their own fig tree, and rear children with stout limbs and colour in their cheeks, and a chance before them of a human existence. Oceana would then rest on sure foundations; and her navy—the hand of her strength and the symbol

of her unity—would ride securely in self-supporting stations
in the four quarters of the globe.

To the magnificence of such an Oceana, were it but attain-
able, the dullest imagination can no longer blind itself. But
how? but how? the impatient politician asks. We may
dream, but he must act. He has heard of no scheme of union
which is not impracticable on the face of it, and because we
cannot give him a constitution ready made he shuts his ears.
He can do nothing better. We do not ask him to act; we
ask him only to leave things alone. An acorn will not expand
into an oak if the forester is for ever digging at its roots and
clipping its young shoots. Constitutions, commonwealths, are
not manufactured to pattern; they grow, if they grow at all,
by internal impulse. The people of England have made the
colonies. The people at home and the people in the colonies
are one people. The feeling of identity is perhaps stronger in
the colonies than at home. They are far away, and things to
which we are indifferent because we have them are precious
in the distance. There is fresh blood in those young countries.
Sentiment remains a force in them, as it is in boys, and has
survived the chilly winds which have blown from Downing
Street: the sentiment itself is life; and when the people desire
that it shall take organic form, the rest will be easy. If
statesmen had not in other days overcome greater difficulties
than any which are then likely to present themselves, the
English nation would have dragged out an obscure existence
within the limits of its own islands, and would not have made
the noise in the world which it has done.

No such commonwealth as Harrington imagined for his
Oceana was, or ever can be, more than Utopia. Harrington,
like the Abbé Sièyes, believed that constitutions could be made
in a closet, and fitted like a coat to the back. But the arduous
part of it is no longer to create : it is an achieved fact. The
land is our possession. We ourselves—the forty-five millions
of British subjects, those at home and those already settled
upon it—are a realised family which desires not to be divided.
If there have been family differences, they have not yet risen
into discord. The past cannot be wholly undone by soft

words and a mere change of tone in political circles. We and
the colonists have lived apart and have misunderstood one
another. They require to be convinced that the people of
England have never shared in the views of their leaders. We
have been indifferent, and occupied with our own affairs; but
we, the people, always regarded them as our kindred, bone of
our bone and flesh of our flesh. They will never submit again
to be ruled from England. The branch is not ruled by the
stem; the leaf does not ask the branch what form it shall
assume, or the flower ask what shall be its colour; but if the
colonists know that as their feeling is to us so is ours to them,
branch, leaf, and flower will remain incorporate upon the
stem, aiming at no severed existence, and all together, indispensable each to each and mutually strengthening each other,
will form one majestic organism which may defy the storms of
fate.

So I, many years ago, as a student of England's history
and believing in its future greatness, imagined for myself the
Oceana that might be. But having no personal knowledge of
the colonies, I could but preach vaguely from the pulpits of
reviews and magazines, and, finding my sermons as useless as
such compositions generally are, I determined myself to make
a tour among them, to talk to their leading men, see their
countries and what they were doing there, learn their feelings,
and correct my impressions of what could or could not be
done. I set out for this purpose. Accident detained me at
the Cape of Good Hope, entangled me in Cape politics, and
consumed the leisure which I could then spare. After an
interval of ten years, finding that I had still strength enough
for such an enterprise, and time and opportunity permitting,
I resumed my dropped intention. I do not regret the delay.
In the interval the colonies have shown more clearly than
before that they are as much English as we are, and deny our
right to part with them. At home the advocates of separation have been forced into silence, and the interest in the
subject has grown into practical anxiety. The union which
so many of us now hope for may prove an illusion after
all. The feeling which exists on both sides may be a warm

one, but not warm enough to heat us, as I said, to the welding point.

Ταῦτα θεῶν ἐν γούνασι κεῖται.

The event, whatever it is to be, lies already determined, the philosophers tell us, in the chain of causation. What is to be, will be. But it is not more determined than all else which is to happen to us, and the determination does not make us sit still and wait till it comes. Among the causes are included our own exertions, and each of us must do what he can, be it small or great, as this course or that seems good and right to him. If we work on the right side, coral insects as we are, we may contribute something not wholly useless to the general welfare.

However this may be, in the closing years of my own life I have secured for myself a delightful experience. I have travelled through lands where patriotism is not a sentiment to be laughed at—not, as Johnson defined it, 'the last refuge of a scoundrel,' but an active passion—where I never met a hungry man or saw a discontented face—where, in the softest and sweetest air, and in an unexhausted soil, the fable of Midas is reversed, food does not turn to gold, but the gold with which the earth is teeming converts itself into farms and vineyards, into flocks and herds, into crops of wild luxuriance, into cities whose recent origin is concealed and compensated by trees and flowers—where children grow who seem once more to understand what was meant by 'merry England.' Amidst the uncertainties which are gathering round us at home—a future so obscure that the wisest men will least venture a conjecture what that future will be, it is something to have seen with our own eyes that there are other Englands besides the old one, where the race is thriving with all its ancient characteristics. Those who take 'leaps in the dark,' as we are doing, may find themselves in unexpected places before they recover the beaten tracks again. But let Fate do its worst, the family of Oceana is still growing, and will have a sovereign voice in the coming fortunes of mankind.

CHAPTER II.

The Children of the Sea—The 'Australasian '—Company on board—Storm in the Channel—Leave Plymouth—Great Circle sailing—Sea studies—Emigrants—An Irishman's experience—Virgil—Metaphysical speculations—Old measurement of time—Teneriffe—Bay of Santa Cruz—Sunday at Sea —Approach to the Cape.

After their own island, the sea is the natural home of Englishmen ; the Norse blood is in us, and we rove over the waters, for business or pleasure, as eagerly as our ancestors. Four-fifths of the carrying trade of the world is done by the English. When we grow rich, our chief delight is a yacht. When we are weary with hard work, a sea voyage is our most congenial ' retreat.' On the ocean no post brings us letters which we are compelled to answer. No newspaper tempts us into reading the last night's debate in Parliament, or sends our attention wandering, like the fool's eyes, to the ends of the earth. The sea breezes carry health upon their wings, and fan us at night into sweet dreamless sleep. 'Itself eternally young, the blue infinity of water teaches us to forget that we ourselves are old. For the time we are beyond the reach of change—we live in the present ; and the absence of distracting incidents, the sameness of the scene, and the uniformity of life on board ship, leave us leisure for reflection ; we are thrown in upon our own thoughts, and can make up our accounts with our consciences.

Thus, in setting out for Australia, I resolved to go by the long sea route—long it is called, but with the speed of modern steamers scarcely longer than the road through the Suez Canal. I should have an opportunity, as we went by, of seeing my old friends at Cape Town. I should make acquaintance with the grand waves of the Southern Ocean ; I should see albatrosses, and Cape hens, and sea hawks, which follow passing ships for thousands of miles ; above all, I should have six weeks of quiet, undisturbed even by a visitor before I reached the colonies, and had again to exert myself. My son was to go with me, fresh from Oxford and his degree. His health, as

well as mine, required change, and before he settled into the
work of his life, I wished him to enlarge his knowledge of
things. Him I shall call A. Glancing over the ship advertisements in the 'Times,' I selected by chance a vessel announced as to sail in a few days, belonging to a small and as yet
little-known line of Aberdeen packets. She was called the
'Australasian,' of 4,000 tons, with improved engines which
were said to promise speed. She was a cargo ship, carrying
170 emigrants. The after-cabin accommodation was limited,
but, as it turned out, amply large enough. In the moderate-
sized but elegant saloon there was convenient room perhaps
for thirty passengers. There were but nine of us, including
the doctor and his pretty, newly-married wife. We had each
a state-room, spacious and well-furnished ;—as we were so few
they could afford to lodge us handsomely. Half the long deck
was appropriated for the cabin passengers' sole use, so that we
could have been no better off in a large private yacht. The
owners modestly warned me that the 'table' was inferior to
what we should have found on the established lines. We
found, on the contrary, breakfasts and dinners superior to what
I ever met with in any steamer in any part of the world. I
paid the cook a compliment on the first evening, which he
never ceased to deserve. We had a cow on board, and new
milk every morning ; bread every day fresh from the oven,
and porridge such as only Scotch cooks and a Scotch company
can produce. In respect of vessel, officers, attendance, pro-
visions—of all things, great and small, on which we depend
for our daily comforts, it had been a happy accident which led
me to the choice of the 'Australasian.' My plan was to
escape the Northern winter, and we therefore sailed at the
beginning of it. We went on board at Tilbury on December 6,
1884, and anchored for the night at the Nore. We had not till
now seen our companions, and as we were to be shut up with
them for six weeks, we looked at them with some anxiety.
Besides the two whom I have mentioned, there was a London
man of business going on a voyage for health, accompanied by
his sister,—both of them quiet, well-bred, and unobtrusive ;
two youths with nothing especial to distinguish them ; and a

C

middle-aged gentleman, who had travelled much and had opinions about many things, with accomplishments, too, which made him both agreeable and useful. He could talk well, play, whist well, play chess tolerably, and the saloon piano with the skill of a professional. Add the handsome captain, some thirty-two years old, with blue merry eyes, gracious, pleasant ; a skilful seaman, willing to talk to us about his own business, making us welcome to his chart room at all fitting seasons, ready to explain the mysteries of great circle sailing ; besides this, a true-hearted, brave, energetic, and really admirable man. . . . These made the party who were collected three times each day for breakfast, luncheon, and dinner, in the ' Australasian's ' saloon.

The new engines being of peculiar construction, there was some curiosity as to how they would work. We were accompanied, therefore, as far as Plymouth, by an accomplished and agreeable naval engineer ; by Mr. Thompson, the chief manager of the company to which our vessel belonged ; by an Aberdeenshire gentleman, who was a director of it ; and by a handsome, athletic, young Glasgow ship-builder. We had reason to be glad that they went with us, especially the Glasgow professional. Sunday, December 7, broke wild and stormy. We left our anchorage soon after daybreak, wind, at W.S.W., blowing hard, and the barometer falling. Short brown waves were breaking round us in dirty foam, and a vessel which had steamed past us in the night lay on a sandbank in the middle of the river, with the water breaking over her. The sky between the clouds was a pale green, sure sign of a gale coming. We had shelter as far as the South Foreland, when we met the heavy Channel sea. A misty rain was falling, the air was cold, and the spray flew over us from stem to stern. The passengers were most of them sick, and, though the engineers were well satisfied and the 'Australasian' herself cared little for the waves, it was a dreary start. In all the world there is no more uncomfortable stretch of water than the British Channel in nasty weather. The day wore on ; the wet drove us below. In the saloon there was an open fireplace, and a bright fire burning. We tried to read,

but it didn't answer; and after dinner, which I was able to
eat in spite of the roll, I turned in early—turned in, but not
to sleep. It is not till one lies down and tries for it that one
becomes conscious of the multitudinous noises which go on
during a gale : the grinding of the screw—a constant quantity
that never ceases—the roar of the wind, the fierce crunch as
the vessel strikes the advancing waves, the slamming of doors,
the rush of feet on deck, and the wild cry of the sailors
hauling ropes or delivering orders. I lay in my berth for a
good many hours, listening to all this, and fancying what it
looked like up above, when off St. Alban's Head I felt that
something had gone wrong. The engines stopped, the ship
lay rolling in the trough of the sea broadside on to the waves ;
loud voices were calling, men in their heavy sea-boots were
trampling to and fro. Passengers are not wanted on deck on
these occasions. I made my way to the foot of the stairs and
called up to know what was the matter. A gruff voice advised
me to stay below. In two hours the screw began to revolve
again, and the mischief, whatever it was, had been repaired.
I slept at last, and in the morning learnt what had happened.
The 'Australasian' was steered by steam from the bridge ;
one of the chains had parted. They had tried to steer with
the wheel, but in fixing the gear the rudder broke loose, flying
to and fro and snapping the ropes, with which they were trying to secure the tiller, like packthread. Mr. R——, our
friend from Glasgow, at last mastered the difficulty, and we
were able to go on. Fortunately we were well off the land
and had ample sea room. The ship had rolled easily in her
temporarily disabled state, and her behaviour had given general
satisfaction. When I came on deck the gale had moderated,
and we were steaming quietly along the Devonshire coast a
few miles from Plymouth.

At Plymouth we had to stay for twenty-four hours repair-
ing damages and taking in coal. Mr. Thompson and his
party took leave of us, and on Tuesday, the 9th, a little before
noon, we took our final departure. The sea was still high.
Our course being now south, and the wind being N.W., we set
canvas to check the rolling, and away we went. Our speed

c 2

was good considering our expenditure of coal. The Cunarders
cross the Atlantic in seven days, burning each day 300 tons
and doing 18 knots an hour. We made from 12 to 13 knots,
and burned only 35. On Wednesday we were outside the
Bay of Biscay, far to the westward of our course, as traced on
a flat chart ; but the captain tells us that we should see it to
be right on a spherical one, and we entirely believed him. In
all healthy work that is done as it should be, we live and move
by faith. Had the passengers been required to give their
independent opinions, they would have voted that we were
going wrong and must change our direction, especially if they
suspected that the captain and officers were interested in the
matter. They were not asked for their opinions, and did not
wish to give them. They were contented, being ignorant, to
be guided by those whom they suppose to know ; this is the
universal rule, and when it is observed, our sums work out
clear, without fractional remainders. Times were when it
held in all departments of human things—when the supposed
wise taught us what to believe, and the supposed ἄριστοι
taught us what we were to do, and we kept in temperate
latitudes in politics and theology. In these two singular
sciences everyone now makes his own creed, and gives his
vote by his own lights as to how he wishes to be governed.
We could not help it, and we had but a choice of evils. There
is no success possible to any man save in finding and obeying
those who are his real superiors. But to follow mock superiors, and to be cheated in the process ! who could wish that
we should submit to that ? If captains and officers were
discovered to have never learnt their business, to be doing
nothing but amuse themselves and consume the ship's stores,
the crew would have to depose them and do the best they
could with their own understandings ; but if the crew were
persons of sense, they would probably look out at their best
speed for other officers, and trust to their own lights for as
short a time as possible.

Anyway we were well assured that Captain S—— would
carry us along his great circles while ship and engines held
together, and that we should arrive infallibly at the port to

which we were bound. Without anxiety on this s
could settle down to our own occupations. The only q
was what these occupations were to be, when we h
duties provided for us save to eat and sleep. Wha_ und
passengers do on long voyages when there were no novels ?
They must bless the man that invented them, for at present
they are the only resource. The ship's bookshelves hold them
by dozens. They stream out of private portmanteaus—yellow
shilling editions, with heroes and heroines painted on the
covers in desperate situations. The appetite for such things
at sea is voracious. Most of them will not bear reading more
than once ; we consume them as we smoke cigars ; and on
second perusal they are but ashes. One only wishes that they
introduced one to better company. Villanous men and doubtful ladies are persons whom one avoids in life ; and though
they are less objectionable in a book than in actual flesh and
blood, their society is not attractive anywhere. At least,
however, there was an abundance to choose from ; each of us
could have a new novel every day, and there was no need to
fall back upon the ashes. But besides these I had a few
volumes of pocket classics which I always take with me in
distant expeditions. Greek and Latin literature is wine
which does not spoil by time. Such of it, in fact, as would
spoil has been allowed to die, and only the best has been preserved. In the absence of outward distractions one can understand and enjoy these finished relics of the old world. They
shine as fixed stars in the intellectual firmament—stars which
never set. My first experience, however, was an unfortunate
one. There are stars and stars. I had not looked into Ovid
since I was a boy. He had survived, and had therefore merited
survival. I had decided to use the opportunity and to read
him through again. I tried and I failed. Ovid, like Horace,
claims at the close of his 'Metamorphoses' to have built a
monument which will be coeval with mankind ; he lives yet,
and can have lived only by excellence of some kind ; but I
found him wearisome and effeminate, an atheistical epicurean
with neither Horace's humour nor Lucretius's grandeur to
make up for his objectionable creed ; very pretty, very un-

manly, a fashionable Roman man of letters, popular in society, and miserable when the unfeeling Augustus condemned him for a time to salutary solitude. Still people read him, read even the least decent of his writings. It was curious to find in the worst of these the lines which are so often quoted in books of theology :—

Est Deus in nobis, sunt et commercia cœli ;
Sedibus æternis spiritus ille venit.

Ovid's Deus, if he had any, may have sipped nectar with the rest at the Olympian tables, but could not have been a respectable form of divinity. I flung my Ovid behind my sofa pillow ; even in the novels I was in better company than with him. There were other things to do besides reading. As we flew south the air grew more balmy and the sea more smooth. The emigrants got over their sickness, and spread themselves about the deck in the sun. The captain was busy among them, chattering and making jokes. Emigrants, he told me, were generally discontented. One very handsome dame had fastened upon him, her tongue running like a shuttle in a cotton mill. He was obliged to be careful, he said, for the ship was under the Board of Trade, where complaints were always listened to, reasonable or unreasonable. But he was exceptionally popular. His art was to keep the women in good humour, and to leave the men to take their chance. I saw him going from group to group, distributing sugar-plums among the children, cramming lozenges into a fresh-looking young mother's mouth whose hands were full of babies. A coil of thick rope had been left lying on the main hatchway ; a pretty group had fitted into it as in a nest, and were knitting and stitching. Boys and girls from infancy to ten years old were scrambling about; happy, and happier than they knew, for they were escaping out of their suburban dirt, and going to a land where the sun could shine and the flowers blow ; where the sky at night was spangled with stars, and the air was unloaded with fetid smoke. No more for them the ragged yard and the broken window, and its scanty geranium-pots—pathetic efforts of the poor souls to surround themselves with objects not wholly hideous. These few elect at least were being snatched away

from an existence in which not to be at all, was better than
to be.

Sitting apart from the crowd, and apparently with no one
belonging to him, I saw an Irishman in the unmistakeable
national costume, the coat-seams gaping, the trousers in holes
at the knees, the battered hat, the humorous glimmering in
the eyes. I made acquaintance with him, gave him a pipe and
some tobacco, for he had lost his own, and tempted him to
talk. He was on his way to Brisbane. His wife and children
had been left behind at Gravesend. The officer of the Board
of Health had found measles among them. They were to
follow by another vessel. He was to go on meanwhile, and
make out some kind of home for them. I asked him why he
was leaving Ireland just at this time when better days were
coming. 'The divil is in the country,' he said, 'there is no
living in it any way. There are good laws now. There is
nothing to say against the laws ; but, do what you will with
them, no one is any the better.' I inquired what specially
had gone wrong with himself. 'Well, your honour,' he said,
· I had a little farm at Kinsale, and there was the boats and
the nets; and, with the fishing and the rest, I contrived to get
a living some way. But the Manx men came down, and with
their long nets they caught all the large herrings and only left
us the little ones. And then there was the bit of land,'—he
paused a moment and went on, 'Thim banks was the ruin
of me. I had rather had to do with the worst landlord that
ever was in Ireland than with thim banks. There is no mercy
in them. They'll have the skin from off your back.' Poor
fellow! No sooner had he got his 'fixity of tenure' than he had
borrowed money on the security of it, and 'thim banks' would
have their pound of flesh. I was very sorry for him ; but
how could it be otherwise ? How many hundreds of thousands
of his countrymen will travel the same road !

In less than a week from Plymouth we were out of soundings, looking round us and down into nothing but the violet-
coloured ocean,—Homer's ἰοειδέα πόντον—violet-coloured where
most transparent, or lightening into turquoise when particles
of matter are floating thickly in it. A light north-east wind

followed us, forming the beginning of the trades. The air on deck was still, the speed of wind and vessel being equal. The sun blazed hot by day. The nights were warm, and one could sit on deck till midnight watching the stars pursuing their stately march from east to west, and shining with the calm lustre of the lower latitudes. I suppose it is owing to our colder climate that we know the stars so much less accurately than the Greeks and Romans knew them, or the Egyptians and Babylonians. The sky to the Latin farmer was a dial-plate, on which the stars were pointers ; and he read the hour of the night from their position on its face. The constellations were his monthly almanack, and as the sun moved from one into another he learned when to plough and when to sow, when to prune his vines, and clip the wool from his sheep. The planets watched over the birth of his children. The star of the morning, rising as the herald of Aurora, called him to the work of the day. The star of the evening, glimmering pale through the expiring tints of sunset, sent him home to supper and to rest, and to his ignorant mind these glorious sons of heaven were gods, or the abode of gods. It is all changed now. The Pleiades and Orion and Sirius still pass nightly over our heads in splendid procession, but they are to us no more than bodies in space, important only for purposes of science ; we have fixed their longitudes, we can gauge in the spectroscope their chemical composition, we have found a parallax for the Dog-star, and know in how many years the light which flows from it will reach us. But the shepherd and the husbandman no longer look to them to measure their times and seasons, trusting to clocks and to printed authorities, and losing, in the negligence of their celestial guide, as much as, or more than, they have gained. The visible divinities who were once so near to our daily lives are gone for ever.

Even Virgil was sighing after a knowledge of the material causes of things. He, if he had felt the strength in himself, would have sung, like Lucretius, of earthquakes and eclipses, of the moon's phases and the lengthening and shortening of the days—of all the secrets, so far as they were then penetrated, of the processes of nature. He complains of the weakness of

his intellect, which could not soar amidst these august mysteries.
He abandons the vast inquiry with a sorrowful sense of inferiority. He says:—

Sin has ne possim naturæ accedere partes
Frigidus obstiterit circum præcordia sanguis,
Flumina amem sylvasque inglorius.

Could he have foreseen the blank vacancy in which science
was to land us, he would have been better contented with what
the gods had bestowed upon him. But even in Virgil's time
the Olympians were growing mythic ; sincere belief in them
was no longer possible, and nothing in which he could believe
had as yet risen above the horizon. By the side of spiritual
negations, democracy, their inevitable comrade, had rushed in
upon his country. He was consoled to feel that this monster
of anarchy at least had been grappled with by Cæsar, and lay
chained and powerless.

Furor impius intus
Sæva sedens super arma et centum vinctus ahenis
Post tergum nodis fremet horridus ore cruento.

Civil order at least was upheld, though it was order maintained by the sword ; and in that compelled interval of calm,
religion passed from nature into conscience and struck root
there. Spiritual belief revived again in Christianity, and
renewed the face of the earth, and kept science at bay for
another era of eighteen hundred years. It seems now that
this era too is closed ; Science has come back upon us, and
Democracy along with her. What next ?

Yet, while change is all around us, there is so much that
never changes : those stars on which we were gazing from the
deck of the 'Australasian,' those seas through which we were
rushing, age after age had looked on them and seen them as
we saw them. How many mariners, each once at the front of
the world's history, had sailed over those same waters !
Phœnicians, Carthaginians, Greeks, Romans, Norsemen, Cru-
saders, Italians, Spaniards, Portuguese, French, English, all in
their turn. To each of these it had seemed once to belong,
and they steered their courses by the same stars which are
now shining on ourselves. Knights and warriors, pirates and

traders, great admirals, discoverers of new continents, of whose names history is full—Columbus and Santa Cruz, Drake and Grenville, Rodney and Nelson—had passed where we were passing, between the Azores and the Canaries ; all burning with fires of hope and purpose which have long since sunk to ashes. Their eyes, like mine, saw Draco winding among the stars of the Bear, and the Bear making his daily circuit round the pole, alone of the Northern constellations unwetted in the ocean bath—very strange to think of. The history of old nations and peoples comes down to us in ruined temples, in parchments, venerable from age, in fading portraits, in models of antiquated war-ships, to be smiled at in modern museums. The generations of man are but the hours of a season a little longer than a single year. The memory of them is trampled in by the million feet of their successors, themselves in turn to be trampled in as swiftly and cared for no more. But the stars which we see are the stars which they saw. Time has not dimmed their brilliance, or age made them loiter on their course. Time for them is not. They are themselves the measures and creators of time. Have they too their appointed end ? 'They shall perish, but thou shalt endure. They all shall wax old, as doth a garment. As a vesture shalt thou change them, and they shall be changed. But thou art the same, and thy years shall not fail.' Is this true ? No answer peals to us out of the abysses of space. No evidence can be alleged to satisfy a British jury. The answer, if it comes at all, must come from the heart of men ; and who put it there, and how can a man's heart know ? In the silent solitude of sea and sky the unanswerable questions thrust themselves upon one unasked. What is it all ? What am I ? What is anything ? Schopenhauer tells me that nothing is of which no idea has been formed by some conscious being, and therefore that nothing existed until some conscious being came into existence capable of forming an idea of it. All that we know of ourselves, or of things outside ourselves, being conceptions or images impressed either on mind or on sensation, where there is no mind or no sensation there can be no conceptions and therefore no existence, and things now perceived will similarly cease to be when conscious beings cease. In other words the material universe is created and sustained by spirit, and without spirit is nothing.

Parallel to this is Kant's question, one over which I have many times puzzled myself to sleep when opiates failed : whether *Da seyn* is a predicate, whether to have had a being subject to space and time is a necessary condition of existence. Has not a character which has acquired a place in the minds of mankind as real an existence, even though a creature of imagination merely, as if the person in question had been born with a material body and had lived a fixed number of years, and had worn clothes and taken his regular meals, and in course of time had died ? Ulysses, Hamlet, Julius Cæsar are real persons. Each of them stands with a clear and fixed form before the minds of all of us. Would Ulysses and Hamlet be more than they are to us if some Greek king having that name had once actually lived and reigned in Ithaca, and Hamlet been a real prince who thought he saw a ghost and killed his uncle ? Would Julius Cæsar be any less to us if we had simply the story of him and his actions as an accepted part of human tradition ? They and he alike are the offspring of the creative intellectual spirit. They have been actually created or they would not be among us. Does the mere fact that they were subject once for a few years to the conditions of time and matter add anything to the truth of the conception of them which we have in our minds ? It is no verbal speculation, for important consequences hang upon it, for in this way Kant establishes the truth of the Christian religion. Nay, in this way only he considers that the truth of it can be established with absolute certainty. Historical facts can never be demonstrated with a completeness of proof which can leave no room for doubt. A religion which takes possession of the convictions of mankind carries with it its own evidence, in its conformity with universal spiritual experience ; and the truth of it lying within the four corners of the conception, is above and beyond the power of historical criticism. The historical truth is a question of space and time which does not touch on eternal verities. The properties of a

circle lie in the definition, and are truths of reason whether in
nature any perfect circle exists or does not exist. The
spiritual truth of a doctrine or a mythology lies in the recognition which the mind gives to it, as conforming to and representing universal experience. It is a convenient theory, convenient for many purposes. No church council has yet
sanctioned it, but it must have been present unconsciously in
the mind of Cardinal Newman when he wrote his 'Grammar
of Assent.' It was present in the ages of faith, when the
miracles of the saints were told as freely as in a novel, with a
belief which looked only to edification. It is implied in the
assertion that belief *per se* is a virtue, and that doubt is a sin.

Yet, after all, facts are something. My Uncle Toby concluded, in spite of all the arguments of the learned lawyers,
that the Duchess of Suffolk must have been some relation to
her own child. Julius Cæsar, as an historical person, is more
to me than he would have been had he existed nowhere save
in Shakespeare's play. The stars had a being before Adam or
Adam's children began to speculate on their movements, and
will be after Adam's race has ceased to perplex itself with
metaphysical conundrums.

To return to the voyage. On Sunday, the 14th, five days
out from Plymouth, we passed Teneriffe. They had called us
up at daybreak for the first sight of the islands, which rose
stern and grand out of the sea in the misty morning air. We
had coal enough and were not obliged to stop; so we swept
slowly round the Bay of Santa Cruz. I know not whether
the famous Marquis, the greatest of the Spanish admirals, took
his title from this place or no. The Peak was white with
snow, though on deck the tar was melting in the sun. The
bay and town were disappointing when I thought of the great
fights which it had witnessed. Between these headlands
Drake met the first of his defeats on his last and fatal voyage,
the story of which is told exultingly in Lope de Vega's 'Dragon-
tea.' Lope had been in the Armada in 1588, and his faith in
Providence had been tried by the good fortune of the heretic
English, and especially of *El Draque,* the pirate, the dragon of
the Apocalypse, who had so long roved the seas with impunity,

plundered the Spanish gold-ships, burnt the fleet in Cadiz, and had shattered and hunted through the English Channel the avenging squadrons of Medina Sidonia. Strange that the wicked one should so long have prospered ; but the hand of God fell upon him at last, and here, in the bay, the first stroke had reached him. There was nothing but the mere locality, nothing to throw light either on the misfortune of El Draquè, or on the great victory of Blake afterwards on the same spot. Santa Cruz is a mere collection of Spanish houses and churches, spread loosely on the hillside, the dark lines and spots being avenues and clumps of oranges and olives. The Great Island is green but bare, and unpicturesquely covered with ugly plants which are grown for the cochineal insect. From the sea it is less beautiful by far than Madeira, though less repulsive than the arid rocks of St. Vincent and the rest of the Cape de Verd group. Close inspection might have improved our impression ; and had we landed I should have heard again the pleasant sound of the Castilian tongue. But it could not be. The captain had his own and his ship's credit to maintain by a quick passage.

Being Sunday we had service on deck after we left the bay. The captain read prayers at a table covered in the usual way with the Union Jack. He was a Presbyterian, and new to this part of his business, so he missed his way in the Liturgy and we had to help him. It was very pretty, however : the officers in full uniform, the emigrants in their best clothes, joining, all of them, some with full, rich voices, in the hymns which have grown among us in such profusion in the last forty years, and have become household songs to the English race all over the world. Otherwise the day was as tedious as we everywhere make it. St. Aldegonde in 'Lothair' exclaims, 'How I hate Sundays !' We mean to be reverent, and we try to force the feelings by forbidding irreverent amusements, while at the same time we provide nothing to help the mind to serious thoughts when service is over, except books, generally themselves tedious, and especially so when they try to be spiritually entertaining. The most stringent rules cannot bind the thoughts, cannot give a tone to conversation. People, as a fact, think as usual and talk as usual, but they must not act as usual. They do not work, because it is a holy day ; yet chess, for instance, is not work, and we are forbidden to play chess. St. Aldegonde's impatience was not entirely because his habits were artificially interfered with. He disliked the inconsistency and the unreality perhaps a great deal more. If Sunday books were the best in the world, all eyes cannot read after sunset, especially in imperfectly-lighted ships. Why may I not play chess ? I must not set a bad example ; but is it wrong ? and, if not wrong, why is the example bad ? I have heard some people say that they go to church for example. They do not need outward observances for themselves ; they are not like the poor publican, and can do without such things ; but church is good for the publican, and it gives them pleasure to encourage him. Such pleasure as this belongs to the *mala mentis gaudia*, the evil pleasures of the soul, which, Virgil says, lie in the vestibule of Orcus.

The engines, at any rate, do not observe Sunday, not being human. We run punctually our 300 miles a day. When we have left Teneriffe under the horizon we reach the north-east trade. The wind barely overtakes the ship. The sun streams hotter upon the deck. The water rises to 80 degrees ; but the air is pure and sweet. An awning is spread over the deck, where I lie by day and read about the pious Æneas. At night we watch Arcturus and the Bear sinking lower and lower, and to the south new constellations appearing above the horizon. The black care which clings behind the horseman cannot reach the ocean. We smoke, we dream, we read, we play quoits on deck. Our star-gazing, as we are without accurate knowledge, costs us no intellectual effort, and we pick up, without difficulty, fragments of nautical science in the captain's chart-room. We stand at his side when he makes it twelve o'clock at noon and notes down the exact point which we have reached. A friend of mine who was to cross the Atlantic in the old sailing-ship days had studied his route on a map formed of the two flat circles representing the two halves of the globe. They touched only at a single point, and he was afraid that the captain might miss it and carry him off into space. Our course

lay happily upon a single hemisphere, so that we had no
anxiety. On December 20 we crossed the line, leaving mid-
winter behind us and entering into midsummer. The weather
continued beautiful. The ship slid on upon an even keel.
Our windows were open day and night, for there was not a
wave to threaten our port-holes. On Midsummer Night the
emigrants got up an entertainment. They sang glees; they sang
solos. One poor fellow tried a dance, but the only fiddle broke
down, and dancing without music is not beautiful. 'The best
in this kind are but as shadows, and the worst are no worse if
imagination mend them.'

I finished the ' Æneid.' It is a beautiful piece of work-
manship, but I can understand why Virgil himself wished it
burnt. He did not believe in his story of Æneas. All that
part of it is conscious invention, and the gods are intolerable.
Lucian himself never equalled the conversation between Jupiter
and Juno, where Jupiter calls her his ' sweetest wife,' and she
him the ' beautifullest of husbands.' The pious Æneas himself, too, save on the one occasion on which he forgot himself,
is immaculate as Tennyson's Arthur, and very like him—not a
genuine man, but an artificial model of a highly respectable
man.

As we approached the Cape I became more and more
anxious to know in what condition I should find it. The
Government at home had taken a new point of departure in
sending Sir Charles Warren into Bechuanaland. To myself it
appeared to be one more step in the same direction which commenced with our taking the Diamond Fields from the Dutch
in 1871, and has led us into such a labyrinth of trouble. For
twenty years before that achievement there had been compara-
tive peace in South Africa. In 1852 we had discovered that
wars with the natives and wars with the Dutch were expensive
and useless ; that sending troops out and killing thousands of
natives was an odd way of protecting them. We resolved then
to keep within our own territories, to meddle no more beyond
the Orange River, and to leave the Dutch and the natives to
settle their differences among themselves. If we had kept to
that policy, a good many thousand people now dead would be

alive. A good many millions of money now spent would be
in the pockets of the taxpayers, and the South Africans, white
and black alike, would have been a great deal happier and
more prosperous. We had set the treaty aside, however ; we
had been seizing territory and then abandoning it, and fighting
and killing and getting bad defeats, and we were now going
into a fresh adventure, in my eyes equally unpromising. The
peace to which we consented after the victory of the Dutch
at Majuba Hill was an act of high magnanimity. Our ac-
quiescence had been misinterpreted, and some step might be
necessary to show that we intended, notwithstanding, to assert
our authority in South Africa ; but in what we were now
doing we were running the risk of plunging the whole country
into civil war ; and success would leave the essential problem
as far from settlement as ever.

Having, as I said, been at one time connected with Cape
affairs, and having some knowledge of the inner bearings of
them, before I describe our arrival there, I will give a brief
account of the colony, how we came by it, and how we have
conducted ourselves in the management of it.

CHAPTER III.

The Cape Colony—The Dutch settlement—Transfer to England—Abolition of
slavery—Injustice to the Dutch—Emigration of the Boers—Efforts at re-
conquest—The Orange River treaty—Broken by England—The war—Treaty
of Aliwal North—Discovery of diamonds—Treaty again broken—British
policy at Kimberley—Personal tour in South Africa—Lord Carnarvon pro-
poses a Conference—Compensation paid to the Orange Free State—Annexation of the Transvaal—War with the Dutch—Peace—Fresh difficulties—
Expedition of Sir Charles Warren.

THE CAPE COLONY, as we ought to know, but in practice we
always forget, was originally a Dutch colony. Two centuries
ago, when the Hollanders were the second maritime power in
the world—perhaps not even second—they occupied and
settled the southern extremity of Africa. They easily conquered the Hottentots and Bushmen, acting as we ourselves

also acted invariably in similar circumstances. They cleared out the wild beasts, built towns, laid out roads, enclosed and ploughed the land, planted forests and vineyards. Better colonists or more successful did not exist than the Dutch. They throve and prospered, and continued to thrive and prosper till the close of the last century. If we compare the success of the Dutch in the management of uncivilised tribes with our own, in all parts of the world, it will be found that, although their rule is stricter than ours, and to appearance harsher, they have had fewer native wars than we have had. There has been less violence and bloodshed, and the natives living under them have not been less happy or less industrious. Holland in the Revolutionary war was seized by the French Directory. The English, at the request of the Prince of Orange, took the Cape under their protection. It was on the high road to India; there was then no alternative route by the Suez Canal; and so important a station could not be permitted to fall into the hands of Napoleon. At the peace of Amiens it was restored to Holland, and the English garrison was withdrawn. On the war breaking out again, our occupation was renewed; a fleet was sent out, with a strong invading force. The Cape Dutch resisted—fought a gallant action, in which they were largely helped by native allies; they yielded only in the belief that, as before, the occupation would be temporary, and that their country would be finally given back to them when the struggle was over. It was not given back. At the Congress of Vienna, they found themselves transferred permanently to the English dominion without their own consent being either obtained or asked for. They had made the country what it was, had set up their houses there, had done no one any harm, and had been in possession for seven generations. They were treated as *adscripti glebæ*, as part of the soil. They resented it; the hotter spirits resisted; they were called rebels, and were shot and hanged in the usual fashion. If we had been wise, we should have made allowance for the circumstances under which the Cape had come into our hands; we should have tried to reconcile the Dutch to an alien rule, by exceptional consideration. We did make an exception,

D

but not in their favour. We justified our conquest to ourselves by taking away the character of the conquered, and we
constituted ourselves the champion of the coloured races
against them, as if they were oppressors and robbers. After
the peace, slave emancipation was the question of the day.
They were slave-owners, but so were we ; we had been sinners
alike. We repented, and voted over twenty millions to clear
ourselves of the reproach. We expected that the Dutch
should recognise as instantaneously as ourselves the wicked-
ness of the institution ; and because they are a deliberate and
slow people, not given to enthusiasm for new ideas, they fell
into disgrace with us, where they have ever since remained.
Slavery at the Cape had been rather domestic than predial ;
the scandals of the West India plantations were unknown
among them. The slaves were part of their families, and had
always been treated with care and kindness. They submitted
to the emancipation because they could not help themselves ;
but when the compensation came to be distributed, the terms
offered them were so much less favourable than had been
allowed to the planters at Jamaica and Barbadoes, were so
unequal in themselves and were embarrassed with so many
technical conditions, that many of the Dutch farmers refused
to accept them. They dismissed their slaves freely, and to
this day have never applied for the moderate sums which they
might with difficulty have obtained.

It was not enough to abolish slavery. The enthusiasm of
the hour could not tolerate the shadow of it. The Hottentots
were then numerous in the colony ; with the emancipated
slaves, they formed a large population ; they had been placed
under vagrancy laws like those which prevailed in England
up to the reforming era of the present century ; like the
'sturdy and valiant beggars' of our statute-book, they were
forbidden to wander about the country, but were forced to
remain in one place and work for their living. These laws
were repealed. The Hottentots were allowed to go where
they pleased ; they scattered through the bush, they took to
drink and thieving, and became a general nuisance to the
Dutch farmers ; for as yet there were few English settlers

outside the towns, and our own position was purely that of
military conquerors. Had the Dutch and the Hottentots
been left to themselves, the latter, most of whom came to a
bad end, would probably now be surviving, and in a fair way
to leading useful lives. Drink and idleness carried them off;
but because the Dutch objected to these measures, they were
regarded in England as slave-owners at heart, as barbarians
and tyrants, as illiterate savages, as the real cause of all that
had gone wrong. The unfavourable impression of them became
a tradition of the English press, and unfortunately of the
Colonial Office. We had treated them unfairly as well as
unwisely, and we never forgive those whom we have injured.

The Cape Dutchman, or Boer, as we call him, is a slow,
good-humoured person, not given to politics, occupied much
with his religion and his private affairs, and if let alone, with
some allowance for his habits and opinions, would have long
since forgotten his independence, would have acquiesced in
the inevitable, and become the most conservative and least
revolutionary of the Queen's subjects. And the Colonial
Office, if free to act by its own judgment, would, for its own
sake, long ago have followed a conciliatory policy. But
colonial secretaries have to consider their party in Parliament,
and members in Parliament have to consider their constituents
and public opinion. Slave emancipation was the special glory
of the English people, and there was no safer road to public
favour than to treat those who were unsound on this greatest
of questions as beyond the pale of consideration. The Boers
had, or imagined that they had, a list of grievances, large and
small, as long as an Irishman's, and sufferers of wrong have
longer memories than the inflictors of wrong. Impatient of a
yoke which calumny made intolerable, a swarm of them, many
thousands strong, took wing in 1835 and 1836, packed their
goods into their waggons, gathered their flocks and herds about
them, and struck off for the unknown wilderness to the north
of the Orange River. The migration left the home ties unbroken. Each family in the colony sent one or more of its
young ones. The history of these emigrants repeats our own
history wherever we have settled, and must be the history of

all settlers in new countries which are inhabited already by an inferior race. Before they went they established communications with various tribes, who agreed to receive them. They were welcome to some, they were unwelcome to others. Disputes arose about land and stolen cattle. There were collisions, and massacres called treacherous, avenged by wars and fresh acquisitions of territory, till they became possessors of all the country now known as the Orange Free State, the Transvaal, and Natal. In England it was represented that they were carrying fire and sword among the innocent natives. Aborigines of other breeds might suffer; we were sorry, but we could sit still. But there was something in the ill-treatment of a negro which fired the English blood. We decided that the Boers could not escape their allegiance by going out of the colony. We pursued them, drove them out of Natal, invaded the Orange Free State, fought battles with imperfect results, got into quarrels with the natives ourselves, notably with the Basuto Moshesh, who taught us that these roving expeditions were unprofitable and might be dangerous. Grown sick at last of enterprises which led neither to honour nor peace, we resolved, in 1852, to leave Boers, Caffres, Basutos, and Zulus to themselves, and make the Orange River the boundary of British responsibilities. We made formal treaties with the two Dutch states, binding ourselves to interfere no more between them and the natives, and to leave them, either to establish themselves as a barrier between ourselves and the interior of Africa, or to sink, as was considered most likely, in an unequal struggle with warlike tribes by whom they were infinitely outnumbered. They, on their side, undertook not to re-establish slavery; and so we left them.

With an exception, which I shall notice presently, these treaties were observed for seventeen years, and 'the land had rest' from its misfortunes. Our own Border troubles ceased. The colony was quiet and had no history. The new states did not sink but prospered. The Boers spread over a territory as large as France. They arranged their disputes with the natives with little fighting. In the Transvaal a million natives lived peaceably in the midst of them, working with them and for them. By far the most thriving native location which I myself saw in South Africa was close to Pretoria. They were rough, but they had rude virtues, which are not the less virtues because in these latter days they are growing scarce. They are a very devout people, maintaining their churches and ministers with excessive liberality. Their houses being so far apart, they cannot send their children to school, and generally have tutors for them at home. Religious observances are attended to scrupulously in their households. The Boers of South Africa, of all human beings now on this planet, correspond nearest to Horace's description of the Roman peasant soldiers who defeated Pyrrhus and Hannibal. There alone you will find obedience to parents as strict as among the ancient Sabines, the *severa mater* whose sons fetch and carry at her bidding, who, when those sons go to fight for their country, will hand their rifles to them and bid them return with their arms in their hands—or else not return at all.

They rule after their own pattern. They forbid idleness and indiscriminate vagrancy. They persuade, and when they can, compel the blacks to cultivate the ground and be industrious. They give them no votes for the Volksraad. They do not allow them even to own the freehold of land, except under white trustees, lest they should reintroduce their old tribal tenures and confound the law. But, on the whole, the management has not been unsuccessful. There have been no risings of blacks against whites in the Transvaal. Authority has been sustained, without panics and without severity. Such scenes as the destruction of Langalibalele's tribe in Natal, or the massacre at Koegas, which disgraced the Cape Colony in 1878, have never been paralleled in the Dutch independent states. They could not, however, earn the confidence of the English Government. Perhaps their unexpected success was an offence. Their methods were not our methods, and were easily misrepresented. Stories were told—untrue generally, but not wholly without foundation—of Boers, on the borders of the Transvaal, kidnapping native children, or purchasing them of plundering tribes, and bringing them up as slaves under the disguise of apprentices. The Transvaal Government severely and successfully repressed these proceedings. I say successfully because, in the years during which the Transvaal was again a British province, cases of the kind would have been brought to light had any then existed, and not a single child was discovered in the condition described. Yet these practices were reported to England as ascertained facts, and were honestly believed. The Boers were held to have broken their engagement, and many excellent people among us insisted that we were neglecting our duty in leaving them uncontrolled.

They were left, however, materially undisturbed. The English Government was in no haste to meddle again. Cape politics had been so disagreeable a subject that persons in authority at the Colonial Office dismissed them from their minds. They hoped that the Dutch difficulties were disposed of altogether; and so little acquainted were they with the character and distribution of the Cape population, that Lord Cardwell, who had been himself Colonial Minister, believed, as late as 1875, that all the Dutch in South Africa had migrated to the Free States, and that the Colony was entirely English. He told me so himself, and was taken entirely by surprise when I informed him that the Dutch were still the majority, and a very large majority, in the Colony itself. Nor were they only the majority, but they were doing all the work which was really valuable. The English were merchants, shopkeepers, artisans; they made railways, managed ostrich farms, dug diamonds and copper, and drove ox-waggons. The Boers almost alone were cultivating the soil, and but for them all the white inhabitants of South Africa would be living on foreign flour, tinned milk, and imported potatoes.

Peace was doing its work. The two races were drawing together, and, if the treaties of 1852 had not been broken, South Africa would have by this time been reunited, and the Dutch farmers would have been loyal subjects of the Crown. I think everyone who knows South Africa will agree with me in this opinion. The Boer is a born Conservative, and the Free States, if let well alone, would have naturally rejoined their kindred. Unhappily the feeling in England continued to be irritated against them by reports not entirely honest. The friends of the coloured races were on the watch, and an occasion rose which enabled them to force a renewal of interference. On abandoning the Orange Free State, we bequeathed as a legacy an unsettled border dispute with the Basutos. We were tired of fighting with them ourselves, and we left the President and Volksraad at Bloemfontein to arrange the differences as they could. They could not arrange them peacefully. In 1865 a war broke out between the Orange Free State and the sons of Moshesh. It lasted four years, and was then ending because the Basutos could resist no longer, when they threw themselves on British protection, and, in spite of our solemn engagements, we interfered with a high hand. It seldom answers to break treaties, even with the best intentions. The Basuto territory was north of the Orange River, and we were doing what we had distinctly bound ourselves not to do. I suppose that neither we nor South Africa generally have reason to be gratified with our action on that occasion. The common interest of all of us would have been better served had we stood by our engagements, and left the Dutch to deal with the Basutos as they could. But the true state of things was not known in England. The Boers had a bad name with us. To protect innocent natives from oppression was a popular cry, and the British Government yielded to the general wish. It was, however, so far a single act; the non-intervention policy was still to be maintained as a whole. To satisfy the Orange Free State we undertook to guarantee that the Basutos should keep the peace for the future, and the treaty of 1852 was renewed at Aliwal North in 1869, with fresh assurances that the breach of it should not be made a precedent for further interpositions. The Dutch of the colony resented what we had done, and there remained a soreness of feeling; but they considered that a new engagement, freshly entered into, would not be again violated.

Perhaps it would not have been violated had no new temptation come in our way. But South Africa, like other countries, is torn by factions. There was a party there who

bore the Free States no good-will, and a step which had been
once taken might be more easily taken a second time. The
ink on the treaty of Aliwal North was scarcely dry when diamonds were discovered in large quantities in a district which
we had ourselves treated as part of the Orange Territory before our first withdrawal, and which had ever since been administered by Orange Free State magistrates. There was a
rush of diggers from all parts of the country. There was a
genuine fear that the Boers would be unable to control the
flock of vultures which was gathering over so rich a prey.
There was a notion also that the finest diamond mine in the
world ought not to be lost to the British Empire. It was discovered that the country in which it lay was not part of the
Free State at all, and that it belonged to a Griqua chief named
Waterboer. This chief in past times had been an ally of the
English. The Boers were accused of having robbed him. He
appealed for help, and in an ill hour we lent ourselves to an
aggression for which there was no excuse. Lord Kimberley
gave his name to the new settlement. The Dutch were ex-
pelled. They did not resist, but they yielded under protest to
superior force, and from that day no Boer in South Africa has
been able to trust to English promises. The manner in which
we acted, or allowed our representatives to act, was insolent
in its cynicism. We had gone in as the champions of the
oppressed Waterboer. We gave Waterboer and his Griquas a
tenth of the territory. We kept the rest and all that was
valuable for ourselves. What could the Dutch have done
worse? We have accused them of breaking their engagements
with us, and it was we who taught them the lesson. A treaty
but a few months old was staring us in the face. Even if
Waterboer's title had been as good as his friends pretended,
we had pledged ourselves to meddle no more in such matters,
in language as plain as words could make it. Our conduct
would have been less entirely intolerable if we had rested
simply on superior strength—if we had told the Boers simply
that we must have the Diamond Fields and intended to take
them ; but we poisoned the wound, and we justified our action,
by posing before the world as the protectors of the rights of

native tribes, whom we accused them of having wronged, and we maintained this attitude through the controversy which afterwards arose.

I had myself to make inquiries subsequently into the details of this transaction, perhaps the most discreditable in the annals of English Colonial History. There were persons ready, if necessary, to depose in a court of justice how Waterboer's case had been got up. It was proved afterwards in a Land Court held at Kimberley, before Mr. Justice Stockenström, that the Griqua chief had never possessed any rights in the Territory at all. But all such inquiries are superfluous. The Treaty of Aliwal is our all-sufficient condemnation. This one action has been the cause of all the troubles which have since befallen South Africa. The Dutch are slow to move, but when moved are moved effectually. We selected this particular moment to pass the Cape Colony over to its own Parliament to manage, and we meant the Diamond Fields to be a present to it on attaining its majority. The Colonial Office could have given no better proof of its own unfitness to govern there than in its last performance, and in that sense perhaps the time was well chosen. There was a general election at the Cape on the occasion of the new constitution. The Dutch electors determined to support the protest of the Orange Free State, and the new members made it at once clear that if the Imperial Government chose to violate treaties it must take the consequences. Instead of accepting gratefully Lord Kimberley's gift, they refused to touch it. They would have nothing to do with the Diamond Fields until the Orange Free State declared itself satisfied with our occupation ; and we were left with a province in the interior of Africa with no communication with it, except through the Free States which we had robbed, or the Cape Colony which we had alienated and which was no longer our own. The mining population who had assembled there was miscellaneous, dangerous, and ungovernable. The frontier between the province and the two Free States was unsettled, and apparently incapable of settlement, since our right to be there was not admitted by the Government at Bloemfontein.

One saving feature there was in the situation : the daring
and able man whom we had selected to govern our precious
new possession. He had no British troops to support him,
nor did he ask for any. Tearing to pieces the shreds of the
now useless treaties, he entered into relations with all the
native chiefs on the borders of the two republics, inviting
them to become British subjects, and promising to protect
them from the Dutch. They sent gangs of their people to
work in the diamond pits. The wages of these people were
laid out in powder and arms, with which we had promised not
to furnish the natives. Tens of thousands of guns and rifles
were distributed in two or three years among the surrounding
tribes as a direct menace to the Dutch, who had now a semi-
circle of armed men drawn outside them from Kimberley to
Zululand. Naturally there was the greatest alarm and the
greatest indignation among them. They were threatened with
invasions and inroads of savages set on and countenanced by
the British Government. They were poor in money, and with
difficulty were able to provide means to defend themselves.
The object was of course to bring them upon their knees, force
them to withdraw their protest, and acknowledge the sovereign
rights of Great Britain. The waggons bringing the rifles up
to Kimberley passed through the Dutch territory. The Free
State magistrates stopped them as illegal, which they were.
To supply the natives with arms was against the law. Re-
paration was instantly demanded. Commissioners were sent
from Kimberley to Bloemfontein to require compensation and
an apology, and forty-eight hours alone were allowed for an
answer. The President was ill at the time and unable to take
part in business. His council paid the money, but paid it
under protest, with an old-fashioned appeal to the God of
righteousness, whom, strange to say, they believed to be a
reality.

Another ultimatum had been sent to the Transvaal Government. The Transvaal being far off was less submissive, and a
state of tension was set up which could only have ended in a
war of races. The native tribes would have been let loose
upon the Dutch farmers. Every Dutchman in South Africa

who could carry a rifle would have gone to the help of his kindred, so justly, so deeply indignant were they. We had been sowing dragon's teeth at the Diamond Fields, and the old harvest was springing from them.

Such was the state of things when, in 1874, I travelled through Natal, the Free States, the Diamond Fields, and the North of the Colony. At Kimberley I inquired privately into the history of Waterboer's claims. The evidence was violently conflicting : but persons who were behind the scenes were ready to come forward and prove that 'the annexation had been a swindle and a trick.' It was impossible for me, as a stranger, to tell who were lying and who were speaking the truth. But the breach of treaty was indisputable ; and I could not reconcile myself to the calm statement of one gentleman high in authority, that as we had broken the treaty in the case of the Basutos we might break it again. If Waterboer's pretensions were as clear as they were doubtful, our action had been extravagantly impolitic. It could be no object to us, even for so precious a possession as a pit of diamonds, to hold a province in the far interior which our own Cape Colony repudiated, and our occupation of which was creating such a temper in the Dutch population all over South Africa. At Cape Town I had a conversation about it with the Premier, Mr. Molteno. He told me that he was as sorry as I could be ; that he had himself opposed the annexation, that he regretted the course which the Imperial Government had pursued and was pursuing, but that Griqualand was beyond the colonial frontier. It was not his business, and he could not interfere.

On my return to England I laid my experiences before Lord Carnarvon, who was then Colonial Secretary. Lord Carnarvon was not satisfied that the annexation had been unjust, but of course he paid great attention to the opinion of the Cape Premier. The Colonial Office had undervalued the Dutch as a fighting power, and had thought that the irritation would be limited to words. Nor had it allowed for the feeling created in the Colony : a war with the Free States, should it come to that, would be dangerous as well as disgraceful, and would lead certainly to complications with the newly established Constitutional Government. Lord Carnarvon resolved to make an effort for a peaceful settlement. It was not easy for the office to acknowledge that it had done wrong ; nor had proof yet been produced that wrong had been done. If a treaty had been broken, there were perhaps exceptional reasons for breaking it. But the impolicy of alienating and exasperating the majority of the constituents of a colony which had just been trusted with self-government was obvious. It had been represented to me at the Cape that a conference of representatives from the various states interested could easily find a solution. Lord Carnarvon considered that the simplest solution would be a confederation of all the South African, Dutch, and English communities into a confederation like the Canadian Dominion, in which minor differences would be merged. I did not think myself that the Dutch, in their existing humour, would listen to this proposal. It was the easiest road, however, for the retreat of the Colonial Office. Lord Carnarvon sent out a despatch inviting a conference to consider various questions, the position of the Diamond Fields among them, suggesting confederation, but not pressing it. A fortnight after the despatch went I followed, with instructions that when the conference met, the dispute with the Free States was to be considered and disposed of before anything else was discussed. I had myself written along with the despatch a private letter to Mr. Molteno, under the impression that he would welcome Lord C.'s proposal as a means of carrying out his own expressed wishes. Since the original appropriation of South Africa no minister had shown so much concern for the Dutch inhabitants as Lord Carnarvon now was showing, and I never doubted for a moment that Mr. Molteno would meet his intentions with the cordiality which they deserved.

I do not know the secret history of what followed. There were persons, I suppose, who were interested in keeping open the quarrel between the Free States and the Imperial Government —who wished the Free States to be brought upon their knees with the assistance of native allies. The despatch was laid before the Cape Parliament with commentaries, which, if the object was to embitter every difference, had the merit of ingenuity. It was represented as an insidious attempt to entangle the colony in responsibilities which it had repudiated —as a treacherous scheme to bring the Free States back under the English flag—as an interference with the colony's private affairs, which it was necessary to check on the spot. The proposed conference was hurriedly, and even insultingly, rejected. The absurd misrepresentation of Lord Carnarvon's objects was spread over the country by the press ; and when I arrived, I found a universal ferment, and the Dutch more furious than ever.

I applied for an explanation to the Premier, and I reminded him of what he had said to me. To my surprise, he went back from his own words. He said now, that we might do as we liked with the Free States. He had no objection. I told him that I must at least explain Lord Carnarvon's intentions. The Governor had suggested that I might address a letter of explanation to him which he could lay before Parliament. But Mr. Molteno positively refused to allow the matter to come before the Parliament again. I took his refusal to mean that no explanation was to be given, and that my own lips were to be closed. The position seemed unfair to me, and the injury from the lies that were put in circulation to be more than serious. If I was silent I should seem to admit their justice. The Dutch, at least, ought to know what Lord Carnarvon had meant, and as the question was between the Free States and the Imperial Government, I could not recognise that I should violate any constitutional principle in telling the truth. In doubtful cases truth is generally the safest policy. I attended a dinner in Cape Town and said a few words. The result was a revulsion of feeling among the friends of the Free States, much abuse of myself in ministerial newspapers, an agitation which spread over the Colony, and finally a recall of the Parliament, which had been prorogued in the interval, when the Colony agreed to assist the Imperial Government in bringing the quarrel to an end. This was all that I wanted. There could be no war after the Colony had become a party to the dispute, and a settlement agreeable to the Dutch colonial constituencies could not be unsatisfactory beyond the Orange River. I went home. Mr. Brand, the President of the Orange Free State, came to London shortly after. It was admitted in general terms at the Colonial Office that he had not been treated fairly about the Diamond Fields, and a sum of 90,000*l*. was allowed him as compensation. The money was nothing : the acknowledgment of wrong was everything. The Dutch of South Africa, though obstinate as mules, are emotional and affected easily through their feelings. It seemed to them that their evil days were over, that an English Government could be just after all, and that a United Africa might still be possible under the English flag.

If Lord Carnarvon, having accomplished one piece of good work, had been contented to let well alone : had he made as fair an arrangement with the Transvaal as he had made with the Orange Free State ; still more, had he lent her a hand in her native difficulties, there would have again been at least a chance of the confederation which he desired. We owed something to the Dutch of the Transvaal. Bechuanas, Matabelies, Amaswazis, Zulus, all had received either arms or encouragement from the Diamond Fields to annoy them. A little help in money to the Transvaal, a few kind words, the concession of a fair western frontier, and an intimation to the border tribes that we and the Dutch were henceforth friends, and that an injury to them would be taken as an injury to the British Crown, and every Dutchman in South Africa would have torn the leaves out of his book of griev-ances and have forgotten them for ever. But Lord Carnarvon mistook the nature of the warm feeling which he had aroused. He supposed it to be in favour of his confederation scheme, with which it had nothing directly to do ; he felt that to bring about a South African Dominion would be understood and admired in England as a brilliant and useful political achieve-ment. The Transvaal appeared the key of the situation. With the Transvaal an English province again, the Orange Free State would be compelled to follow. He had recovered in some degree the Dutch confidence. It was a plant of tender growth, but he believed that it would now bear pressure. The life of English ministries is short. If they are to achieve anything they must act promptly, or they may leave the chance to their successors. The Transvaal treasury was empty, and an occupation of the country would at the moment be unresisted. He was assured by the South African English—at least by many of them—that the Transvaal farmers were sick of their independence, and would welcome annexation. He could count on the support of both parties in Parliament. Mr. Courtney, I believe, was the only English member of the Legislature who protested. I myself was certain that to take over (as it was called) the Transvaal would undo the effect of his past action, and would bring back the old bitterness. I gave him my opinion, but I could not expect that he would believe me when so many persons who must know the country better than I could do insisted upon the opposite. The step was taken. The 'South African Republic,' so proud of its independence that it had struck a coinage of its own, was declared British territory. 'Confederation,' which had been made absolutely impossible, was next to follow, and Sir Bartle Frere was sent to the Cape as governor, to carry it out. How he fared is fresh in our memories. His task was from the first hopeless. Yet he could not or would not understand it to be hopeless. He was not even told the truth. It was said that the native tribes were too strong; that if South Africa were confederated they would have to deal with the Caffres, Basutos, Zulus, &c., single-handed, and that they were not equal to it. If this was the difficulty Sir Bartle could sweep it away. Hitherto we had at least affected a wish to protect the coloured races. Now all was changed. He found an excuse in a paltry border dispute for a new Caffre war. He carried fire and sword over the Kei, dismissing his ministers, and appointing others who were more willing to go along with him in his dangerous course. He broke up the Zulus after a resistance which won for them more credit than the ultimate conquest brought honour to ourselves. South Africa was wet with blood, and all these crimes and follies had been committed for a shadow which was no nearer than before. The Zulus had

been enemies of the Boers, but their destruction had not re-
conciled the Boers to the loss of their liberty. They demanded
back their independence in dogged, determined tones. Sir
Garnet Wolseley's campaign against Secocoeni, who had once
defeated them, made no difference. The Liberal party in
England began to declare in their favour. They learnt at last
that the Liberal leader had condemned the annexation as
adopted under false pretences ; and when the Liberals came
into power in 1880 they counted with certainty that their
complaints would be attended to. We could at that time have
withdrawn with dignity, and the Boers would have perceived
again that when we were convinced of a mistake we were willing to repair it. But I suppose (and this is the essential difficulty in our Colonial relations), that the Government knew
what it would be right to do, but were afraid to do it in fear
of an adverse vote in the Parliament to which they were responsible ; and party interests at home were too important to
be sacrificed to the welfare of remote communities. It was
decided that before the complaints of the Transvaal Boers
could be heard they must first acknowledge the Queen's authority. They had taken arms for their freedom, and did not
choose to lay them down, when the rulers of England had
themselves admitted that they were in the right. Then followed the war which we all remember, where a series of
disasters culminated on Majuba Hill and the death of Sir
George Colley.

I, for one, cannot blame the Government for declining to
prosecute further a bloody struggle in a cause which they had
already condemned. I blame them rather for having entered
upon it at all. To concede after defeat what might have been
conceded gracefully when our defeat was on both sides thought
impossible, was not without a nobleness of its own ; but it
was to diminish infallibly the influence of England in South
Africa, and to elate and encourage the growing party whose
hope was and is to see it vanish altogether. Had we persisted,
superior strength and resources must have succeeded in the
end. But the war would have passed beyond the limits of the
Transvaal. It must have been a war of conquest against the

whole Dutch population, who would all have taken part in it. We should have brought a scandal on our name. We should and must have brought to the verge of destruction a brave and honourable people. We should have provoked the censure —we might, perhaps, have even provoked the interposition— of other Powers. For these reasons I think that Mr. Gladstone did well in consenting to a peace, although it was a peace which affected painfully the position and feelings of the English South African colonists, and could not fail to leave a dangerous sting behind it. The peace was right. It was a pity only that, as a balm to our wounded pride, we insisted on stipulations which could not or would not be observed, while we had left ourselves no means of enforcing them. Some concession, I suppose, was necessary to irritated pride at home, but the conditions which we inserted in the treaty were a legacy from our earlier errors, and that they came to be mentioned at all was a pure calamity. Having swallowed the draught, we might as well have swallowed it completely, without leaving drops in the bottom of the cup. The origin of all the anger in the Transvaal had been the arming the native chiefs against them from the Diamond Fields. These chiefs had remained our allies in the war. We could not, or thought we could not, leave them without taking security for them and their territories. I think it would have been better, though it might have seemed unhandsome, to have fallen back on the principle which had worked so well while it lasted, of the Orange River Treaty, and had resolved to meddle no more in the disputes between the Boers and these tribes. Had we maintained our authority we could have maintained the tribes by our side ; but to abandon the country, and to insist at the same time that the inhabitants of it should not fall into their natural relations, was to reserve artificially a certain cause of future troubles. The chiefs whom we called our friends had been drawn into an attitude of open menace against the Boers. The Boers were not to be blamed if they preferred to form settlements of their own in those territories, that they might not be exposed again to the same danger.

However, they agreed to our terms, and they did not

E

observe them. We had broken the treaty of Aliwal North.
They broke the later treaty, or rather their Government did
not prevent individuals among them from breaking it. We
took note of their faults; we forgot our own. A clamour
rose against the Boers' perfidy. The missionaries, who have
never loved them—the English in the colony, who were smart-
ing from a sense of humiliation—the army, sore at an un-
avenged defeat—politicians, jealous for the honour of their
country—philanthropists, whose mission in life is the cham-
pionship of innocent negroes, all joined in the cry; while 'her
Majesty's Opposition' was on the watch to take advantage of
any opening which the Government might give them. The
Cabinet was called on to send out an expedition to expel the
Boers by force from our allies' territories, and they dared not
refuse. Yet what was the expedition to do? The Knight of
La Mancha delivered the lad from his master's whip, made the
master swear to pay the wages which the boy claimed, and
rode on his way, rejoicing at the wrong which he had redressed·
When he was out of sight, the master again bound the lad to
the tree and flogged him worse than before. When we had
driven the Boers out of Bechuanaland, were we to stay there?
to maintain an army there? If yes, who was to pay for it?
If not, the tide would flow in again when we retired. Between
an evil to be remedied and the cost of the remedy, there must
always be some proportion. The best to be looked for was that
we should send our troops up, at an expense of, perhaps, a million
of money to the taxpayers, that they should find no enemy,
that the troops should remain till we were tired of paying for
them, and then go back with a confession of impotence. To
raise a revenue in such a country would be impossible. To
establish an authority there which could be self-maintaining
would be equally impossible. And what were we to do with
a province, productive of nothing but an opportunity of spending money indefinitely, of which we could make no use, and to
which we could have no access except through Cape Colony,
while the Cape Colony would do nothing to make our presence
there more easy to us? The Cabinet might hope that when
Bechuanaland was cleared of Boers, the Cape Colony would

. take charge of it. The Cape Colony, it was certain to those who understood the question, would do nothing of the kind. If we chose to take Bechuanaland, we should have to keep it till we were tired, and then to go away like fools. This was the best which we could look for. The worst was a renewal of the war which would turn to a war of races between the Dutch and English in South Africa. The slightest imprudence, or the mere refusal of the Boers to retire without being forced, might bring it on. And the consequence would be incalculable. The danger was the greater, because many of those who were the most active in promoting the expedition hoped eagerly that war would be the issue of it. They were longing to wipe off the stain of Majuba Hill, and to raise the English flag at Pretoria again.

The prospect was so alarming that to prevent the expedition from being despatched, the present Cape Premier, Mr. Upington, went himself in the autumn to the frontier, and made some kind of arrangement with the Transvaal Government—an arrangement satisfactory to the majority of the whites in the colony. As we have chosen to establish constitutional government there, the views of the majority ought to be accepted. If we wish South Africa to be governed not according to the views of the majority, we must govern it ourselves. The English Cabinet rejected Mr. Upington's agreement as too favourable to the Dutch. The preparations were continued ; 8,000 men were sent out, under the command of Sir Charles Warren, to proceed to Bechuanaland. The Cape Government was invited to co-operate. The Cape Government declined respectfully, and we were thus again launching into an enterprise inconsistent with the constitutional principles on which we had determined that South Africa should be governed. South Africa can only be ruled constitutionally by conciliating the Dutch people there, and we had persisted from the beginning, and were still persisting, in affronting them and irritating them. I conceive that Mr. Gladstone's Cabinet, if left to their own judgment, would have declined this adventure. But the step was taken. The last detachment had sailed before I left England, and the prospect seemed to me to be as

unpromising as our worst enemy could wish. The Boers might.
have no right to the farms which they were occupying; but
was the expulsion of them worth the consequences which it
might involve? The territory in dispute was an almost water-
less wilderness. A week's cost of the delivering army would
have sent the complaining chiefs away rejoicing. Some measure
there must always be between an object to be gained, and
the cost of gaining it. The object to be gained, so far as there
was an object which had reality in it, was revenge for Majuba
Hill. The cost might not improbably be the loss of the South
African colonies. Public opinion in England would certainly
not permit a war of extermination against the Cape Dutch,
and the alternative might easily arise between a war of this
description and the evacuation of the country. As little
would it allow the suppression of the Cape constitution and a
military government there. Yet what other government would
be possible, if we persisted in a course of violent action which
the Cape Parliament and Ministry disapproved? I could see
no light at all. The only prospect that had hope in it was
that Sir Charles Warren would march up, and eventually
march down again, having driven his plough through a morass
which must close again behind it. If this was the issue it
would be only ridiculous. But just now we could hardly afford
to seem ridiculous.

It is of course certain that if we choose, and if we act
consistently with conscientious resolution, we can govern South
Africa as we govern India; we can have a native policy of
our own, and distribute equal justice to white men and black
under our own magistrates responsible only to English opinion.
Under such a rule the country might be peaceable and fairly
prosperous. It is equally certain that if South Africa is to
rule itself under a constitutional system, we must cease to
impose English views of what is expedient on a people unwilling to act upon them. We cannot force them at once to
govern themselves and to govern in the way which we ourselves
desire. You can take a horse to the water, but you cannot
make him drink; and attempts to combine contradictory
methods will lead in the future, as they have led in the past,

to confusion and failure. As an imperfect believer in the value of popular suffrage, I incline myself to the first alternative. But it must be one thing or the other. Inconsistency is worse than either. I was approaching the Cape with anxious curiosity to learn the prospects of our latest adventure.

CHAPTER IV.

Arrive at Cape Town—A disagreeable surprise—Interviewers—State of feeling—Contradictory opinions—Prospects of Sir Charles Warren's expedition—Mr. Upington—Sir Hercules Robinson—English policy in South Africa.

WE steamed into Table Bay at dawn on December 30. The air, though it was early, was sultry with the heat of midsummer ; fishing-boats were gliding away to the offing before the light morning breeze. The town was still asleep in the shadow of the great mountain, over whose level crest a rosy mist was hanging. In all the world there is perhaps no city so beautifully situated as Cape Town ; the grey cliffs seem to overhang it like Poseidon's precipice which threatened the city of Alcinous ; from the base a forest of pines slope upwards wherever trees can fasten their roots, and fills the entire valley to the margin of the houses.

The docks had been enlarged and the breakwater carried far out since I had seen the place last. A few ships were at anchor in its shelter, otherwise there were no signs of growth or change. Business thrives indifferently in a troubled political atmosphere. We went in alongside the pier. One of the first persons who came on board thrust into my hands the ' Argus ' of the previous day. I opened it and was in consternation. A week or two before I left England, a gentleman whom I knew slightly and was inclined to like, had called on me and asked me a number of questions, which I had answered with the unreserve of private conversation. Among other things we had talked of the prospects of South Africa, and I had spoken freely, because I supposed myself to be

speaking in confidence, of colonial factions and tempers out of
which so much evil had arisen and might again arise. I had
complained especially of the misleading information which had
been supplied to the English Government, and of the unscrupu-
lous character of part of the Cape press. To my horror, yet
to my amusement also, I found the whole of the conversation
in print (so far as my friend had remembered it), filling two
columns of the newspaper, and a furious leader attached, holding me up to indignation. Interviewers who are taking down
one's words ought to give one notice. The system anyway
is questionable, but when unacknowledged is intolerable. If
you know what is before you, you can at least be careful what
you say, and make sure also that your friend understands
what you say, and so can report it correctly.

Apology was hopeless, and explanation impossible. There
was no time for it, for one thing ; and, for another, I believed
what I had said to be true, and therefore could not unsay it,
though it had never been meant for the public.

The 'Argus' people, I suppose, had seen the report
accidentally in a London paper, and having heard that I was
coming, had prepared this pretty reception for me. It was a
neat and characteristic stroke, which, provoked as I was, I
could not refuse to admire. M. ——, the oldest friend I had
in the Colony, came on board while I was reflecting. The
whole town, he told me, was in a rage. But, after all, it
mattered little, except to myself, and the three or four persons
whom I wished to see would perhaps forgive me. The political situation was precisely what I expected. M. —— had
accompanied the Premier to Bechuanaland when making the
arrangement with the Boers which Lord Derby had declined to
ratify. Had it been accepted the Premier would have been
prepared to advise the Cape Parliament to annex the Bechuana
territory to the Colony, and the party who wished for peace
would have been all satisfied. But the English Government
would not have it so. Sir Charles Warren had arrived and
had gone to the front ; part of the troops had gone up with
him, the rest were to follow as fast as possible. The Colony
had no more to say in the matter, and were waiting to see the

result. The English were in high spirits, they were looking confidently to another war in which the misfortune of Majuba Hill would be wiped out and their own position made more tolerable. Two thousand of them had volunteered to serve in this expedition. The Dutch as a party of course approved of the Premier's arrangement. The Dutch were the large majority in the Parliament and out of it, and what was to become of constitutional government? It was true that the scene of Sir Charles's operations was outside the colonial frontier. But the Colony was the right arm of South Africa; and how were England and the Colony to get on together, if we persisted in a policy which three-fifths of its white inhabitants detested?

After breakfast we went up the town and I paid my visits. As to my delinquencies, I could not deny them, so I let them take their chance. Time and change had made large gaps in my old circle of acquaintances. Paterson was drowned, Sir John Molteno had retired from public life, and was absent at a watering-place. The Barrys, Charles and Tom, were both gone; De Villiers—not the Chief Justice, but another—was dead; Saul Solomon, one of the best men I ever knew, I had left behind me in bad health in London; but there were still a few remaining for whose judgment I had a high respect, of all shades of opinion. I called on one man of great eminence, unconnected politically with party, yet intensely colonial, and related personally both to Dutch and English, whom I found, to my surprise, not only approving of Sir Charles Warren's expedition, but professing to believe that if we meant to retain our position in South Africa we had no alternative. This gentleman said that after our surrender to the Transvaal, it had been taken for granted that we were weary of South Africa and had intended to retire altogether. The future had been a blank on which no one had dared to calculate. They were to be a republic. They were to be under the protection of Germany; anything was possible. The English in the Colony had lost heart; some were preparing to leave the country; others, who could not leave, were making terms with the winning party. He for one, whose home was at the

Cape, had been depressed and disheartened. South Africa, he was convinced, could not stand alone, and could never be so free under any other sovereignty as it had been under the English Crown. Till within the last few weeks, and till the resolution of the English Government was known, he had looked at the prospect with dismay. All was now changed. The Cape English knew that they were not to be deserted. The Dutch —the sensible part of them—would acquiesce when they saw that we were in earnest. I asked him what would happen if there was fighting. He said he hoped that there would be no fighting, though he could not be sure. His reason for thinking so appeared to me a weak one. The troops, he said, were to go as police, not as soldiers. The sight of a red jacket affected Boers as it affected bulls. They were to wear corduroys and not their uniform. Perhaps there was more in the distinction than I was able to understand. He did not conceal, however, that he thought that the English, both Government and individuals, had behaved extremely ill in South Africa. They had brought their troubles on themselves ; and he trusted that they would have learnt their lesson, and would do better for the future. They had despised the Boers —had not treated them with ordinary honesty, and in illustration he told me of a recent incident which he knew to be true. An Englishman had called at a Boer's farm in the Orange Free State, pretending to be starving. The Boer took him into his service out of charity, and sent him to Kimberley in charge of two waggon-loads of timber. The man sold the wood, went off with the money, and left waggon and bullocks, not daring to dispose of these, to find their own way home. This discreditable story was only too representative. The Boers had been so systematically abused and misrepresented that the English scarcely regarded them as human beings to whom they owed any moral consideration. It made a deeper impression upon me than the approval of Sir Charles Warren's mission, although it was something to find that a wise and temperate man who knew the circumstances thoroughly, and had no prejudice, could express such an opinion. Events may prove that he was right, little as I could believe it then, little

as I believe it now. I fear that the English have not learnt
their lesson. The 2,000 volunteers may be useful if there is to
be a war of conquest, and if the minority are to rule the
majority. Otherwise I cannot see that their coming forward
has improved the prospect. If we could think more of the
wrong things which we have done ourselves, and less of the
wrong things which we accuse the Boers of having done,
I believe that would be considerably more effective.

I do not know whether I should have ventured to call on
the Premier. Ten years ago Mr. Upington had just arrived
at the Colony, to practise at the bar. I had occasionally met
him, with his brilliant and beautiful wife, and had liked what
I had seen of both of them ; but I had no acquaintance which
would have entitled me to intrude upon him in his present
position. I was told, however, that he wished to see me, so I
went to the office. How many things had changed since I was
last there, and how much was not changed ! The players were
altered ; the play was the same : the old problems, and the
old suspicions and rivalries. The ten years had greatly improved Mr. Upington's appearance. He was still young-looking,
with a light active figure, black hair and moustache, black eyes
with a genial lively expression, a well-set mouth with courage
and decision in the lines of it—a man who knew what he
thought right, and was not to be frightened out of his purpose.
To me he was frank and cordial ; he had not much time to
give me, and I had less ; so he spoke at once and freely on
the situation. He had been opposed, he said, to Sir Charles
Warren's expedition, because it could not fail to widen the
existing breach between the English and the Dutch ; and he
regretted that his proposals for Bechuanaland had not been
accepted. He said, and with evident sincerity, that the Dutch
as a body did not desire to break the connection with Great
Britain. He repeated what —— had said, that they could
not be independent, and that Germany, if they fell under
German influence, would not leave them as much political
liberty as they were allowed by England. It was in loyalty,
therefore, and not in disloyalty, that he deprecated our present
action. We could not hope to retain our influence in South

Africa under constitutional forms, if we persisted in disregard-
ing Dutch feeling, and an armed interference in opposition to
their avowed wishes was irritating and extremely dangerous.
He himself and the Presidents of the two Republics would do
their best to prevent a collision. They might not succeed.
Tempers on both sides were excited and inflammable. The
whole country was like a loaded magazine which an accidental
spark might kindle, and all South Africa would then be in a
blaze. But he trusted that the Boers would see that there
was no need of fighting. They had only to sit still. In that
case Sir Charles Warren would take possession of the disputed
territory without opposition. Plausible grounds might be
found for expelling nineteen or twenty Boer families who had
settled there. These would retire into the Transvaal, and
Sir Charles would then, if he pleased, fix the boundaries of
such part of Bechuanaland as he chose to occupy, and declare
it a Crown colony. A Crown colony it would have to be.
The Cape Parliament would decline to have anything to do
with a province so acquired except on their own conditions.
If we took it we must keep it and must govern it ourselves,
since no material existed out of which a local government
could be formed. The soil was too barren to invite colonisa-
tion ; the natives too poor and wretched to yield the smallest
revenue. A small garrison would be useless and would invite
attack ; we should therefore have to maintain a large one.
On those terms we could stay as long as we liked, but he pre-
sumed that the English taxpayer would tire in a few years of
so expensive an acquisition.

This was common sense, so obvious that the promoters of
the expedition could not have been blind to it. Their desire
was probably to promote a general war, provoke the Dutch
into striking the first blow, and force England to put out its
strength to crush them. I cannot believe that English
ministers had any such intention ; they had yielded to clamour
and done the least which they could be allowed to do ; but
none the less they have entered a road which must either end
in impotence or in the suppression of the constitution which,
when it suited us, we forced South Africa to accept.

The history of Ireland is repeating itself—as if Ireland was not enough. Spasmodic violence alternating with impatient dropping of the reins; first severity and then indulgence, and then severity again; with no persisting in any one system—a process which drives nations mad as it drives children, yet is inevitable in every dependency belonging to us which is not entirely servile, so long as it lies at the will and mercy of so uncertain a body as the British Parliament.

Of all persons connected with South African administration, the most to be pitied is Sir Hercules Robinson, the Governor, and I think he knows it and pities himself. He has been accused in England of having imperfectly supported Sir Charles Warren. When I was at Cape Town he was supposed to belong to the extreme war party, and to wish to see the question of Dutch or English supremacy fought out once for all in the field. Poor Sir Hercules! he is too upright a man to belong to any party, and therefore all in turn abuse him. He is simply an honourable English gentleman, endeavouring to do his duty in a position of divided responsibilities. He is the constitutional Governor of the Colony, and he is High Commissioner. As Governor of the Colony he has to be guided by his ministers, who are responsible to the Cape Parliament. As High Commissioner he has an undefined authority all over South Africa, extending even to the independent states, as protector of the native tribes. But, like the Amphictyonic Council, he has a voice only, without a force of any kind to carry his orders into effect; and for his conduct in this capacity he is responsible to his employers at home, to the English press, and to every dissatisfied member of the House of Commons who chooses to call him to account. As High Commissioner he has charge of the interests which Sir Charles Warren was sent to protect, yet Warren's command was made independent of him. If he pleased his responsible advisers, he would be rebuked by opinion at home If he threw himself into the quarrel on the English side, he would strain his relations with the Cape Parliament. If Warren's arrival had restored his consequence as British representative, it had aggravated the tension between himself and his ministry. He could if he pleased dismiss Mr. Upington, dissolve the legislature, and appeal to the colony ; but the effect could only be a larger majority, which would bring Mr. Upington back, and make his situation more difficult than ever. He explained his embarrassments most candidly when I called upon him. He said that they would perhaps be less if those who had the real power had the responsibility along with it. But the Dutch leaders held personally aloof, being content to dictate the policy which the ministers were to follow, without choosing to come personally into contact with himself. I left him with the most sincere compassion. No English colonial governor had ever been in a more cruel position, and perhaps none has ever acted with more prudence. I augured well from the stoic endurance which was written in his face. Good perhaps he would be unable to do, but at least he would not lend himself to evil.

I met afterwards one of those 'Dutch leaders' to whom he had referred—a cool, determined gentleman, with faultless temper and manners, who knew what he meant himself to do if no one else knew. The Dutch can abide their time and wait the issue of our blunders. President Kruger (President of the Transvaal) said to me in London, that every step which the English had taken in South Africa during the last twelve years had been what he would have himself recommended if he had wished the connection with England to be terminated, with the single exception of the admission of wrong which Lord Carnarvon had made to the Orange Free State, and the compensation which he had granted for the Diamond Fields. The effect of that concession had been to keep the Free State back when the Transvaal was fighting for its independence ; everything else had been what the most advanced Africander could have desired. I mentioned this to Mr. H——, the gentleman of whom I am speaking. He smiled ominously, as if he was himself of the same opinion. There was no likelihood of the exception being repeated.

I concluded from all that I heard that we have now but one hold left upon the South African Dutch, and that is their fear of the Germans. The efforts of their chiefs to prevent the peace from being broken have been successful. The Boers in Bechuanaland have retired from before Sir Charles Warren, who is in possession of his vast province, and is now asking what is to be done with it. The Cape Parliament has refused to annex it except on its own conditions, as the Premier said that it would refuse. No blood has been spilt, and no excuse has been given for a march upon Pretoria. The war party have not perhaps altogether abandoned hope. There is now a cry to drive the Boers out of Zululand, and this they will probably resist. If it comes to a war they will perhaps ask for German protection before they submit, and in some form or other they may perhaps obtain it. But they prize their individual freedom, and for this reason, if for no other, they will seek German aid only at the last extremity. If English Governments, if the English Parliament and press, will try to make the best of the Boers instead of the worst, if they can make up their minds to leave the Cape alone, as they leave Australia and Canada, the unfortunate country may breathe again ; and with their fine soil and climate and wealth of minerals and jewels, English, Dutch, Basutos, Caffres, and Zulus may bury the hatchet, and live and prosper side by side. Our interferences have been dictated by the highest motives ; but experience has told us, and ought to have taught us, that in what we have done, or tried to do, we have aggravated every evil which we most desired to prevent. We have conciliated neither person nor party. Native chiefs may profess to wish for our alliance, but they have not forgotten the Zulu war or the fate of Waterboer. We cannot afford to be permanently disinterested, and when they too turn round upon us, as they always have and always will, we shall have brought it to a point where white and coloured men alike of all races and all complexions will combine to ask us to take ourselves away.

This is the truth about South Africa. I, for my part, shall see it no more, and this book contains the last words which I shall ever write about it. The anchor is up in the ' Australasian,' the whistle screams, the bell rings to clear the ship of strangers ; we steam away in the summer twilight, the gray precipices of the mountain turning crimson in the glow of the sunset. We have added to our list of passengers some thirty English and Scotch, who are flying from a land which, like Ireland, seems lying under a curse. We are bound now for brighter and happier regions, beyond the shadow of English party factions. So far, I had been in waters that I knew ; we were entering now into the Southern Ocean, on the Great Circle, and into high latitudes and polar cold. Australia lies due east of the Cape, but our course from Cape Agulhas is south. The nearest road would lie through the South Pole and the great barriers of ice. This way there is no passage ; we are to keep within ' the roaring forties ; ' but though it is midsummer, and the nights are but two hours long, we are warned to prepare for the temperature of an English winter. The thick clothes must come out of our boxes again ; the fire will be relighted in the saloon ; we may fall in with icebergs and see snow upon our decks ; and then in three weeks we shall be again in tropical sunshine amidst grapes and flowers.

CHAPTER V.

The Indian Ocean—New Year's night at sea—Extreme cold—Wave and currents—The albatross—Passengers' amusements—Modern voyages—The 'Odyssey'—Spiritual truth—Continued cold at midsummer.

If cold weather lay before us we had not yet reached it. After a brilliant sunset the sky clouded, and wind came up from the west. The air was thick and close ; the sea rose, the ports were shut, and as the waves washed over the deck, the skylights were battened down. I tried the deck myself, but was driven back by the wet. The saloon, when I went down again, smelt of dead rats or other horrors. I took shelter in the deck-house, and lay there on a bench till morning, snatching such patches of sleep as were to be caught under such conditions. It continued wild all next day, but the temperature cooled and brought back life and freshness. This was the last day of the year, and at midnight the crew rang in its successor. All the bells in the ship were set swinging ; the

cook's boys clanked the pots and pans; the emigrants sang
choral songs. The exact moment could not be hit. Time is
'made' at midday, and remains fixed, so far as man can fix it,
for four-and-twenty hours. In itself it varies, of course, with
every second of longitude. 1885, however, had arrived for
practical purposes. I slept when the noise was over as I had
not slept for months, till late into the morning. 'Adsit
omen,' I said to myself; 'here is the new year. May I and
those belonging to me pass through it without sin!' As a
book for the occasion as a spiritual bath after the squalor
of Capo politics, I read Pindar, the purest of all the Greek
poets, of the same order with Phidias and Praxiteles, and as
perfect an artist in words as they in marble. Hard he is, as
the quartz rock in which the gold is embedded; but when you
can force your way into his meaning, it is like glowing fire.
His delight is in the noble qualities which he can find in man,
and of all the basenesses which disfigure man he hates φθόνος,
'envy,' the worst: as admiration of excellence is the finest
part of our nature, so envy and the desire to depreciate excellence Pindar holds to be the meanest. Great souls, he says,
dwell only with what is good, and do not stoop to quarrel with
its opposite. The backbiting tongue waits upon illustrious
actions, soiling what is bright and beautiful, and giving honour
to the low. But he prays that his tongue may not be like
any of these; and he desires that when he dies he may leave
his children a name unstained. He has no complainings or
gloomy speculations. Life to him is a beautiful thing, to be
enjoyed as in the presence of the gods who made it—a wholesome doctrine, good to read in doubtful or desponding hours.
'If,' he says, 'a man has wealth and fortune and can add to
these honour, let him be content and aspire to no more. Let
him feast in peace and listen to the music of song. Let the
voice rise beside the goblet; let him mingle the cup, the sweet
inspirer of hymns of praise, and pass round the child of the
vine in bowls of silver twined with wreaths woven out of
righteousness.' We, too, on board the 'Australasian,' had not
been without our orgies and inspiring draughts. One of the
emigrants at our New Year's festival, a Mrs. ——, a Mænad

with flashing eyes, and long, black, snaky hair, had plunged
through the ship, whisky-bottle in hand, distributing drams.
Her catches certainly were not hymns of praise; her bowl
was not wreathed with righteousness; and the dame herself,
though in Corybantian frenzy, was redolent of Billingsgate.
From Pindar to Mrs. —— was a long road in the progress of
the species; but she did what she could, poor woman, to cele-
brate the occasion.

Fellow-passengers in a ship soon become intimate. Meeting hour after hour in a small space, and sitting at the same
table, they pass first into acquaintance and then into fami-
liarity. They like to have some one to talk to, and communicate freely their adventures and their purposes. Among those
who had joined us at the Cape, there was a gentleman who
was really interesting to me. He had been thirteen years at
the Diamond Fields, had witnessed all its distractions, had
made some kind of fortune, and was now flying from South
Africa as from a country past saving. He filled gaps in my
own information with many details; but they all set in one
direction. He told me nothing which at all affected my already
formed opinions.

When we had been three days out the weather rapidly
cooled. The temperature of the water sank to within ten
degrees of freezing. When we were in 45° south—the latitude corresponding to Bordeaux—we saw no actual ice, but
ice could not have been far from us. We shivered in the
saloon in spite of the fire; we piled blankets over ourselves at
night, and took our walks on deck in our heaviest ulsters.
From winter to the heat of a forcing house, from the tropics
back into winter, and then again into the tropics, are transi-
tions but of a few days in these days of swift steamers, and
are less trying than one might have expected. The Great
Circle course from the Cape to Australia is adopted chiefly to
shorten the distance, but it has another invaluable advantage
to sailing vessels which are bound eastward; for between
latitude 40° and the ice of the South Pole a steady draught
of air from the west blows perennially all through the year
and all round the globe. It may shift a point or two to north

of west or south, but west it always is, never sinking below what we call a stiff breeze, and rising often to a gale or half a gale, and constantly therefore there is a heavy sea, nearly a thousand miles broad, rolling round the earth from west to east. The waves were magnificent : I believe the highest ever fallen in with are in these latitudes. Vessels for Australia under sail alone accomplish often 300 miles a day on the course on which we were going. If they are bound west they keep within the tropics, which these winds do not reach. To steam in their teeth would be impossible, even for the most powerful ships afloat. It struck me that a series of enormous waves for ever moving in one direction over so large a part of the earth's surface might in some degree counteract the force which is supposed to be slowly stopping the rotation of our planet. The earth turning under the moon generates the tidal wave, which, as the earth's rotation is from west to east, moves itself from east to west. A certain resistance is thus set up which, within a vast but still calculable period will check the rotation altogether, and earth and moon will wheel on together through space, the earth turning the same face to the moon, as the moon does now to the earth. Long before this consummation is reached the human race must have ceased to exist, so that the condition matters little to us to which this home of ours is eventually to be reduced ; but in the system of nature many forces are in operation which have threatened to make an end of us, but which are found to be neutralised by some counterbalancing check. Waves propagated steadily in any direction create a current ; and these great waves in the Southern Ocean, for ever moving in the opposite direction to the tidal wave, may at least so far counteract it as to add a few million years to the period during which the earth will be habitable.

From the Cape to Australia the distance is 6,000 miles, or a quarter of the circumference of the globe. Our speed was thirteen knots an hour, and we were attended by a bodyguard of albatrosses, Cape hens, and sea-hawks—the same birds, so the sailors said, following the ship without resting, all the way. I know not whether this be so, or how the fact has been ascertained. One large gull is very like another, and the islands in the middle of the passage are their principal breeding-places. Anyway, from fifty to a hundred of them were round us at sunrise, round us when night fell, and with us again in the morning. They are very beautiful in the great ocean solitude. One could have wished that Coleridge had seen an albatross on the wing before he wrote the 'Ancient Mariner,' that the grace of the motion might have received a sufficient description. He wheels in circles round and round, and for ever round, the ship—now far behind, now sweeping past in a long rapid curve, like a perfect skater on an untouched field of ice. There is no effort ; watch as closely as you will, you rarely or never see a stroke of the mighty pinion. The flight is generally near the water, often close to it. You lose sight of the bird as he disappears in the hollow between the waves, and catch him again as he rises over the crest ; but how he rises and whence comes the propelling force is to the eye inexplicable ; he alters merely the angle at which the wings are inclined ; usually they are parallel to the water and horizontal ; but when he turns to ascend or makes a change in his direction the wings then point at an angle, one to the sky, the other to the water. Given a power of resistance to the air, and the air itself will do the rest, just as a kite flies ; but how without exertion is the resistance caused ? However it be, the albatross is a grand creature. To the other birds, and even to the ship itself, he shows a stately indifference, as if he had been simply ordered to attend its voyage as an aerial guardian, but disdained to interest himself further.

The Cape hen is an inferior brute altogether. He, too, is large. One that flew on board us was seven feet across the wings. He is brown, hungry-looking, with a powerful hooked beak, and there is no romance in his reasons for pursuing us. So bold is he that he sweeps past the stern within reach of a stick, looking on the water for any scraps which the cook's mate may throw overboard, and glaring on crew and passengers with a blue, cruel eye, as if he would like to see them overboard as well, and to have a chance of making his breakfast upon them. Besides these, Mother Carey's chickens skimmed over the water like swallows, with other small varieties of gull. The passengers' chief anxiety was to shoot these creatures, not that they could make any use of them, for the ship could not be stopped that they might be picked up, not entirely to show their skill, for if they had been dead things drifting in the wind they would not have answered the purpose, nor entirely, I suppose, from a love of killing, for ordinary men are not devils, but from some combination of motives difficult to analyse. The feathers of the large birds were too thick for the shot to penetrate. My acquaintance from the Diamond Fields had a rifle and emptied case after case of cartridges at them, for the most part in vain. A dancing platform to stand on, and an object moving sixty miles an hour, are not favourable to ball practice. One albatross, I am sorry to say, was hit at last. It fell wounded into the water, and in a moment the whole cannibal flock was tearing it to pieces—not a pleasant sight ; but how about the human share in it ? The birds were eating their brother, but after all it was for food ; wild animals never kill for sport. Man is the only one to whom the torture and death of his fellow-creatures is amusing in itself.

I heard Cardinal Manning once say that there could be no moral obligation on the part of man to the lower animals, he having a soul and they none. He was speaking of vivisection and condemning it, but on the ground not that it was unjust to the dogs and horses, but that it demoralised the operators. Our passengers, I suppose, would have taken the risk of being demoralised. Being lords of the creation they were doing as they pleased with their own.

> He prayeth well who loveth well
> Both man and bird and beast ;
> He prayeth best who loveth best
> All things both great and small,
> For the dear God who loveth us
> He made and loveth all.

So says Coleridge. We admire and quote—but we hunt and shoot notwithstanding. We have a right to kill for our dinners ; we have a right perhaps to kill for entertainment, if we please to use it ; but why do we find killing so agreeable?

The days went rapidly by. The cold might be unpleasant, but it was wholesome ; we were all ' well '—how much lies in that word !—but we had no adventures. We passed St. Paul's Island and Kerguelen Island, one to the south, the other to the north, but saw neither. The great ocean steamers are not driven into port by stress of weather, but go straight upon their way. Voyages have thus lost their romance. No Odyssey is possible now, no ' Sindbad the Sailor,' no ' Robinson Crusoe,' not even a ' Gulliver's Travels,' only a Lady Brassey's Travels. The steam boiler and the firm blades of the screw are stronger than the elements. We have yoked horses of fire to our sea-chariots ; the wire-imprisoned lightning carries our messages round the globe, swifter than Ariel ; the elemental forces themselves are our slaves, and slaves, strange to say, of the meanest as well as of the noblest, as the genius of the lamp became the slave of the African magician. What, after all, have these wonderful achievements done to elevate human nature? Human nature remains as it was. Science grows, but morality is stationary, and art is vulgarised. Not here lie the things ' necessary to salvation,' not the things which can give to human life grace, or beauty, or dignity.

Mankind, it seems, are equal to but one thing at a time. Dispositions change, but the eras as they pass bequeath to us their successive legacies. Though the conditions of an Odyssey are gone for ever, it was, it is, and cannot cease to be, and of all reading is the most delightful at sea. I had tried to combine Homer and Shakespeare, reading them alternately. But they would not mix. The genius was different. Shakespeare interprets to us our own time and our own race. The Odyssey is a voice out of an era that is finished, and is linked to ours only by the identity of humanity. Man is the same at heart, and the sea is the same, and the fresh salt breeze breathes through its lines. I escaped from the gull-shooting to my cabin sofa, back into the old world and the adventures of the Ithacan prince. A fairy tale we should now call it, but it was no fairy tale to those who listened, or

to those who sang the story. When Ulysses tells Alcinous of
his descent into hell, the old king does not smile over it as
at a dream. 'Thou resemblest not,' he answers, 'a cheat or
a deceiver, of whom the earth contains so many—rogues who
trade in lies. Σοὶ δ' ἔπι μὲν μορφὴ ἐπέων. Thy words have
form, and thy brain has sense. Thou tellest thy experience
like a bard.' Where were the lines which divided truth from
falsehood in the mind of Alcinous? The words of Ulysses
had *form*. Lies of the accursed sort have no form, and cannot be shaped into form. Organic form is possible only when
there is life, and so the problem returns which so often haunts
us. What is truth? The apple falls by gravitation. Whether
Newton ever watched an apple fall and drew his inference in
consequence, has nothing to do with the universal reality
which remains unaltered if the rest is a legend. The story of
the apple is the shell. The truth is in the kernel or thing
signified. Sacred history, in like manner, busy only to convey spiritual truth, is careless as Alcinous of inquiring into
fact. It takes fact or legend or whatever comes to hand, and
weaves it into form. The beauty of the form, and the spirit
which animates the form, are the guarantees of truth and
carry their witness in themselves. Thus we are rid for ever of
critical controversies. The spirit is set free from the letter,
and we can breathe and believe in peace. Too good news to
be true! Perhaps so. In a long voyage, where we can do nothing but read and reflect, such thoughts come like shadows
upon water when it is untouched by the breeze. The air ruffles
it again and they are gone. 'We shall know all about it in
another and a better world,' as the American storekeeper said,
when so many shots were fired and no one was hit.

κακὸν ἀνεμώλια βάζειν.
It is ill to speak windy words.

The cold weather persevered, even after we had left 'the
forties' again and turned north. The temperature of the
water would not rise; the icy currents flow right on to the
great Australian bight, and there is no sense of warmth till
the air comes heated off the land. The wind being behind

us, the deck was tolerable, as there was no draught. The
ports were kept closed because of the swell ; but the fire and
a windsail kept the cabins fresh. We were well provided
for every way, but the sameness of day after day became
monotonous. The forward passengers drove the time away
with cards, the cabin passengers with backgammon. At each
noon there was an excitement to know where we were, and
there was a raffle over the number of miles which the ship
had run since the noon preceding. The Cape emigrants interested me more and more. They all seemed of opinion that
the Dutch meant to try conclusions with us on the first fair
opportunity, and that the Caffres, Zulus, and all the warlike
tribes would be found on their side. The English reader may
think it strange ; to them it did not seem strange at all. We
were growing weary, however, every one of us, and counting
the hours before we should hear the cry of land.

By the middle of January the cold slightly relaxed. The
sun shone with unusual warmth, and tempted us to lay off our
overcoats. We could venture into the bath in the mornings
again. For many nights it had been cloudy, but now the sky
again cleared. The nebula in Orion shone like a patch of the
Milky Way. The black chasm at the south-west angle of the
Southern Cross showed blacker from the contrast, the more
brilliant the stars. So black it was that one would have
called it a passing cloud ; but the clouds went and came, and
the inky spot remained unchanged, an opening into the awful
solitude of unoccupied space.

At length the last day came. In a few hours we were to
sight Kangaroo Island. Books were packed away, and preparations made to leave—my last reading was ' Œdipus
Coloneus,' the most majestic of all the Greek plays. Human
imagination has conceived nothing grander, nothing so grand,
as the mysterious disappearance of the blind old king, the
voice calling him to come which no mortal lips had uttered,
the sight which only Theseus was allowed to look on, and
Theseus, shading his eyes with his hand before a scene too
awful to be described. It was the highest point achieved by
the Greek branch of Adam's race The Australians, among

whom I was so soon to find myself, were the latest development of the same family. Among them there would be no Œdipus, no Theseus, no Sophocles, yet whatever has come out of man has its root in man's nature ; and, if progress was not a dream, who could say what future of intellectual greatness might not yet lie before a people whose national life was still in its infancy ?

CHAPTER VI.

First sight of Australia—Bay of Adelaide—Sunday morning—The harbour master—Go on shore—The port—Houses—Gardens—Adelaide city—The public gardens—Beauty of them—New acquaintances—The Australian magpie—The laughing jackass—Interviewers—Talk of Confederation—Sail for Melbourne—Aspect of the coast—Williamstown.

FROM the Cape to Australia—from political discord, the conflict of races, the glittering uniforms and the tramp of battalions—from intrigue and faction, and the perpetual interference of the Imperial Government, to a country where politics are but differences of opinion, where the hand of the Imperial Government is never felt, where the people are busy with their own affairs, and the harbours are crowded with ships, and the quays with loading carts, and the streets with men, where everyone seems occupied, and everyone at least moderately contented—the change is great indeed. The climate is the same. The soil, on the average, is equal ; what Australia produces, South Africa produces with equal freedom. In Australia, too, there is a mixture of races—English, Germans, and Chinese ; yet in one all is life, vigour, and harmony ; the other lies blighted, and every effort for its welfare fails. What is the explanation of so vast a difference ? One is a free colony, the other is a conquered country. One is a natural and healthy branch from the parent oak, left to grow as nature prompts it, and bearing its leaves and acorns at its own impulse. No bands or ligaments impede the action of the vital force. The parent tree does not say to it, You shall grow in this shape, and not in that ; but leaves it to choose its own. Thus it spreads and enlarges its girth, and roots itself each year more firmly in the stem from which it has sprung. The Cape, to keep to the same simile, is a branch doing its best to thrive, but withering from the point where it joins the trunk, as if at that spot some poison was infecting it. It is pleasant to turn from shadow to sunshine, from a gangrene in the body politic of Oceana to a country where the eye sees something fresh to please on whichever side it turns, where the closest acquaintance only brings out more distinctly how happy, how healthy English life can be in this far off dependency. We were bound for Melbourne and Sydney, but the first point at which we were to touch was Adelaide, named after William the Fourth's queen, the capital of South Australia. We passed Kangaroo Island before dawn on January 18, thirty-nine days after leaving Plymouth. January there corresponds to our July, and when we anchored it was on a soft warm summer morning.

The bay of Adelaide is a long broad estuary, with a small river running into it behind a sandbank, which forms a port like the harbour at Calais. The broad Murray falls into the sea at no great distance to the westward; but is cut off from Adelaide by a line of mountains, and loses itself in shoals and sand before it reaches the ocean. The site for the town was chosen on the only spot upon the coast where vessels have a safe basin in which to load alongside a wharf. The town itself is seven miles inland in a hollow below the hills. The port, which is growing fast into a second city, is connected with it by a railway and by an almost unbroken series of villas. Adelaide is not more than fifty years old. It grew first into consequence through the Burra Burra copper-mine—a hill of virgin metal, which was brought there by sea and smelted. Burra Burra is worked out, and mine and smelting furnaces lie deserted; but Adelaide has found a safer basis for prosperity, and is the depôt of an enormous corn and wool district with which it is connected by arterial railways. Five years ago South Australia had between two and three million acres under the plough. There has been again a further increase. The crops are light, but the grain is of peculiar excellence,

We dropped anchor at breakfast-time. The bay was shallow, and we were a mile and a half from the shore. In front of us were long lines of houses, churches, towers, big hotels, and warehouses ; wooden jetties ran far out into the sea, and across the sandbank were forests of masts, where ships were riding in the river behind. The land seemed level for ten or twelve miles inwards, and in the background rose a range of mountains looking brown and bare from the heat, but clothed at intervals with heavy masses of timber, and divided by ravines which in the winter are copious watercourses.

The wheat had been cut, and the fields, which three months earlier had been green as an English meadow, looked as arid as Castile. It was Sunday and all was quiet. A steam launch came off, bringing a port official, a rough-spoken but good-natured gentleman, who took me in charge. Our stay was to be brief : he undertook that I should make the best use of the time which the captain could allow. He had been out fishing with the Controller of the Customs when we hove in sight. They had caught a bream or two and a mackerel or two, one of these like the mackerel of the Channel ; the other, which I cannot find in the book of Australian fish, a mackerel evidently, from the tail, the skin, and the opal tints, but short, broad, and shaped like a tench. They saw us coming and had hauled their anchor to be ready for us. The first thing that struck me—and the impression remained during all my stay in Australia—was the pure English that was spoken there. They do not raise the voice at the end of a sentence, as the Americans do, as if with a challenge to differ from them. They drop it courteously like ourselves. No provincialism has yet developed itself. The tone is soft, the language good, the aspirates in the right places. My friend talked fast about all sorts of things on our way to the pier. When we landed he took me first to his house adjoining it—a sort of bungalow, with a garden, and a few trees to keep off the heat. He produced a bottle of Australian hock, light and pleasantly flavoured, with some figs and apricots. We then walked out, to look about us under the shade of our umbrellas. There were cottages and villas everywhere ; the business people in the city bringing their families to the sea in the hot weather for bathing. They were low, generally of one story, shaded with large india-rubber trees, the fronts festooned with bougainvillæas, the hedges of purple tamarisk, and the small garden bright with oleanders and scarlet geraniums. After walking for a mile we reached the port. Thirty years ago the spot where it stands was a mud swamp. Piles were driven in ; stone, gravel, earth, and shingle were laid on in tens of thousands of tons. The area was raised above the tideway, made firm and dry, and is now laid out in broad quays, and covered with broad handsome streets and terraces. The harbour was full of ships : great steamers, great liners, coasting schooners, ships of all sorts. Among them a frigate newly painted, and seeming to be intended rather for show than use, like a suit of armour with no one inside it. My guide growled out, 'There is our harbour defence ship, which the English Government insists on our maintaining. It is worth nothing, and never will be. Our naval defences cost us 25,000*l.* a year. We should pay the 25,000*l.* to the Admiralty, and let them do the defence for us. They can manage such things better than we can.' This seemed likely to be true ; and I heard more of it afterwards, as will be told in its place.

After looking round the port, we stepped into the railway station. Being Sunday and a holiday, there was a crowd of clerks on their way to the town, and the carriages were rapidly filling. We found seats in one of them along with half-a-dozen young lads, very English in look and manner, not lean and sun-dried, but fair, fleshy, lymphatic, and fresh-coloured ; for the rest, well-dressed, good-natured, and easy-going, all with pipes in their mouths, all polite and well-mannered. The fields on each side of the line were as brown as the Sahara, but wheat crops had been reaped upon them a month before. When the rain came they would grow green again ; and even, burnt up as they were, cattle and sheep were grazing in the stubble. We ran along through an avenue of stone pines, which had been planted eight years back, and were now handsome trees. You could see how fertile the soil would be if continually irrigated, by the country houses which were buried in foliage.

There needs but a great reservoir in the mountains, such as they have made for Melbourne, and the plain of Adelaide might be as the gardens of Ephraim.

We rose slightly from the sea, and at the end of the seven miles we saw below us in a basin, with the river winding through it, a city of a hundred and fifty thousand inhabitants, not one of whom has ever known, or will know, a moment's anxiety as to the recurring regularity of his three meals a day.

Adelaide is already a large child for its years. Its streets are laid out in anticipation of a larger future—broad, bold, and ambitious. Public buildings, law courts, Parliament house, are on the grand scale. Churches of all denominations are abundant and handsome—symptoms all of a people well-to-do, and liking to have an exterior worthy of them. It was busy England over again, set free from limitations of space. There were the same faces, the same voices, the same shops and names on them ; the same advertisements making hideous wall and hoarding, the same endless variety of church, chapel, and meeting-house. I asked my guide what a building was, a little different from the rest. 'Another way to heaven,' he answered impatiently. The Governor being absent, and being without acquaintances in Adelaide or time to form any, I had no calls to pay. We hired a carriage and drove round the environs ; and then, as it was midday and hot, we went for shelter to the Botanical Gardens.

It was my first experience of the success of the Australian municipalities in this department. Whether it be the genius of the country, or some development of the sense of beauty from the general easiness of life, or the readiness of soil and climate to respond to exertion, certain it is that the public gardens in the Australian towns are the loveliest in the world, and that no cost is spared in securing the services of the most eminent horticulturists. The custodian at Adelaide, Dr. Schomberg, has a worldwide reputation, and he is allowed free scope for his art. Ornament is more considered than profit, and flowers and flowering shrubs than fruit trees. He follows Goethe's rule in taking care of the beautiful, and leaving the useful to take care of itself. I was sorry to miss

Dr. Schomberg; we looked for him at his house, but he was absent. The gardens not being open to the public on Sundays till the afternoon, we had them to ourselves, and could wander at leisure. Trees from all parts of the world are gathered together in that one spot, of the rarest kinds. The flowers with which we are familiar as exotics in our forcing-houses luxuriate as in their natural home. The oleander towers and spreads in pale pink glory. The crimson hibiscus glows among the bananas ; passion-flowers—blue, purple, and scarlet—hang in careless festoons among the branches. The air is loaded with perfume from datura, orange-flowers, stephanotis, and endless varieties of jessamine. Araucarias, acacia-trees, Norfolk Island pines, tulip-trees, &c., are dispersed over the lawns, grouped, not as science would order them, but as they would be arranged by a landscape painter. Avenues of dense evergreens, the Moreton-bay fig-tree conspicuous among them, invite you under their shade. I missed two things only : for our delicate grass there is buffalo-grass, whose coarse fibre no care in mowing can conceal ; worse than that was the water—there was a pond on which Dr. Schomberg had done all which his art could accomplish with water-lilies white, pink, and blue, swans black and white, and particoloured ducks and geese ; the banks were fringed with weeping willows growing to the dimensions of vast forest trees ; but the water itself was liquid mud, so dirty that the pure blue of the sky turned brown when reflected on it. Such is the nature of the rivers and pools in that country, and such it must remain till the engineers have made dams across the mountain valleys, and preserved the rain as it falls from heaven, in artificial lakes. All in good time : even Australians cannot do everything at once.

Thanks to my guide I had seen the outside of Adelaide; the inside, the ways and characters of the men who had made it, I had no leisure to see. An interviewer found me out, and fired questions into me which I had no inclination to answer ; so we made our way to the station again, and in half an hour were sheltered at our friend's bungalow, with a handsome luncheon before us. The home of his fishing companion of the morning—the Controller of the Customs—was a few yards distant. Luncheon over, I was taken across, to be introduced. I found an agreeable and intelligent gentleman in an airy room with cool mats instead of carpets, opening into a verandah, where his ladies were engaged over the national five-o'clock tea. We were 12,000 miles from England; yet we were in England still, and England at its best, so far as I could gather from the conversation. The Controller showed me his curiosities, his fish which he had caught in the morning, his garden, his poultry-yard, and his aviary, in which last I made two acquaintances with whom I afterwards grew into more intimacy. The first was the Australian magpie—a magpie certainly, with the same green, cunning eye, the same thievish nature, the same mottled coat; the difference between him and our magpie being that he has no long tail, that he is rather larger, and that, instead of the harsh cry of his European relation, he has the sweetest voice of all Australian birds, a low crooning but exquisitely melodious gurgle, which he intensely enjoys. A dozen of them will gather in a tree together and hold a long morning concert. My second new acquaintance was a much stranger being—the laughing jackass of the forest. This creature may be a piece of metamorphosed humanity, so subtle is his humour, so like a spoilt child he is in many of his ways. He is the size of a crow with the shape of a jay, and is of a greenish-brown colour. His throat is thick, his beak large and strong, and in the woods his chief amusement is to seize hold of snakes and bite their heads off. This is a human trait in him, as if he knew something about our first mother's misfortune. And he has no shyness about him. He willingly exchanges his liberty for good quarters in a yard or on a lawn, and likes well to have human beings about him. He knows his master and mistress, knows what they say to him, knows what he is expected to do, and if he doesn't choose, which is usually the case, he is as determined as a naughty boy not to do it. His laugh is exactly like a man's—not the genial sort, but malicious and mocking. He was told to laugh, that I might hear him. Not a note would he utter. He was rebuked, taken in hand, and admonished. No laugh came from him, nor can I construe literally the words which he used in reply; but it was perfectly clear to me that he was swearing worse than a Spanish muleteer, and he went through his whole vocabulary before he would stop.

In the club garden at Melbourne I had afterwards another chance of observing the temper of these curious birds. A jackass lived there, with a wing clipped, to keep him out of mischief. He used to march up and down on the grass, chat with the members as they sat in the verandah with their newspapers, and was a universal favourite for his wit and readiness. One day, as I was alone there, I saw my friend sunning himself under a wall, and I walked up to talk to him. He liked generally to have his head scratched, as parrots do, so I tried to ingratiate myself in this way. He affected to be bored, submitting with an indifferent languid air, as if telling me that he cared nothing about me and would much prefer to be let alone. A cat who had been basking in the distance observed what was going on, and seeing how ungraciously my advances were received, came sloping over and pushed her head into my hand, intimating that she at least would like to be stroked very well. It was delightful to see the jackass. His wicked little eye flashed; he glanced at the cat, went for her with his beak, and drove her off the field.

I had a pleasant conversation with the Controller and his family, who had many questions to ask about 'home' and what was going on there. I would gladly have stayed longer; but the evening was wearing on and I was obliged to return to the ship. On the jetty, before I could reach the launch, I was fairly captured by an interviewer and put through my paces. Another came alongside at midnight and insisted on seeing me, but was warned off by the kind care of the watch on deck. They wanted my opinions on the federation of the Australian Colonies with one another, on the federation of the whole of them with the mother country,—most of all, on the sudden squall which had blown up since we left England over the German occupation of part of New Guinea, and the supposed delinquencies of the Colonial Minister. Of the latter I knew nothing, and had never heard of them. On federation of either kind I had come to learn the opinions of the Colonists, not to offer opinions of my own. Such views as I had myself formed were tentative and provisional, subject to correction in every detail by fuller information. Earnestly desirous I was and always had been to see a united Oceana - united as closely as the American States are united—but of how the union was to be brought about I had not a notion which I did not hold with the utmost diffidence, and I was particularly unwilling to set my crude ideas flying in the newspapers. I evaded my cross questioners as well as I could, and I regretted afterwards the few humble sentiments which I allowed to be drawn out of me. However, as I found eventually, the good people meant no harm. Their object generally seemed to be the same as my own. I had nothing to complain of, except a curiosity which, in itself, was innocent enough.

We sailed for Melbourne the next morning, where we intended to land finally and remain. The day was still bright; the sea blue-green in the shallow water. The albatrosses had left us : we were attended now by flights of the small, beautifully white Australian gull. The coast was generally bold, but it opened at intervals into wooded valleys with sandy beaches, where were solitary cottages of fishermen who supplied the Adelaide market. The fish are not of the highest order, but good enough and abundant. Oysters were everywhere ; no crabs or lobsters, but crayfish in plenty, which are an excellent substitute. We passed a point where a steamer had been lately run ashore. The captain, I was told, had been agitated by having an English duke on board, and had not been entirely himself. When we drew clear of the islands the character of the rocks altered, and the coast became like the coast of Suffolk—low perpendicular cliffs of pale brown sandstone, which was unequally yielding to the unresting wash of the waves, and was shaped by light and shadow into buttresses and bastions. Behind the crags the land was green and undulating, and extremely rich. They call it the Potato Land ; all the Australian sea-towns are supplied from it.

One more night, and the day following was the last of our

voyage, the finish of an undisturbed six weeks, the sea all round me, and the blue sky by day and the stars by night over my head, and the fresh clean breezes to blow away dust and care. I hope I was properly grateful for so blessed a relief. A few more hours and we were to bid adieu to the 'Australasian,' her light-souled but good and clever captain, her ever kind and attentive officers. She had carried us safely *down under*, as the Square gardener put it to me afterwards in London, scarcely able to believe it could be reality. I was asleep when we passed between the 'Heads' at Port Phillip, and was only conscious of the change from the long ocean roll outside to the calm of the great bay. When I woke and went on deck we were alongside the wharf at Williamstown, with Melbourne straight before us five miles off, and the harbour reaching all the way to it. In my life I have never been more astonished. Adelaide had seemed a great thing to me, but Melbourne was a real wonder. Williamstown is the port, from which vessels outward bound take their departure. The splendid docks there were choked with ships loading and unloading. Huge steamers—five, six, or seven thousand tons —from all parts of the world, were lying round us or beside us. In the distance we saw the smoke of others. Between us and the city there seemed scarcely to be room for the vessels anchored there ; from their masthead or stern the English flag blowing out proud and free, and welcoming us to Australia as to a second home. Steam launches, steam ferry-boats, tugs, coasting steamers were flying to and fro, leaving behind them, alas ! black volumes of smoke, through which the city loomed large as Liverpool. The smoke is a misfortune. The Sydney coal, cheap as it is, and excellent for all useful purposes, is fuliginous beyond any coal I have fallen in with, and on windless mornings, like that on which we arrived, a black cloud envelops harbour and town. But it is seldom thus, and there is generally a breeze. Even the smoke itself means business, life, energy ; and along the shore for miles and miles rose the villas and plantations of the Melbourne magnates—suburban, unromantic, but all the more reminding one of England, and telling of wealth and enjoyment.

CHAPTER VII.

Landing at Melbourne—First impression of the city—Sir Henry Loch—Government House—Party assembled there—Agitation about New Guinea—The Monroe doctrine in the Pacific—Melbourne gardens—Victorian Society—The Premier—Federation, local and imperial—The Astronomer Royal—The Observatory—English institutions reproduced—Proposed tour in the Colony —Melbourne amusements—Music—The theatre—Sunday at Melbourne— Night at the Observatory.

WE landed at our leisure at Williamstown, from which a railway train was to take us to the city. We were in no hurry, for the day was still early, and we had no plans, save to find an hotel in the course of it. A 'nigger,' who must have weighed thirty stone, wheeled our luggage to the station in a hand cart. As at Adelaide, I was impressed by the good English and good manners of the station officials. There was an American smartness about them, but it was American with a difference. Something might be due to the climate. Manners soften of themselves where tempers are never ruffled by cold. The line makes a long circuit by the shore ; we had ten miles to go. The fields were inclosed all the way with the Australian rails one hears riding men talk about—heavy timbers four feet and a half or five feet high. Clusters of wooden houses were sprinkled about, growing thicker as we advanced, and painted white to keep off the sun. Gardens and flowers were, as usual, universal. Melbourne station was, like other metropolitan stations in the world, vast, crowded, and unbeautiful. Again some ingenuity was needed to escape the newspaper people ; we extricated ourselves only at last by a promise of future submission, and got away in a cab with our luggage. I was disappointed, after Adelaide, with the first appearance of the streets. Melbourne is twice as large, and many times more than twice as rich. The population of it is 300,000, who are as well off as any equal number of people in the whole world. But the city has grown hastily, and carries the signs of it on the surface. The streets are broad. There are splendid single buildings : Town Hall, University, Parliament-

G

houses, public offices, besides banks, exchanges, and again churches, &c. There are superb shops too, gorgeous as any in London or Paris. But side by side with them you see houses little better than sheds. People have built as they could, and as their means allowed them, and they have been too busy to study appearances. But they have boundless wealth, and as boundless ambition and self-confidence. They are proud of themselves and of what they have done, and will soon polish up their city when they can look about them at their leisure.

At the hotel to which we were taken we found a message that we were not to remain there, but were expected at Government House. I had already a slight acquaintance with Sir Henry and Lady Loch—an acquaintance which I was delighted to think that I should improve into intimacy, while, as the Governor's guest, I should see everyone that I wished to see. I said there could be no Odyssey now, but Sir Henry Loch has passed through at least one adventure which Ulysses might have been told in Alcinous's hall, and to which the Phæacian youth would have listened with burning interest. He had been a prisoner in the Chinese war, sentenced to be executed, and taken out every morning for a fortnight in the belief that he was to be killed then and there—a unique experience, enough in itself to have killed most men without the executioner's assistance. The composure with which he had borne the trial marked him as an exceptional person. He was taken into the public service, and had been made at last Governor of the Isle of Man, where he ruled long as the constitutional sovereign of a singular people, and achieved the highest success nowadays possible—the success of being never spoken of outside his dominions. His Manx subjects had been devoted to him ; his reign lasted fifteen years ; he had been like a Greek βασιλεύς, *pater patriæ*, or father of his people ; and when the authorities in Downing Street began to feel that they must change their ways with the colonies and raise the quality of the governors, he had been selected to preside over Victoria—a choice most commendable, for a fitter man could not have been found. There was a time when men were selected to represent their sovereign in the colonies for other reasons than fitness. I am an old man now, and my memory goes a long way back. I remember asking a noble duke why Lord —— had been made governor of a certain colony. He answered, 'Because he is a bankrupt peer.' 'They asked me,' the duke continued, 'whether I would undertake such a thing. I said I was not qualified ; I was still solvent.' Now of course under our reformed Parliament such appointments are impossible. Sir Henry Loch at Melbourne is a fit representative of the better order of things.

Government House stands in a commanding position on a high wooded plateau a mile from the town on the opposite side of the Yarra, overlooking the park and the river valley. In the great days of the gold digging, when Victoria was first rising into consequence, and the State had not settled into its saddle, no official residence could be provided for the Governor, and the Colony had munificently allowed, I believe, 15,000*l.* a year, out of which he was to furnish himself as he pleased. When the parliamentary constitution was conceded, a more dignified arrangement was resolved upon, better suited to the Colony's ambitions. An architect was selected, a site was chosen, and the architect, as I heard the story, was directed to produce a plan. He sketched a Gothic construction, which was wisely disapproved as out of character with the climate. The minister of public works asked to look at his book of designs. On the first page was Osborne. 'Something like that,' the minister said, 'on a scale slightly reduced ; ' and the result was the present palace, for such it is—not a very handsome building, in some aspects even ugly, but large and imposing. There is a tower in the centre of it a hundred and fifty feet high, on which waves the Imperial flag. There are the due lodges, approaches, porticoes, vast reception rooms, vast official dining-room and drawing-room, and the biggest ballroom in the world, all on a scale with the pride of the aspiring little State, with the private part of the house divided off by doors and passages, and having its own separate entrance. The expense was great, and the Governor was the principal sufferer. The big ball-room and the accompanying entertainments are a heavy demand on his now reduced allowance.

We found Sir Henry surrounded by his aides-de-camp,
among whom were two young aristocrats sent to study colonial
institutions under him ; and a house full of distinguished
visitors, among whom was E——, a Scotch representative
peer, quiet, humorous, sensible, slightly scornful as you began
to see when you knew him better, and rather proud of being
known at home as 'the worst-dressed man in London.' Besides E—— there were several others—a really brilliant party ;
Sir Henry being hospitable, and anxious to promote acquaintance between English travellers and the leading colonists.   He
was himself just then in warm water from the excitement
caused by the German invasion of New Guinea, as it was
called, of which I had heard at Adelaide.   The Australians
naturally enough regard themselves as the leading power in
the South Pacific, and besides their own immense continent
look on the adjacent islands as their proper inheritance.   The
Americans have their Monroe doctrine, prohibiting European
nations from settling on their side of the Atlantic, except as
American subjects.   Australia—especially the ambitious, pushing Melbourne—which claims to be the leading State, had unconsciously come to a similar conclusion respecting all the
neighbouring territory.   The Australians meant it to be theirs
as soon as they had leisure to occupy it ; and to learn that
close at their doors, as they said, the dreadful Bismarck contemplated a rival establishment had stirred them into a temper
at the moment of my arrival.   A German colony 2,000 miles
away did not seem likely to hurt them, but it was a beginning
which might lead to consequences, and was the violation of a
principle.   We at home take such things more coolly ; but
young nations are like young men, sensitive and passionate ;
and even their most experienced statesmen do not escape the
contagion.   The irritation over the French convict station in
New Caledonia had but half subsided.   The French concessions
in that matter were held to be far from sufficient.   Their
grievances on this point had been legitimate enough ; but now
on the back of it came looming a danger which touched their
dignity and their imagination.   They saw at their doors, in
the intended New Guinea settlement, German soldiers, Ger-

man fleets, German competition with their trade, a great rival German influence menacing their wealth, their institutions, their independence. It was a thing too horrible to contemplate, a thing to be instantly denounced and resisted. Our Home Government has been trying for some time past to federate the Australian States into a Dominion like the Canadian, as a saving of trouble to Downing Street. Part of the scheme was to be the formation of a Dominion fleet, in which the separate ship of the now divided colonies were to be united under a flag of their own, to relieve the English Navy of the burden of defending them. In the condition of mind in which I found Melbourne about New Guinea I thought it really fortunate that the federation was still incomplete.

If Australia had been a single State with a fleet of its own and with the Melbourne statesmen at its head, as they would probably be, it is not at all impossible, so angry were they, that of their own motion they would have sent their ships round to warn the Germans off. Of course a step like this would be equivalent to a break-up of the British Empire. Australia is part of that empire, or it is not. If it is part, the mother country is responsible for the doings of its dependencies, and the peace or war of the empire will lie in the power of each of its branches. No State can preserve its unity with two executives. The Australians do not contemplate separation. They desire nothing less ; but hot-headed men do not always pause to calculate the consequences of their actions. I understood better after hearing the language used in Victoria the meaning of my friend at Adelaide, who wished the colonies to exchange their war-ships into a subsidy to the Home Government. Of course I do not mean that the conduct which I speak of was likely. Of course it was not likely ; but it ought not to be possible. Where there is strong provocation the possession of means to resent an imagined wrong is a temptation to use those means ; and on the first news of the German movement (for they became cooler afterwards) the provocation in the press, in society, and among

the responsible authorities in the colonies was very strong
indeed.

As matters stood, the anger was directed as much at
England as at Germany. As they could not act for themselves
they thought that England ought to have acted for them,
to have claimed New Guinea at once as British territory,
and to have ordered the Germans out of it as peremptorily
as the Americans ordered the French out of Mexico.   They
blamed the Gladstone ministry ; they blamed especially the
Colonial Secretary, the unfortunate Lord Derby.   Impatient
people talked of petitioning the Crown for his dismissal. To
them as to all of us their own affairs were nearest, and the
maintenance of the British Empire was made to turn upon
this particular point.   In the ablest, coolest, and best-disci-
plined colonial politicians there is an enthusiasm of youth
bound up with their highest qualities.   We ought to allow for
such feelings : to respect, admire, and perhaps envy them,
though we cannot allow them to influence our imperial action.
Lord Derby may have been too cold in manner.   They complained bitterly that he had no sympathy with them.   Kind
words cost nothing, and the Australian impatience was, after
all, but an exaggerated jealousy for the honour of Oceana.
But, so far as action went, Lord Derby did all that was
possible, as I, when I was asked my opinion, always tried to
show them.   In the United States a Monroe doctrine is
possible because the political union is complete.   The States
are one and indivisible, and each is bound to support the
central authority. If England and her colonies were organised
as the States are organised, we too might, if we pleased, have
our Monroe doctrine in the Pacific.   It is unreasonable to
require us to challenge a great European power in the interest
of countries which, if they liked, might leave us to-morrow,
and who meanwhile contribute nothing to the fleets and
armies which would be required to maintain their pretensions.
On cooler reflection those who had been most angry began to
see that their fears had been excessive, and that a German
colony on the far side of the far-distant New Guinea could not
do them much harm after all.   A military station it could never

be. A colony would be free, like their own, and, if it prospered, would probably, in the end, assimilate with themselves.

The storm, however, had been as sudden as it was violent. Not a word had been heard of it before I left England, and some days had to pass before I comprehended what it was all about. Meantime I was looking round me and enjoying the delightful quarters in which I found myself. Our windows on the north overlooked the park, which was planted with clumps of pinus insignis and eucalyptus. Between and among them roofs rose of handsome houses, and, apart from the rest, the scattered buildings of the Observatory. At the park gate was the Yarra River, and Melbourne beyond it, in the distance; and when the smoke was off, and the fine buildings stood out conspicuous, the town looked really fine with its domes and steeples, Houses of Parliament, and Courts of Justice like the Four Courts in Dublin. To the west was the Harbour, and Williamstown where we had landed, with its crowded shipping; in the distance was the western ocean into which at evening we saw the sun set in crimson splendour. The private gardens surrounding the house were fairly kept by the Colonial authorities. Bright in such a climate they could not fail to be, and there was the usual lawn-tennis ground, where the aides-de-camp and the Melbourne young ladies played with as much enthusiasm as at home. The trees, however, wanted the English softness, both of form and colour. The coarse buffalo-grass eats, like a destroying monster, into its delicate English rival and kills it out of the way. More may and should be done in the ornamental garden department if it is to be worthy of such a mansion. In the kitchen garden I saw pear and apple trees destroyed by the burden of fruit which they were allowed to endeavour to ripen—large branches literally broken off, some of them, by a weight which they could not carry ; others, which could not so relieve themselves, dying of exhaustion. Melbourne, Sydney, and even more, I believe, Tasmania, can grow apples and pears enough to supply the world with cider and perry, and plums, apricots, and peaches enough to surfeit us with preserves.

Adjoining the grounds of Government House and con-

nected with them by a private walk down a picturesque
ravine, are the public gardens of the city, which eclipse even
those of Adelaide in size and the opportunities of the situation.
The Melbourne gardens are on the slope of a valley, at the
head of which, and where the incline is nearly precipitous,
the tower and battlements of the house stand out conspicuous.
The gardens themselves extend for a mile with a large sheet
of winding water in the middle of them. As at Adelaide no
expense has been spared : and I think I observed more attention to scientific arrangement in the grouping of the trees.
Broad lawns, kept carefully watered, open out at intervals
with flower-beds blazing with splendour. The lake has islands
in it, approached over pretty bridges, and it will be one day
beautiful when the water is filtered. Here was all which
heart of visitor could desire : avenues to stroll in which a
vertical sun could not penetrate ; with the glory of colour
which nature lavishes on leaf and petal to look at. Alas ! that
in all things in this world there should be a something one
could wish away. The something here was the flies, of all
sizes and hues, who were in millions, and who, like the giant
in ' Jack and the Beanstalk,' 'smell the smell of an Englishman,' and fasten on him and devour him. A cigar would be
a remedy but for the stern ' No smoking allowed in these
precincts.' The gardeners happily are more humane than their
masters, and do not see the forbidden thing when it is not
flourished in their faces. With the help of tobacco I contrived
to protect myself, and thus guarded I had the most charming
place to walk in all the time of my stay, and a great many
curious things to observe. They are trying hard to introduce
English trees, and succeed tolerably with some. The elms
and planes thrive best ; of oaks they have fifty varieties, I
think, and none of them do really well. They grow vigorously
for a year or two, then lose their leading shoot, which dies
away, and they throw out branches horizontally. I noticed,
however, that they bore the largest acorns which I had ever
seen. They are perhaps acclimatising themselves, and out of
these acorns may come true monarchs of the forest, grander
than our own.

Meanwhile indoors we were studying the Victorians and Victorian society. Party followed party, and it was English life over again : nothing strange, nothing exotic, nothing new or original, save perhaps in greater animation of spirits. The leaves that grow on one branch of an oak are not more like the leaves that grow upon another, than the Australian swarm is like the hive it sprang from. All was the same—dress, manners, talk, appearance. The men were quite as sensible, the women as pretty, and both as intelligent and agreeable. I could not help asking myself what, after all, is the meaning of uniting the colonies more closely to ourselves. They are closely united ; they are ourselves ; and can separate only in the sense that parents and children separate, or brothers and sisters ; and until symptoms have actually appeared of a wish on our part to throw them off, or on theirs to desert us, the very talk of such a thing ought not to be. Nor need any other straiter bond exist between us, were there but one executive among us, or even but one fleet, since in no other way can the colonies come in collision with a foreign power. Parents and children do not enter into articles of compact. If the natural tie is not strong enough, no mechanical tie will hold. And it is on account of this existing relationship between us that the sting has lain of the late suggestion of parting with the colonies. They have felt as a child would feel who was trying to do his best, and was conscious that he was no discredit to the family, yet was told by his father that the family had no wish to keep him, and that the sooner he took himself off the better. It was treating close kinsmen as if we acknowledged no relationship with them except of interest, and kinsmen are apt to resent such *un*human indifference.

Several of the Victorian ministers dined with the Governor while I was there, and other gentlemen of past or present distinction. They seemed all to be persons who would have been distinguished anywhere—made of the same material as our public men at home. They would have gone to the front in the English House of Commons as easily as in their own legislature, and have become members of Cabinets in London instead of at Melbourne. I was introduced to Mr Service, the Premier, sat next him at dinner, and liked him well. He is a spare, lean man, rather over the middle height, with a high, well-shaped forehead, grey eyes (so they seemed to me by lamplight), fine in their way; a manner quiet but dignified; a mouth that indicated a capacity for anger if there was occasion for it. In this last indication his mouth, I believe, does not belie him. He is the representative of the ambition of Victoria to be the chief state in a federated Australia, and is an ardent supporter of the colonial federation policy. The Australian colonies have grown with a rapidity which justifies extensive expectations for them. Mr. Service sees before him at the end of half a century an Australia with fifty million inhabitants : a second United States of itself, in the Southern Hemisphere. I have no right, and certainly no wish, to throw a doubt on this. If the several provinces continue to increase their numbers at the present rate, there will be more than fifty millions then. There is a proverb that 'nothing is certain but the unforeseen,' and in fact few things turn out as we expect them.

ταῦτα θεῶν ἐν γούνασι κεῖται.

But it is well to be sanguine, and we are the better off for our hopes even if they are never realised. In the distance and when it has reached these dimensions, Mr. Service probably looks forward to Australian independence. But for the present and for a long time to come, he said that he thought the continuance of the connection absolutely essential to the peaceful growth of the Colony, and that the politico-economic view of the matter, if carried into action, would be as injurious to them as it would be degrading and dishonourable to England. He hoped to see England grow more conscious of the value of the colonies to her, and the colonies of the consequence attaching to them as members of a great empire. Their technical relations to each other might adjust themselves in different forms as time went on : prudent statesmen did not let their conduct be influenced by remote possibilities. They looked to the present and the circuit of the visible horizon ; and their duty now, in all parts of the empire, was to draw closer together, and recognise their common interest in maintaining their union.

For this reason he deprecated the language so often lately heard from influential Liberal politicians at home. If the colonies continued to be told by the press and by platform speakers that we did not care about them, and that they might leave us when they pleased, and if official communications continued cold and indifferent, indifference might produce indifference. A separatist tendency, which had as yet no existence, would grow up. The links might be broken in a fit of irritation and impatience, and once gone could never be mended. They resented—knowing that they were as English as ourselves—being treated by English ministers as if they were strangers accidentally connected with us, as if blood and natural affection were to go for nothing.

This may sound sentimental, but the chief part of the reality in questions of this kind is sentiment. Family affection is sentiment ; friendship is sentiment ; patriotism is sentiment. A nation with whom sentiment is nothing is on the way to cease to be a nation at all. I decidedly liked Mr. Service : he expressed what I thought myself more clearly than I could do, and I considered him, in consequence, a sensible man.

On other subjects, too, he talked well, like a man as much accustomed to reflect seriously as if he had been a profound philosopher or an Anglican bishop. He, the popular chief of a great, modern, progressive, middle-class community, began, to my astonishment, to raise a question whether, after all our scientific discoveries, our steam-engines and railways and newspaper printing-offices and the other triumphs of the revolutionary period, mankind were really superior, morally and spiritually, to what they had been two thousand years ago ; whether, if we were to meet Ulysses or Pericles, Horace or Lucian, we should be conscious of any steep inequality in our own favour. He argued his point very well indeed, brought out all that was to be said on either side, and left the conclusion open.

On the other side of me at the same dinner sat the Astronomer-Royal, Mr. Ellery. Not knowing at the moment who he was, I could only be agreeably pleased with a gentleman evidently so highly cultivated, and wonder whether I was to take such a man as a type of Australian society. I was introduced to him afterwards. He graciously invited me to visit the Observatory, and the next morning Lady Loch, Lord E——, I, and two or three more, walked across. The instruments were said to be specially worth seeing—a magnificent reflecting telescope, and several others, with all the latest inventions.

The Observatory was but a quarter of a mile distant, but in the forenoon, and under a Victorian sun, we had a *mauvais quart d'heure* in getting there. On the way, amidst some coarse grass, I beheld a scarlet pimpernel, the veritable 'poor man's weatherglass' of northern Europe, basking wide open in the rays. If I had been studying the language of the New Hebrides, and had found imbedded in it a Greek verb, perfect in all its inflexions, I could not have been more surprised. How in the wide world came a highly organised plant of this kind to be growing wild in Australia? Had the seed been brought by some ship's crew, or in a bird's stomach, or been wafted over in the chambers of the air? To what far-off connection did it point of Australia with the old world? I gathered my marvel, and carried it to Mr. Ellery to be explained. How idly we let our imagination wander! He laughed as he said, 'Many weeds and wild flowers from the old country make their first appearance in this garden. Our instruments are sent out packed in hay.'

I remember Mr. Joseph Hume objecting once to a grant in the Budget for an observatory at the Cape. Had we not an excellent observatory at Greenwich? and if the globe revolved, what use could there be for a second? Had he seen what the Melbourne people were willing to do or give to promote astronomical science, he would have been shocked at their extravagance. They are not going to be left behind in any department of things, and have spared neither thought nor money. Mr. Ellery showed us all his equipments : his great telescope, and his transit instruments, and these were tho least of his wonders. In every vacant space, in the passages, against the walls of the rooms, under the roof, or under the sky, there was something strange, of which we had to ask an explanation. Gravefaced clocks were turning barrels everywhere, round which paper was rolled, and all the properties of the atmosphere—motion, temperature, density, electricity, &c.—were authentically and deliberately writing down on these rolls in what degree they were present. A generation back a special assistant was required to draw and write down each of these things, and he could do it but imperfectly. Here they were patiently recording themselves in lines upon the paper coils. Most curious of all to me was the breed of spiders, which are carefully and separately brought up, fed, and protected from contamination with others of their race. In transit and other delicate observations, where the period at which a star passes this point or that must be noted to the fraction of a second, the inner surface of the glasses used is crossed by minute lines, dividing it into squares, to assist in measuring the precise rate of movement across the field. For these lines no thread is fine enough which man can manufacture. Spider web is used, and not even this as the spider leaves it : for the spider makes a rope, and it is the strands of the rope, when untwisted, which alone will answer. The common spider's thread, such as we see him stretch from point to point on a bush, is a rope of eight strands, the untwisting of which to human fingers is a difficult operation. But a variety has been found at Melbourne whose thread has only three strands, and the precious creatures are among the Observatory's rarest treasures. Looking at all this elaborate apparatus, I said it made me wonder the more at the old Alexandrians, who, with their imperfect instruments, had discovered the precession of the equinoxes. 'Yes,' Mr. Ellery answered, 'and the best work now is being done by men who have imperfect instruments. It is the eye of the observer, and not the telescope, which makes the difference.' Some day, I suppose, all human necessities will be supplied by mechanical demons ; but I doubt whether man himself will be much the better for it. Aladdin remained a poor creature for all his genii.

In the afternoon Lady Loch took me to the park to hear the band play, and to see the rank, beauty, and fashion of Victoria. In the hot weather the rank, beauty, and fashion migrate to cooler quarters at Hobart Town, so the show was not impressive ; even the horses disappointed me after what I had heard of the Australian breed. Here and there I saw a handsome carriage, with smart appointments, and well-dressed ladies in it ; but horses, riders, phaetons, curricles, tandems, were of a scratch description, and the scene was gipsy-like and scrambling, like what one sees at an English country racecourse.

We drove afterwards round the environs of Melbourne, among endless suburban residences, like ours at Wimbledon, in fair modern taste, and all indicating a carelessness of cost. A sense of beauty, however, everywhere indicated itself in the gardens, in striking contrast with the United States, where the ordinary suburban house rises bare in the midst of indifferently kept grass, and even the palaces of the million-aires stand in ground poorly laid out. In Melbourne, and in these colonies universally, there seemed a desire among the owners to surround themselves with graceful objects, and especially with the familiar features of their old home—oaks, maples, elms, firs, planes, and apple-trees. Almost every one of our trees, except the oak, grows easily and luxuriantly.

Other English organisations are also reproducing them-selves, of a kind which some philosophers regard as the rank growth of European civilisation, to be made war against and extirpated. They appear, however, to be natural productions, natural in new countries as well as in old. A landed gentry is springing up in Victoria, with all its established charac-teristics. Sir ——, a baronet with 160,000*l.* a year and an estate as large as Dorsetshire, called afterwards at Govern-ment House—a distinguished highbred-looking man, who invited us to a cruise in his yacht, and kindly pressed me to pay him a visit at his country house, see his picture gallery, &c. There is room in Australia for all orders and degrees of men. I travelled afterwards through Sir ——'s property. His 'tenants' spoke favourably of him, and had no wish to change their occupancy into ownership. Mr. George and socialistic despotism will find no audience in these colonies. Perhaps before long they will lose their audience at home.

At dinner, the same evening, I met, with very great pleasure, a son of Edward Irving's : long Professor, and now, I believe, Rector of Melbourne University. His face reminded me of his father's : there were the same finely-cut features, the same eager, noble, and generous expression ; but he was calmer and quieter. Enthusiasm had become tempered down into rational and practical energy. He was educated at Balliol, and highly distinguished himself. He was among the first men of his year, and would have succeeded, as a matter of course, to a fellowship, but for the religious tests which were then unrepealed. Perhaps—I do not know, it is but my own conjecture—he might have conformed to those tests if he had followed his personal convictions. He was, and is, entirely orthodox, and had no agnostic tendencies, like some of his contemporaries ; but, with a fine filial piety, he would not separate himself from his father's Catholic and Apostolic Church. His career at home was obstructed ; he emigrated to Australia many years ago, and few men have done better service to the land of their adoption. The spiritual interests of the colonies have thriven upon English exclusiveness. It was peculiarly agreeable to me to meet him. I had seen his father once, I had heard him preach, and the impression had never left me.

We had been already presented with free passes on the Victorian railways, the Government being anxious to give us all facilities in their power to learn what was going on in the Colony ; but, as if this was not enough, they were still more exceptionally generous. Mr. Gillies, a member of the Cabinet, proposed, in the name of his colleagues, to conduct us himself over their principal wonders, show us the country, the gold mines, the farms, the vineyards, the scenery. They wished us to see things ; they wished, with most kind consideration, to spare me, as an old man, the fatigue of ordinary travelling. A special train therefore was to be provided with the luxuries of a drawing-room car. There were to be carriages at the

stations for us, rooms at the best hotels, &c., and all this was
to cost us nothing. We were to look on ourselves as the
guests of the Colony, and as a companion we were to have one
of the best informed and ablest of its public servants. The compliment was partly to me, but a good deal more to Lord E——,
with whom we were grouped into a party. My son was to
go with us, and as a fourth we were to have the charming and
accomplished Mr. Way, Chief Justice of South Australia, who
happened to be at Melbourne on a visit. Notice had to be sent
to Ballarat and to the other places to which we were to go,
and the arrangements required a few days' preparation. The
interval was spent on the chief sights of the city, libraries,
galleries, museums, public halls, and such like. To make a
profitable use of such a study requires a special organisation,
which in my case has been left out. My senses lose their perception when many objects of many kinds are thrust upon
them one after the other. It is like flying through a country
on a railway, or tasting successively a number of different
wines. The palate loses its power of distinction, and one
flavour is like another. I can spend a day over a single case
in a museum : one picture at a time is as much as I can
attend to. A day spent in walking from room to room,
from books to paintings, from paintings to sculpture, from
sculpture to crystals and minerals and stuffed birds and
beasts, leaves me bewildered. I remember once taking a
poor lady over the British Museum. She would see everything : printed books and MSS., engravings and illuminated
missals, beetles and butterflies, ichthyosauri and iguanodons,
Greek and Roman statues, Egyptian gods and mummies,
Assyrian kings on the alabaster tablets. It was over at last ;
we passed out between the great winged bulls from Nineveh.
She observed to me, 'Those, I presume, are antediluvian.' I
was reduced to the same state of mind after being taken
through the Melbourne treasures, and I can give no rational
account of them, save that they were abundant and varied,
and had been collected regardless of expense ; that the
managers were full of knowledge, and were most polite in
communicating it.

More intelligible to me was the magnificent Concert Hall, large as the Free Trade Hall at Manchester, but constructed less for public speaking than for music. The organ, which was built at Melbourne, is one of the finest in existence. The organist, who is worthy of his instrument, plays in the afternoon two or three times a week, and workmen, workmen's wives and children, ladies, gentlemen, all sorts and conditions, call indiscriminately to listen. Our own visit was out of hours. For a time we had the hall to ourselves, and the organist let us choose whatever we wished to hear. I have rarely heard any organ-playing more severely grand.

There are amusements, however, suited to all tastes. There was a theatre, of course, and the Governor and his suite were invited to a special performance. We had an operatic pantomime, much like other pantomimes, and a troop of ballet-girls with the usual indecent absence of costume. Poor things! I was sorry to see *them* in this new land of promise, and I wished them a better occupation. The audience was English to the heart. There were the English cat-calls from the gallery, the English delight in animal fun which can be understood without an effort. Two monsters pulling each other's noses in the background, while the chief actors in the play were discoursing in front of the stage, brought down the house. Clown and harlequin tumbled over pantaloon, knocked down the policeman, robbed the shops, jumped in and out of windows —all in the approved style. Satisfaction turned to exuberant delight when one or the other was thrown on his back. It was English without a difference ; no other people in the world have the same enjoyment of rough-and-tumble joking. Some improvised singing, with allusions to local politics, was good natured and well received. The Governor came in for his share of wit-pellets, and laughed as loud as anyone. I observed him while it was going on, and something in his look reminded me, I know not why, of the late Lord L——, with the difference of expression due to a life spent in chivalrous work instead of a life of idleness. Lord L——, the more highly gifted of the two perhaps, being born in the purple, lounged through his existence, shot deer, won notoriety in fast

London society, wrote a few lyrics to show the genius that had been wasted upon him, and died mad. Sir Henry, more happy than he in being without the things which most men covet, not being able to do as he liked and being forced to work, will leave a noble name behind him, and will not die mad.

On Sunday we walked across the public gardens, a mile and a half, to church. It was a church of the most modern English type, ornamental, ritualistic, chorister boys in surplices corresponding to the home pattern as closely as the young ladies at the theatre, an intoned liturgy and a somewhat ambitious sermon on the English race and its destinies. We were to regard ourselves as the salt of the earth—as a nation chosen above all the rest to represent the spirit of Christ. It was good to tell us to exhibit Christ's spirit; but was flattering our vanity the best way to bring us to it? There was once a sternness in the English character, a hatred of insincerities and half-sincerities, a contempt for humbug of all sorts and degrees. Where is it now? Extinct? or only sleeping and by-and-by to wake? On returning we found letters &c. from home which were a singular comment on the address to which we had been listening. They brought news of the dynamite explosions in the Tower and in the Houses of Parliament, another response, I suppose, to the intimation that the Clerkenwell business had brought the wrongs of Ireland within the range of practical politics. There will now, I suppose, be another dose of remedial legislation. Truly it has been a notable medicine for Irish disaffection to destroy the only part of the population there whose loyalty can be depended upon—like feeding a man who has delirium tremens with fresh draughts of the 'water of life.' I, for my own part, believe that the old English character *is* only sleeping, and will rouse itself up at last to see the meaning of all that.

The day after, I spent in wandering alone about Melbourne. I went into the handsome public library, which was fairly filled with readers. They were studying, I was told, books of solid worth. It might be so; but I saw a curious spectacle afterwards. In one of the principal streets there was a large archway leading into a kind of arcade, over which was written,

in large letters, the Book Pavilion. It was divided into
sections. The first and most important was a roomy saloon
with shelves all round and a table in the middle, shelves and
table being completely filled and covered with thousands of
the cheap editions of modern novels and magazines, the backs
of them shining with illustrations of human life as depicted
in the pages inside : despairing lovers at the feet of their
mistresses, corsairs, brigands, forgers, midnight murderers.
What a business our 'life' would be if these were a real
representation of it. There were French and German novels
in translations, English novels in the vernacular tongue, in
their yellow and pink bindings ; and over them and about
them were crowds—literally crowds—of children ; those who
could possess themselves of the precious volumes swallowing
them as if they contained a message of salvation ; the less
fortunate devouring the pictures, exactly like so many flies
round the poisoned tartlets in a pastrycook's shop. In the
rooms beyond were a few units of readers, looking into or at
graver works, arranged under heads, 'Science,' 'Divinity,' &c.
In the books of divinity there was strict impartiality :
Bishop Butler stood peaceably by the side of Renan, and
Canon Farrar's 'Life of Christ' beside Strauss's 'Leben Jesu,'
One could not but feel misgivings for the state of spiritual
digestion in the innocent, eager creatures turned out to browse
in such a pasture. But it was typical of our present condition,
and is worse perhaps, after all, at home than in the colonies.
If this is what comes of sending everybody to school, would
not our boys and girls be better employed as apprentices
learning useful trades and handicrafts?

The last evening before we started on our expedition was
given to the Observatory again. Mr. Ellery had promised to
show us some of the Southern stars. The 'cross' had been
familiar to us ever since we passed the line. To the eye it is
disappointing, the notable feature about it being the black
chasm I spoke of ; but Mr. Ellery showed us, through a
strong refracting telescope, the beautiful cluster in the middle
of it called 'the Gems.' We saw Saturn well, and Sirius like
a brilliant electric light. I had been once shown a blue star,

and wished to renew my acquaintance with it. I had to
learn that there were no really blue stars, and the colour had
been due to an imperfectly achromatic lens—a type perhaps
of some other celestial truths of which we fancy ourselves
perfectly certain.

The night was unfortunately windy and misty, and Mr.
Ellery himself was, after all, the most interesting object in
the exhibition. I had some further talk with him, and wished
it had been more. He considered that the drag on the earth's
rotation from the tidal wave was far from proved. The fact
of the retardation, to begin with, was only conjecture, and if
the tidal wave had a retarding action, it might be corrected
by other influences unknown to us. I did not venture to
propound my own wave theory about it. I asked him about
the sub-tropical plants lately discovered in coal-measures in
latitude 83° north, and how such plants could have grown when
they were half the year in darkness. He seemed to think
that there must have been some great difference, greater far
than our present knowledge can explain, in the inclination of
the earth's axis. I read, since my return, in a French scientific
journal, an assertion that the earth's axis had at one time been
at right angles to the ecliptic, that it had slowly inclined, as
we see a spinning top incline, till it had reached an angle of
45° or more, and was now half-way back to the perpendicular.
This, if true, would explain all the changes of climate which
the north part of Europe has evidently passed through from
tropical heat to the cold of the glacier epoch. It would
explain the plants in those coal-measures. It would explain
everything, if true. But is it true? How many times must
we outsiders learn up our science, and then unlearn it? Each
new generation of philosophers laughs at the conclusions of its
predecessors.

CHAPTER VIII.

Expedition into the interior of the Colony—Mr. Gillies—Special train—Approaches to Ballarat—The rabbit plague—A squatter's station—Ercildoun and its inhabitants—Ballarat—Gold-mining—Australian farms—A cottage garden—Lake and park—Fish and flower culture—Municipal hospitality.

WHO has not heard of Ballarat, the Eldorado of forty years ago ? the diggings where adventurers from all parts of the world flew upon the soil with their picks and shovels, some to light on nuggets which made them into millionaires, some to toil for months unrewarded, yet toiling on as if possessed by a demon ! Ballarat was then an arid treeless hollow lying between low hills, with a scanty brook trickling down the middle of it. Valley and hillside were then dotted over with tiny tents. Each tent held its two mates, for they worked in pairs always ; and altogether there were collected in that spot tens of thousands of human beings, flinging up soil and sand-heaps like the Bactrian ants of Herodotus, the bushrangers watching in the forest to waylay the gold on its way down to the sea. There is not a yard of earth where Ballarat now stands which has not, within the memory of many of us, been dug over and passed through the sieve. It is now the second city in Victoria, a prosperous town with 40,000 inhabitants, created in the wilderness as if by Aladdin's lamp. Ballarat and the Ballarat district was our first destination. I disliked the notion of it, expecting to find merely an unlovely spectacle of insatiable hunger for gold. In this, as in many other things, I was to find myself mistaken.

Mr. Gillies was waiting for us at the station, with Chief Justice Way. We were conducted to a superlative carriage lined with blue satin, with softest sofas, cushions, armchairs, tables to be raised or let down at pleasure. A butler was in attendance in a separate compartment, with provision-baskets, wine, fruit, iced water, and all other luxuries and conveniences. Thus accommodated we shot out of Melbourne, and for the first fifty miles were carried along the shores of the great inlet of Port Phillip. The soil was bare and little cultivated—

generally unoccupied and uninteresting. I was struck indeed
with the extent and solidity of the inclosures—strong railings
of eucalyptus wood—but there was little apparently to inclose
except a few cattle. All was changed as we entered the hills.
Here the land had once been densely wooded. The trees in
many places had been cleared off. Along with the railings we
found thick-set hedges of thorn and gorse ; we passed pretty
farmhouses with solid outbuildings, cornfields, and potato-fields,
cottages with their plots of vegetable grounds, park-like
pastures, cows and sheep abundantly scattered over them,
signs everywhere of vigorous and successful industry. At
intervals the ‘bush’ remained untouched, but the universal
eucalyptus, which I had expected to find grey and monotonous,
was a Proteus in shape and colour, now branching like an oak
or a cork-tree, now feathered like a birch, or glowing like an
arbutus, with an endless variety of hue—green, orange, and
brown. The ground where it had been turned by the plough
was dark and rich. It was harvest time. The corn-shocks
were standing English fashion, red and yellow, out of the
stubble, or were being carted away and raised into stacks. On
the low meadows there was hay. The dark-leaved potatoes,
untouched by blight, were in full blossom. It seemed incredible
that I was in a new country ; that within half my own life all
this had been a wilderness. Every moment I thought of
Midas—Midas reversed—not wholesome things turned to gold,
but gold transmuted into earth's choicest treasures.

We were ascending an incline, and had risen at least 1,500
feet. The air became perceptibly cooler, the fertility more and
more conspicuous. After reaching the highest point we ran
along through an undulating country, chiefly pastures, with
large trees left standing. There was no undergrowth, no
rocks or stones, only green fresh grass on which sheep were
grazing. Here, for the first time, I saw the meaning of the
rabbit plague which has so troubled Australia. Some years
ago an enthusiastic gentleman, wishing to reproduce there all
the features of his home life, introduced a few couples of
rabbits. They have multiplied enormously—injure the farmers'
young crops, and have become a general nuisance. The Vic-

torians perhaps exaggerate the mischief yet done. They are so angry at Melbourne, I was told, that they will no longer eat rabbits, regarding them as vermin, like rats. Mr. Gillies had checked my satisfaction at seeing the gorse fences by denouncing them as a harbour for the enemy. Had their numbers been so vast as has been alleged, had they really been eating the sheep off the pastures, I must and should have seen more of them than I did see. In an open glade of the forest a few miles from Ballarat, there were, perhaps, a hundred of them playing about, a third of these, by the by, being black. One might see as many, however, on a summer evening outside any wood in England where game is preserved. I suppose the Australian farmers want the traditionary reverence for the *feræ naturæ* which are bred for sport.

As we approached Ballarat we left the forest and came among plantations. As the town began to rise, they planted pinus insignis, eucalyptus, magnolia, Moreton-bay fig-trees in all directions and in all convenient places. As the houses grew, the trees grew which were to shade them. A few years in Australia will raise a tree to a size which it will hardly reach in ten times as many years in our islands. They were everywhere—in yards and courts, in streets and squares. They out-topped the chimneys, and in spite of the common-place architecture—no better at Ballarat than at most other places—they gave it an air of grace and even of beauty, as unlooked for as it was agreeable. There were, of course, the inevitable engine-works, great heaps of rubble and cinder, high scaffoldings of mine-works, with wheels revolving, and the black arms of the cranks rising and falling. Mining is still the principal industry of the place. The surface diggings have been long exhausted ; but the quartz rock, of which the hills are chiefly made, is charged with gold. The rock is quarried and crushed, and the gold is washed out of the gravel. This is not, however, the only industry. The city of Midas is a great agricultural centre, and is growing more and more so.

Gold-mining still pays its way. The annual yield of the Victorian mines is from four to five millions, and the cost of producing it about as much. This implies a great many people

earning high wages, the local trade and business prospering,
and thousands of families maintained in comfort ; but other
occupations are spreading by the side of it, and changing the
character of Ballarat externally and internally.

We had left Melbourne early and it was not yet noon.
We were to sleep at Ballarat, but were not immediately to
stop there ; we were engaged to a luncheon party at a squatter's
station, twenty miles beyond, from which we were to return in
the evening. We have all heard of squatters' stations. We
imagine (at least I did) a wild tract of forest, a great pastoral
range ; a wooden hut run up in the middle of it ; men, dogs,
horses, cattle, semi-savage all ; bushrangers perhaps skulking
not far off ; the native and naked blacks of the soil retiring
slowly before advancing civilisation and hovering on the white
man's skirts ; and for the rest the rude hospitality of nomad
settlers amid a life like that of the ancient Scythians. This is
what I looked for when I was told that I was to be taken to
a squatter's station, and the reality was again unlike the
anticipation.

The train stopped at a solitary halting-place in the midst
of a desolate expanse of rolling ground, a large lake in the
distance with barren shores, and something like a village in
the extreme distance. Roads led out straight in several directions, all at right angles with one another, for the country has
been laid out in surveyors' offices as the Roman provinces
probably were, and the highways run direct from point to point
with small regard to local convenience. A carriage was waiting for us ; we drove in a cold wind (for we were still 1,500
feet above the sea) along one of these lines passable enough in
dry weather, and fenced in by stout posts and rails for some
twelve miles. The scene had gradually become less dreary.
Trees became more frequent and there were stubbles where
crops had been reaped. We came at last to a gate, which
needed only a lodge to be like the entrance to a great English
domain.

The park-like character was more marked when we drove
through—short grass, eucalyptus trees, and blackwood trees
scattered over it like the oaks at Richmond ; the eucalypti,

ancient and venerable, with huge twisted trunks and spreading branches, being exactly like oaks at a distance, while the dark green blackwoods glowing picturesque between them might have passed for yews. Sheep were browsing in hundreds, perhaps in thousands, and on a wooded ridge which was behind I was told that there were deer.

The only exotic features were the parrots, small and large, which were flying like cuckoos from one tree to another, flashing with blue and crimson.

After passing a second gate we found more variety. There were plantations which had been skilfully made. English trees were mixed with the indigenous, eucalypti still preponderating however, some towering into the sky, some, as before, fantastically gnarled; here and there a dead one stretching up its gaunt arms as perches for the hawks and crows. High hills stood out all round us, covered with forest. The drive was broad, level, and excellently kept. The plantation gradually became thicker. A third gate and we were between high trimmed hedges of evergreen, catching a sight at intervals of a sheet of water overhung with weeping willows; a moment more, and we were at the door of what might have been an ancient Scotch manor house, solidly built of rough-hewn granite, the walls overrun with ivy, climbing roses, and other multitudinous creepers, which formed a border to the diamond-paned, old-fashioned windows. On the north side was a clean-mown and carefully-watered lawn, with tennis-ground and croquet-ground, flower-beds bright with scarlet geraniums, heliotropes, verbenas, fuchsias—we had arrived, in fact, at an English aristocrat's country house reproduced in another hemisphere, and shone upon at night by other constellations. Inside, the illusion was even more complete. The estate belonged to a millionaire who resided in England. Ercildoun, so the place was called, was occupied by his friends. We found a high-bred English family—English in everything except that they were Australian-born, and cultivated perhaps above the English average—bright young ladies, well, but not over-dressed; their tall, handsome brother; our host, their father, polite, gracious, dignified;

our hostess with the ease of a *grande dame*. Two young English lords on their travels were paying a visit there, who had been up the country kangaroo-shooting. Good pictures hung round the rooms. Books, reviews, newspapers—all English—and 'the latest publications' were strewed about the tables—the 'Saturday,' the 'Spectator,' and the rest of them. The contrast between the scene which I had expected and the scene which I found took my breath away.

We had luncheon, and went afterwards for a walk. Skirting the lake, and following the stream which fed it, we ascended a highland glen, amidst antique trees, great granite crags, and banks of luxuriant fern. The stream was divided into ponds, where trout were bred. Cascades fell from one pond to another—not too full of water at that season—with rockeries and gravel walks. A strange black fish-hawk rose from a pool where he had been feeding. Parrots flashed and glittered. Alas! there was no laughing jackass. I wished for him, but he was not there. The rest was perfect, but so strange that I could hardly believe it was not a dream. Some of the party had guns. The Australians have a mania for rabbit-killing, and shoot them in season and out. A few were knocked over, and were left lying were they fell. The only game brought home was a kangaroo-rat, as large as a full-sized hare, and for which it had been mistaken.

It was a day to be remembered, and a scene to be remembered. Here was not England only, but old-fashioned baronial England, renewing itself spontaneously in a land of gold and diggers, a land which in my own recollection was a convict drain, which we have regarded since as a refuge for the waifs and strays of our superfluous population for whom we can find no use at home. These were the people whom our proud legislature thought scarcely to be worth the trouble of preserving as our fellow-subjects. It seemed to me as if at no distant time the condescension might be on the other side.

Our stay could be but brief. We were under orders, and our minister, who had charge of us, was peremptory. There was to be a dinner at Ballarat in the evening, where we were to meet the leading citizens. We had twenty miles to go, and wo were to drive the whole distance, as there was more to bo seen off the line of the railway. I for one left Ercildoun with a feeling that I would gladly have remained a little longer among such pleasant friends and such charming surroundings; reflecting, too, how this particular form of life, which radical politicians denounce as an artificial product of a disordered society, is the free growth of the English nation, and springs up of itself wherever Englishmen are found. Let me also mention that the eldest son of this luxurious family had, till within a month or two, been herding cattle in Queensland, doing the work for four years of the roughest emigrant field hand, yet had retained the manners of the finest of fine gentlemen—tall, spare-loined, agile as a deer, and with a face which might have belonged to Sir Launcelot. I have ungratefully forgotten his name, and even the name of the family. It was the type which struck me.

Three hours of driving brought us back to Ballarat, and to our rooms and our banquet at the hotel. The evening had been chilly as in an English May. The changes of temperature in these highlands are trying. Mr. Gillies proved a most agreeable companion. He entertained us with stories of the political adventures of the Colony since the establishment of responsible government, in many of which he had himself borne his part. Government by parties is an historical growth of English development due to causes peculiar to ourselves. The meaning of it has been the orderly transition from one state of civilisation to another; and now that the transition has been accomplished, and party lines no longer correspond to natural lines, it has become doubtful whether, even among ourselves, it works with perfect success. Every wise English politician is both Radical and Conservative. He has two eyes to see with and two hands to work with, and to condemn him to be one or the other is to put one eye out and to tie one hand behind his back. To colonies where it has no natural appropriateness at all, where party is purely artificial, and party politics therefore are not a contest of principles but a contest of intrigues, only an English conviction that what is good for ourselves must be good for all mankind could have induced us to think of applying it. General good sense has happily neutralised in a great degree the anomalies of the system. When the moral health is sound, the political health cannot be seriously disordered.

The morning and evening were but one day, since we left Melbourne. If time is measured by sequence of impressions it had been far the longest in my life. We were hardly equal to the dinner in which it was to end. But our Ballarat friends were very good. They talked to us instead of expecting us to talk to them, and soon left us to rest in the sumptuous quarters which had been provided for us.

The day following was to be given to gold mines. The surface diggings, as I said, are exhausted, for the present, everywhere, and at Ballarat there were no longer any alluvial diggings whatever. The gold now raised there was entirely from the quartz rock. But there were deep alluvial mines worked by companies and machinery some twenty miles off. It was in these only that the large nuggets were found, and we were to be taken to see one of the richest of them, which had been lately opened. The weather had become hot again. The roads in dry weather are six inches deep in dust. But we were to go ; our entertainers were our masters, and indeed we were all glad to go. The mine itself was a thing to be seen once at any rate.

We were started after an early breakfast. Our way led through primitive forest, through farms in all stages of progress, through towns so called, but plots of ground rather, intending by-and-by to be towns. At these places a visit from a Cabinet Minister was as a visit from an Olympian god. Notice of our coming must have been sent forward. Wherever we stopped to change horses groups of gentlemen were waiting, with preparations of fruit and champagne ; we might have floated in champagne, they were so liberal to us. The country was tolerably level, but at intervals were singular circular hills, rounded off at the top, like sections of oranges which have been cut in two in the middle. These hills were five or six hundred feet high, and perhaps a mile in circumference. Whether they had a rock base or were merely earth-heaps, I could not learn, but the soil on them was extremely rich, as we could see from the colour of the furrows and the care with which they were cultivated. Before arriving at the mine we passed through a location of Chinese, whose business it was to raise vegetables for the workmen, and wash their clothes. Very good, useful people, as far as I could learn, and as I afterwards found them to be when I fell in with them. We came at last to the foot of a steep hill, rising out of a valley which was crowned by a high aqueduct. The aqueduct brought water to the mine-shaft, which we saw above us on the hillside, with great wheels, platform, chimneys, and miscellaneous buildings. The horses took us up with difficulty. We alighted dust-powdered at the office, cleaned ourselves, and were then conducted to the workings. When a vein of alluvial gold has been once struck, an experienced eye can tell, by the lie of the ground, the direction in which it will run. It flows like an underground stream, following laws of its own, which the miners have generally made out. Sometimes they make a mistake, and fortunes are staked and lost in sinking shafts in vain. In this happy instance they had struck not only into the gold vein, but into some deep pockets in it, and the shareholders were dividing splendid profits. The shaft was 700 feet deep, from the bottom of which the auriferous gravel was brought up by the wheel to a platform where the buckets were emptied into trucks. The trucks are sent along a rail to the washing troughs. There a rush of water is let loose upon the dirt-heap, violent enough, it would seem, to sweep everything before it, but it only sweeps away the stones and gravel. The gold, from its great weight, sinks to the bottom and there remains. We saw two or three cartloads of gravel washed, and a hundred and sixty pounds' worth of gold taken out of it. The directors gave us each a nugget worth a couple of sovereigns as a remembrance. The romance of the digging is gone ; the rough independent life, the delightful trusting to luck, the occasional great prize drawn in the lottery ; the long fever of hope generally, but not always, disappointed. It is now a regular industry. The men have their

regular wages—twelve and fifteen shillings a day. The capitalists have the risk and, on the whole, neither lose nor gain.

I had seen the thing, and it was enough. I could not care
a great deal for it. If they had been *making* the gold it
would have been interesting, but they are only finding it ; and
the finding, when it lost its uncertainties and was reduced to
averages, had lost its chief human charm. If one was bored,
however, one was bound to try to conceal it. I was repaid
for everything on my way home. I felt like Saul, the son of
Kish, who went to seek his father's asses and found a king-
dom. We were taken back through what was called ' the
fertile district ' of Ballarat. The wheat was gone ; the thick
stubble only remained to show where it had been ; but oats,
barley, peas, beans, potatoes were in the fields, and after the
sight of them I could believe Herodotus's account of the crops
grown on the plains of Babylon. E——, who knows what
agriculture is, and had been all over the world, said that he
had never seen the like of it. An oat crop was half cut.
Where the reaping machine had stopped, it was standing like
a wall—so thick that a horse could scarcely have forced a way
through it, and so clean of weeds that there was nothing like
one visible. Weeds indeed are said to be a product of high
civilisation, and not to exist in a state of nature. For seventeen years they have been cropping this land without manuring
it, and there is no symptom of exhaustion. Each harvest is
as rich as the last. When earth is so kind, men cannot choose
but be happy. The human occupiers of these farms live each
on his own freehold, or, if tenants, with no danger of disturb-
ance. They have pretty houses, smartly kept and bright with
paint ; and trellis-vines creep over the verandahed fronts, and
the slopes or lawns are bright with roses. The orchards round
them reminded me of the Boers' orchards in the Free State ;
peaches and apricots, almonds, figs, pears, and apples—all
thriving as if they had taken fresh life in the new land where
they found themselves ; and the men and women seemed as
thriving too, with the courteous manners of independent
gentlemen and ladies. If English farmers and farm-labourers
could but see what I saw that day (and I am informed that

other parts of the colony were as much richer than this as
this was richer than my own Devonshire) there would be swift
transfers over the seas of our heavy-laden 'agricultural population.' The landed interest itself—gentry and all—will perhaps one day migrate *en masse* to a country where they can
live in their own way without fear of socialism or graduated
income-tax, and leave England and English progress to blacken
in its own smoke.

Drought is the worst enemy in Australia, but rain falls
sufficient for all necessities, and only asks to be taken care of.
In a gorge among some high hills the Ballarat corporation
have made a reservoir as big as a large lake. The embankment
across the neck of the valley is a fine piece of engineering
work, and on our way back we made a circuit to see it. Mr.
Ruskin complained of Thirlmere being turned into a tank;
Glasgow has laid down pipes to Loch Katrine; yet Loch
Katrine's beauty has not been vulgarised, has not been affected
at all, for the pipes are out of sight. I could never see that
Ravenscrag would hang less grandly over the lower lake at
Thirlmere, or the birch sprays float less freely over the becks
that foam down its glens because the Lancashire millions were
to be supplied with unpolluted water from it. Here, however,
there was nothing to spoil. The useful has created the
beautiful. There is a sheet of water produced by a mere
desire to prevent Nature's best gift from running to waste,
which, with the pine-groves planted round its shores, will look
as well as any other inland lake in future water-colour art
exhibitions. We stopped for a few minutes at a roadside
hotel, near the end of the embankment, to rest our horses. It
was tidily kept and picturesquely situated. The little wicket
gate was open. I strayed in and found myself in the garden
of an English cottage, among cabbage-roses, pinks, sweet-
williams, white phlox, columbines, white lilies and orange,
syringas, laburnums, lilacs. Beneath the railings were beds
of violet and periwinkle, and on a wall a monthly rose was
intertwining with jessamine and honeysuckle. The emigrants
who had made their home there had brought with them seeds

and cuttings from the old home. They were 'singing the Lord's song in a strange land.'

A second dinner party wound up the evening. The leading men in Ballarat were brought together to meet us, and we were filled with information as freely as with champagne. The Australians in one point are agreeably different from our cousins west of the Atlantic. The American puts you through a catechism of interrogatories. The Australian talks freely, but asks few questions, and does not insist on having your opinion of him and his institutions—a commendable feature in him. But he does insist that you shall see what he has to show. The ambitious young community does not import its rails or engines or machinery. It supplies its own. Next day, with a temperature of 90° in the shade, we were taken to the workshops and foundries, and were set to roast before the furnaces. I bore it, but didn't like it. I had seen other works of the same kind. Thence we went to the town-hall, which, though the town is proud of it, is very like other town-halls. From the town-hall we went to the 'Mills.' The quartz-crushing was at least new, and had a certain clangorous significance. Thirty huge cylinders of steel stood vertically in a row, in oiled sockets. A powerful steam engine lifted them and let them fall, like hammers of the Cyclops. They were fed with quartz blocks trom boxes behind each, and the smashed particles fell into a trough, as at the alluvial diggings, where a rush of water purged away the lighter stone and left the gold behind.

Deafened by the noise, fainting with the heat, and wearied with the endless talk about gold, I made my escape, and was taken possession of by a kind Samaritan who had a carriage and a pair of horses. He drove me about the town, showed me sumptuous-looking palaces, and described the fortunes of their owners, the lucky survivors of the race of original diggers. Finally, he brought me to the gates of the park, where we found the rest of our party assembled. It then appeared how skilfully our entertainment had been arranged. We had been passed through Purgatory in the morning that we might enjoy Paradise afterwards—literally Paradise—for

Paradise means Park, and here was a park worth the name. I have already expressed my admiration of the Australian gardens, but this at Ballarat excelled them all. It was as if the town council had decided to show what gold and science could do with such a soil and climate. The roses which bloom ill on the hotter lowlands were here, owing to the height above the sea, abundant and beautiful as in Veitch's nurseries at midsummer. Besides roses, every flower was there which was either fair to look upon or precious for its fragrance. There were glass houses to protect the delicate plants in the winter ; but oranges and camellias, which we know only in conservatories, grow without fear in the open air, and survive the worst cold which Ballarat experiences. A broad gravel walk led up the middle of the grounds, with lateral paths all daintily kept. Dark shadowy labyrinths conducted us into cool grottoes overhung by tree-ferns, where young lovers could whisper undisturbed, and those who were not lovers could read novels. Such variety, such splendour of colour, such sweetness, such grace in the distribution of the treasures collected there, I had never found combined before, and never shall find again. Even this lovely place had its drawbacks. There were snakes there, and bad ones, though I did not see any. I did, however, see an enemy whom the gardeners hate worse than snakes. I was stooping to examine a bed of carnations, when a large buck rabbit jumped out of the middle of it. No fence will keep them out. If they cannot fly over it they will burrow under like moles, and nothing is safe from them.

The wonders of the Park, however, were not exhausted. Following a winding path through a thicket, we came on a stream of water, not very clear, which ran into and filled a pond. This, I was informed, was a breeding-place for trout. As the pond in question was of the colour and consistency of a duck-pond in an English farm-yard, all the marvels which we had witnessed could not prevent us from being sceptical about the trout. No form of Salmonidæ known in Europe could live five minutes in such a hot, filthy puddle. But the Salmonidæ must change their nature in the antipodes. To satisfy our doubts a net was drawn through the water, and

I

several hundred fish the size of minnows were brought out—
fat, and in perfect health, with the pink spots upon them—un-
mistakable trout. Nor was the destination of them much less
curious. The stream led on to a broad green meadow shaded
by the large weeping willows which I have already spoken of
as so fine and so common—great trees with trunks three feet
in diameter. The meadow bordered upon an artificial lake
four times the size of the Serpentine, and supplied with water
from the reservoirs in the hills.

The park and the lake are the recreation-ground of the
youth of Ballarat. In the meadow the children were playing
in hundreds, looked after by the nursery maids, while the
elders sat on the benches in the shade. Well-dressed ladies
lounged up and down, while barges, bright with flags and
ladies' parasols, were passing along the shore. Here the lads
have their boat-races. Dandy little yachts of eight and ten
tons, like those at Windermere, lay at anchor, to enter for the
cup on regatta days. Across the lake is the shortest cut to
the city, and steam launches, with awnings spread and music
playing, ferried their human freight backwards and forwards.
Wild swans, wild ducks, large coots with crimson heads, which
found shelter in the reed-beds, rose trumpeting or crying, sailed
round and settled down again. The water has been stocked
with fish : perch, roach, and trout. Those which we had just
seen were to be turned in. For some reason, I know not
what, they thrive in an extraordinary way. I saw a trout of
twelve pounds' weight which had been lately taken out. The
citizens have free leave to fish, subject to certain conditions.
I forget how many tons were taken out last year, chiefly
perch, which are also of unusual size. Certainly this was a
singular thing to have been created in the middle of a desert.

While we were admiring, a steam launch came for us to
the landing pier. The head gardener, who had accompanied
us to the water, presented us each with a bouquet of exotics,
the like of which could hardly be put together at Kew or
Chiswick. The engineer blew his whistle; we stepped on
board, and were carried across in time for a luncheon at the
mayoralty. We made our acknowledgments for the hearty

and kind hospitality which we had met with ; and thus closed
our stay in the Golden City, which we left with admiration
and regret. On the whole Ballarat had surprised and charmed
me. There may be, there doubtless are, aspects of colonial life
less agreeable than those which I have described. Most of the
sight-seeing, most of the champagne, might very well have
been dispensed with. But the people had but one wish—to
make us feel, wherever we went, that we were among our own
kinsmen. Personally I was grateful to them for their kindness. As an Englishman I was proud of what they had
accomplished within the brief limit of half my own years.
Of their energy, and of what it had achieved, there can be no
question, for the city and its surroundings speak for themselves. People have written to me to say that we were purposely shown the bright side of things, that we let ourselves be
flattered, be deluded, &c. Very likely ! There was mud as
well as gold, in the alluvial mines. The manager pointed out
the gold to us and left the mud unpointed out. The question
was not of the mud at all, but of the quality and quantity of
the gold. All things have their seamy aspects. If there is
gold, and much of it, that is the chief point. The mud may
be taken for granted. But for myself I can relate only what
I myself saw, and the impression which it made upon me.
Readers may make such deductions as they please.

CHAPTER IX.

Bendigo—Sandhurst—Descent into a gold mine—Hospitalities—Desire for
confederation—Mount Macedon—Summer residence of the Governor—
Sir George Verdon—St. Hubert's—Wine-growing—Extreme heat—Mr.
Castella—Expedition to Fernshaw—Gigantic trees—A picnic—A forest fire
—Return to Melbourne.

BALLARAT is not the only gold-centre. We all remember to
have heard of Bendigo, or the New Rush. Bendigo is now
the town of Sandhurst, a thousand feet below Ballarat, a
hundred miles from it on the interior watershed where the

streams run towards the Murray. To Sandhurst we were
next to go. After the Ballarat luncheon the special train
received us again. It was a hot afternoon, which grew hotter
as we descended. The surface of the country through which
we travelled had been scratched and scored by the old diggers;
pits, holes, long trenches, with broken wheels and timberwork,
indicating where the departed ant-swarms had been busy. All
this is over now; 'companies' have been taking the mining
business everywhere into their own hands, some splendidly
successful, some falling to pieces in bankruptcy, and instantly
commencing again. It is a gigantic gambling system, which
however, the Colony can afford. The community prospers.
Individuals who are down to-day are up to-morrow, and the
loss, when there is loss, is spread over so large an area that it
is not seriously felt. Nothing can go seriously wrong when
the common labourer's wages are 8s. a day.

Hot as the weather was, the land did not seem to suffer
much from drought. The forest was thick where the diggers
had not destroyed it. For the last thirty miles we passed
through a continuous, well-wooded park, the grass green under
the trees and the richer soils inclosed and cultivated. Rabbits
in plenty were running about. Sheep were lying down contented, in the long evening shadows; and though the air was
like a furnace, it was all very pretty and peaceful. In building Sandhurst, as in building Ballarat, the people had thought
first of shelter from the heat. The pine-trees towered above
the houses as we approached, and stretched out in long lines
till we lost the end of them in the distance. The mayor of
the city was waiting for us at the station. He took me off
with him at once in his carriage. In the first minute he told
me that they had planted a hundred miles of avenue, ' and all
paid for.' In the second minute he told me that they had
30,000 inhabitants there, but were crying out for more. He
was a Scotchman, I suppose, for he said, ' We want more
Scots. Give us Scots. Give us the whole population of
Glasgow; we will take them in, and find work for them, and
make Sandhurst the world's wonder.' We were set down at
the ' Grand Hotel,' a fine airy mansion looking out upon a

broad street, with porches, verandahs, and long overhanging balconies. Flowers and flowering trees were all around us. The moon was rising full over the roofs, and the still slowly cooling atmosphere was loaded with perfume. Mosquitoes, 'sweet companions of our midnight solitude,' unfortunately swarmed ; but we kept them at bay with curtains, and heard only the grim notes of their trumpets as they struggled to make their way to us through the network. There had been none at Ballarat, and we had forgotten the existence of such things.

Ballarat had entertained us handsomely ; the mayor of Sandhurst was not to be outdone. In the morning we found that he had watered the roads for us, that we might not suffer from the dust—the mayor, or perhaps the three mayors ; for Sandhurst like other places, is 'a city divided against itself.' There is an Upper Sandhurst and a Lower Sandhurst, each with its own town-hall and corporation, and a superior opinion of itself in comparison with its rival. And there is a suburb four miles out, called Eaglehawk, with another corporation, the principle of local self-government being in full development. Eaglehawk is the latest-born of the group, being the offspring of the exceptionally rich gold veins which have been found in the quartz rock there. The mines at Eaglehawk were the jewels of the district, and as we could not see all, we went to see them. It stands high, on the crest of a ridge, and looks higher than it is, from the white piles of stone raised out of the shafts, and the huge chimneys and wheels and engine-works. Orders had evidently been issued that we should be received with distinction. Mine-captains and miners were waiting our arrival ; we were invited to go down into the mine itself. A rough suit of clothes was provided for each of us, and I and two or three others squeezed ourselves into a lift, and with candles in our hands descended easily and rapidly 700 feet. We were landed in a gallery which had been the track of a gold seam through the rock. The white quartz glittering with iron pyrites in the light of our candles, the gold crystals sparkling on the splintered surface, was like a scene out of the 'Tales of the Genii.' Gnomes or trolls

should have been grinning at us from the black shadowy
corners ; but neither gnome nor troll is known, so far, to have
emigrated into these regions. The floor was clean and dry
under foot. There was no afterdamp or mephitic vapour to
threaten explosions ; we wandered about collecting specimens
till we were tired, and then were lifted into the upper air
again, as easily (in spite of Virgil) as we had descended.
The mine was a thing to be remembered. Back in daylight
and restored to our own clothes, we had to be conducted over
the crushing mills. They were identical with those which we
had seen already—the same row of cylinders thumping down
upon the stone, the same roar of machinery, and the same
results ; but the good people were proud of them and we
could not be impatient after the trouble which they had taken
to please us. Champagne and fruit were laid out in a work-
shed, and out of a tray of quartz fragments bright with sprays
of native gold we were invited to take what we pleased and
carry them home with us. We made such acknowledgment
as we could, and our words said less than we felt. A set
luncheon followed, with more champagne, and we had to
make speeches.

Eaglehawk, however, was not to be preferred to Sandhurst, so we had to be brief and hurry down to a second
luncheon, and more champagne and more speeches. The occasion was used for very warm expressions on the confederation
with the mother country. The general feeling was that there
had been enough of jealousy and distrust. England and the
Colonies were one race, and ought to be politically one. I felt
myself challenged to say something at one of these feasts, I
think it was at Eaglehawk ; so I was as enthusiastic as they
were, and laid the fault on the politicians, who brought people
into quarrels when the people themselves wished for nothing
so little. I told a story of two gentlemen who, after some
small difference, had been drawn into a duel by their friends,
the friends declaring that the matter could not be settled
without an exchange of shots. As the principal parties were
being led to their places, one whispered to the other, ' If you
will shoot your second, I will shoot mine.' There was much

laughing, and a voice called out, ' Do you want us to shoot our Ministers ?' As Mr. Gillies was present I had to be careful, but indeed it was not Colonial Ministers that I was thinking of at all, but one or two whom I could mention at home. Though in superabundance, the champagne was good, and we suffered less from it than might have been expected. All was heartiness and good humour, and as I look back upon those scenes, I see, in the warm welcome which was extended to us, less a compliment to our personal selves, than a display of their affection for the mother country, and a determination not to be divided from it.

This was our last experience with the gold mines ; and I can only say that if all the gold in the world was turned to as good account as the Victorian colonists are turning theirs, reformers and friends of humanity might wrap themselves in blankets and sleep.

Once more to the railway and to a change of scene. It was now the 31st of January, the hottest part of the Australian dog-days. At this time of year Melbourne, generally cool and pleasant, becomes oppressive, especially to children. Those who can be absent go for the season to Tasmania. Sir Henry Loch, who was obliged to remain within reach of his advisers, had removed with his family to a cottage in the mountains, 3,000 feet above the sea, forty miles only from Melbourne, and near the Sandhurst and Melbourne line. Here he had kindly requested us to rejoin him. It was called Mount Macedon from the hill on which it stood. How the hill came by its title I do not know. The native names are shapeless and ugly. The first European owner perhaps took the readiest designation which he found in his classical dictionary. At a roadside station we parted from our escort and his sumptuous carriage, he to go on to Melbourne and prepare another excursion for us, we to make our way in a post-cart to the mountain which we saw rising before us, clothed from foot to crest with gigantic gum-trees. There was forest all about us as far as eye could reach. We had been warned that we were going into a wilderness ; but it was a civilised wilderness, as will be seen. After driving four or five miles we came to the foot of Mount Macedon, up the side of which the horses had to crawl. After ascending four hundred feet we found a level plateau, laid out prettily with cottages, a good-looking house or two, and an English-looking village church. A short descent again, and then an equal rise, brought us to the gate of the summer residence of the Governor, a long, low, one-storied building with a deep verandah round it clustered over with creepers. As at Madeira, where the climate changes with the elevation, and an hour's ride will take you from sugar-canes into snow, so here we found the flora of temperate regions in full vigour, which refuse to grow at all at the lower levels. We had still the gum-trees about us, shooting up freely, two hundred feet or more; some magnificent, in full foliage; others naked, bare, and skeleton-like, having been killed by bush fires; but round the house, oaks and elms, cypress and deodara seemed at home and happy; filbert-trees were bending with fruit too abundant for them to ripen, while the grounds were blazing with roses and geraniums and gladiolus. The Australian plain spread out far below our feet, the horizon forty miles away; the reddish-green of the near eucalyptus softening off into the transparent blue of distance. Behind the house the mountain rose for another thousand feet, inviting a climb which might be dangerous, for it swarms with snakes—black snakes and tiger snakes—both venomous, and the latter deadly. In open ground nobody minds them, for they are easily avoided or killed; but no one walks unnecessarily through long grass or bushes in their peculiar haunts.

The situation is so beautiful and so healthy that it is a favourite with the wealthy Melbourne gentlemen. Seven hundred feet above us the accomplished Sir George Verdon, long agent-general for Victoria, in England, and remembered and regretted by all who knew him, has built himself a most handsome mansion surrounded by well-timbered grounds which he has inclosed and planted.

In the winter, which he spends in Melbourne, this highland home of his is sometimes swathed in snow. In summer the heat of the sun is tempered by the fresh keen air of the mountain ; and were it only a little easier of access, Sir George Verdon's hermitage would be a place to be envied.

He is not the Governor's only or nearest neighbour. A quarter of a mile from Sir Henry Loch's cottage, and on the same lower level, there is another large residence, belonging to a Mr. Ryan, originally from Ireland, I believe, but an old settler in Victoria and a gentleman of very large fortune. Having the colonial passion for gardening and means for indulging it, Mr. Ryan has created what in England would be a show place, for its beauty and curiosity. Tropical plants will not of course grow there, but all else seemed to grow ; there was scarcely a rare flower belonging to the temperate regions of any part of the world of which he had not a specimen, and his fruit garden would have supplied one side of Covent Garden.

The Governor had not such grounds as Sir George Verdon, nor such flower-beds as Mr. Ryan, but what he had would have been counted beautiful anywhere else. The landscape surrounding was perfection ; and in this delightful situation and in the doubly delightful society of the Governor's family, we lingered day after day. He himself was called frequently to Melbourne on business, but he could go and return in the same day. We walked, sketched, lounged, and botanised, perhaps best employed when doing nothing except wandering in the shade of the wood. One night upon the terrace I can never forget. The moon rose with unnatural brightness over the shoulder of the mountain ; the gorges below were in black shadow ; the foliage of the gum-trees shone pale as if the leaves were silver, and they rustled crisply in the light night-breeze. The stillness was only broken by the far-off bark of some wandering dog, who was perhaps on the scent of an opossum ; we stood ourselves silent, for the scene was one of those which one rather feels than wishes to speak about. A week after, when we were far away, Mount Macedon was the centre of a bush-fire ; the landscape on which we were gazing was wreathed for miles and miles in smoke and flame, and the forest monarchs, which stood so serene and grand against the starry sky, were charred and blackened stumps.

While we were thus resting at Mount Macedon, Mr
Gillies had arranged another expedition for us to see a vineyard at a place called St. Hubert's, where the only entirely
successful attempt to grow fine Australian wine had been
carried out, after many difficulties, by a Mr. Castella, a Swiss
Catholic gentleman from Neufchatel. The visit was to be
partly on our account, that we might see what Victorian
energy could do besides raising gold. It was also official,
for Sir Henry Loch was to go with us as a recognition of
Mr. Castella's merits to the colony. Australian wines had
failed hitherto, as they had failed at the Cape, either from
excess of sugar in the grapes, or from an earthy flavour contracted from the soil. The hock which we had tasted at
Adelaide had been palatable but commonplace. Only experiments protracted through generations can determine in what
situations wine deserving the name can be produced. The
flavour of a grape tells you nothing of the final flavour of the
fermented juices. The same vines grown in two adjoining
fields, where the stratification or the aspect is different, yield
completely different results. The wine, too, must be kept for
several years before the flavour into which it will ripen is
defined. The best, therefore, which can be attained in a new
country is tentative and imperfect.

Mr. Castella, however, had received honourable recognition from the best European authorities at the Sydney Exhibition for his hocks and clarets. The Governor was to go over
his manufactory and congratulate him on his triumph.

St. Hubert's was fifty miles from Melbourne, in the valley
of the Yarra. The blue satin railway carriage took us to the
nearest station. There we clambered upon an old-fashioned
four-horse coach, and after a dusty drive of eight miles we
reached a large, roomy, straggling house, built with attempts
at ornamental architecture, high-gabled roofs, a central tower
with a flying outside staircase and gallery, the inevitable deep
verandahs, and, as Mr. Castella's guests were often numerous,
detached rooms, run up with planks, scattered in the shrub-
beries. The Yarra wound invisibly between deep banks across
the plains in front of the windows. Behind it, far off, was a

high range of mountains, from which columns of smoke were rising in half a dozen directions, from forest bush-fires ; either lighted on purpose to clear the ground, or the careless work of wood-cutters or wandering natives. The fields immediately adjoining were the most brilliant green. The vines were all in full-leaf. There were three hundred acres of them standing in rows, and staked like raspberry bushes, each bush powdered with sulphur, and smelling strongly of it. Our host himself was a vigorous, hale-looking man of sixty or upwards, with lively French features, light grey merry eyes, with a touch of melancholy at the bottom of them—to be recognised at once as an original person well worth attention. He was an artist, I found, as well as a vine-grower. His rooms were hung with clever Australian landscapes in oils, his own work in the idle season. He had come to the colony thirty years ago, when Australia was the land of promise to so many ardent European spirits who had been dispersed by the collapse of the revolutions. After many ups and downs of fortune he had married a Sydney lady, very handsome still, and moderately rich. She would have been very rich, I believe, if she had pleased her friends better in the choice of a husband, but she showed no signs of being discontented with her lot, as, indeed, so far as I could judge, she had no cause to be.

We were a large party, and the extensive house was full. Sir George Verdon had descended from his eyrie to accompany us. There was a New Zealand member of council, whose name I did not catch ; Mr. Langton, a high Victorian official, steady, calm, and sensible, with a pretty daughter ; Mr. Rowan, a partner in Mr. Castella's firm, a tall, athletic, fresh coloured, and evidently successful gentleman, who told us that he was a relation of the not yet forgotten Irish conspirator, Hamilton Rowan, whose life was saved by the devotion of the Dublin fishermen. Besides these, there were several others, but I had no opportunity of becoming personally acquainted with them.

We were walked over the estate under our umbrellas, for the sun was blazing down upon us. We saw the vines growing, the presses, the rows of hogsheads in the cellars, the vats in which the grapes were trodden. I learnt here, as a fact now to me, that if fine wine is wanted, the human foot is still in requisition. Machinery crushes the grape-stones and taints the flavour. We had to taste from various casks, and profess to appreciate the differences, which we none of us could ; for the palates of the uninitiated soon lose the power to discriminate. Mr. C., however, offered to supply us with what seemed as good as we could desire, in any quantity, at twenty-five shillings a dozen, and so far as I can tell, I could be contented to drink nothing better, if I was never to have worse.

The worst of the business was the heat. Evening came, but the thermometer did not fall. The air was still and stifling, with a smell of smoke in it. The temperature was 90° in the verandah at eight o'clock when we went in to dinner.

I sat next to our host, and I have rarely met a more amusing companion. He had been in the French army under Louis Philippe. He had been a detective officer, and knew for one thing the secret circumstances of the murder of the Duchesse de Praslin. He had fought in the streets in February 1848. He had served after that revolution in Caussidière's famous police, and had again been in the great battles of June in the same year. I myself knew something of that remarkable time, and some of the principal actors. It was very pleasant, and strange too, in such a place and scene, to hear the old story over again from so competent an authority.

After dinner we sat out on the lawn, trying in vain to cool ourselves. Some of us adjourned to the top of the tower to smoke, where we heard anecdotes from Mr. Rowan of Smith O'Brien's rebellion ; among others, that five hundred Catholic Irish had been killed by the Orangemen in a battle in Ulster. He perhaps meant only 'kilt.' I had been in Ireland myself all that summer observing what was going on, yet had never heard of such a battle. The events which occurred must have been very imperfectly recorded. Perhaps the newspapers were in a conspiracy to suppress untoward incidents. Finally we went off to bed, I to a comparatively cool outbuilding among the bushes, where I was not without uneasiness about snakes. There were no snakes, but in the morning I found a dead Australian wild cat lying against the door, which had been worried in the night by the dogs. I walked out before breakfast among the fruit trees. Delicious ripe greengages hung in thousands within tempting reach. The ground underneath was yellow with them, left to rot as they fell, but the boughs were bending under the weight of those which remained. I found Sir Henry and two or three more of our friends had been attracted by the same magnet. We were tempted and we all fell, but in that climate Nemesis is merciful, and does not exact too severe a penalty for light indulgence.

It was hotter than ever, 98° now in the shade, but our day's work had been laid out for us. Mr. Gillies was a man of business, and was not to be denied. We were to be shown the giant trees at Fernshaw, the largest as yet known to exist anywhere, higher by a hundred feet than the great conifers in the Yosemite valley. They were twenty miles off, in a mountain glen near the rise of the Yarra. We were to picnic among them, and return to St. Hubert's the same evening. One wished to be forty years younger, but the Colony is itself young; age and its infirmities are not recognised, and at Rome we must do as the Romans.

Away we went, squeezed together again on the coach-top, between the vine-rows and across the dusty plains. Neighbours who had been forewarned joined our procession on ponies or in carriages. Matters mended a little when we were over the Yarra. We were then in the forest at the foot of the hills. There was at least shade, the road winding among the valleys and slowly ascending. A railway from Melbourne is expected in these parts shortly, when the mountains will be the summer haunt of lodgers and excursionists. To us the solitude was broken only at a single interval, when the country opened, and there was a scattered hamlet. There wo changed horses, and again plunged into the woods, the ravines growing wilder and wilder, the gum-trees grander and grander, the clean straight stems rising 200 feet, like the tall masts of some great Amiral,' before the lowest branch struck out from them. Unique as these trees are they ought to be preserved ; but the soil which nourishes them is tempting from its fertility, and they are being rapidly destroyed.   The Government makes laws about them, but in a democracy people do as they please.   Custom and inclination rule, and laws are paper.   A notch is cut a yard above the ground, the bark is stripped off, the circulation of the sap is arrested, the tree dies, the leaves at the top wither, the branches stand for a few years bare and ghostlike, and then it rots and falls. Sometimes the forest is wilfully fired ; one sees hundreds of trunks, even when there is still life left, scorched and blackened on one side.

The eucalyptus is a fast grower, and can be restored hereafter when the loss of foliage begins, as it will, to affect the climate ; but the blackwood trees and acacias, which, though dwarfed by their immense neighbours, grow to what elsewhere would be a respectable size, mature only in centuries.   The wood is valuable, and is everywhere being cut and carried off. The genius of destruction is in the air.   In the Fernshaw Mountains, however, no great impression has been made as yet.   One drives as through the aisles of an immeasurable cathedral, the boughs joining overhead to form the roof, supported on the grey columns which rise one behind the other all around.   There is no undergrowth save tree-ferns, fine in their way, for some of them were thirty feet high, but looking like mere green mushrooms among the giant stems. We passed a pretty-looking mountain valley farm or two. One of them in a sheltered hollow had a garden stocked with raspberries, so productive that the owner made last year 450*l.* by them in the Melbourne market.   At length we reached the bottom of the last hill, where stood a picturesque hotel, the Yarra running at the back of it, reduced in volume, but improved in colour—a clear pebbly stream, with blackfish, trout, and eels in it.   Here were lodgings for romantic tourists, as well as visitors' books with doggerel verses of the usual kind.   E—— and I were asked for our autographs, the mistress flattering us into consent by saying that they did not want common names.   The hotel itself seemed nicely kept, the rooms clean, the gardens well attended to, the credit being due more, I think, to the lady of the house than to the master, who looked as if he preferred enjoying himself to work of any kind. Here, too, for the first time, we saw a lyre-bird, which someone had just shot, the body being like a coot's and about the same size, the tail long as the tail of a bird of paradise, beautifully marked in bright brown, with the two chief feathers curved into the shape of a Greek lyre, from which it takes its name. Of other birds we saw none, not a jackass to my sorrow, not even a magpie or a parrot. Two young ladies, however, joined us—from Galway ; both pretty, one quiet, the other of the Baby Blake type, who amused herself, and perhaps him, by flicking one of the aides-de-camp with a riding whip.

The hill was steep. We walked up, skirting the ravine where the objects were growing which we had come in search of, their roots far down in the hollow, their heads towering up as far above our heads. Three hundred and fifty to four hundred feet is their average height, and one was measured which reached four hundred and sixty. In the position in which they stand they are sheltered from all possible winds. To this and to the soil they owe their enormous development. I myself measured rudely the girth of one which stood near the road ; at the height of my own shoulder it was forty-five feet round. We had left the Yarra and were ascending a tributary brook, which was falling in tiny cascades below. The carriage with the hampers followed slowly ; at length we all stopped at a convenient place for the further ceremonies—a sheltered slope by the side of the stream, which was rushing along amidst ferns and rocks, crags hanging over us and the great trees hanging over the crags. The young ladies made themselves conspicuous by posing in picturesque attitudes on a point above a waterfall ; the young gentlemen by springing to rescue them from imaginary perils. The baskets were unpacked, and we settled to our luncheon as chance and convenience of seats disposed us. Three sorts of wine from Mr. Castella's cellars were cooled in the sparkling pools, and in such an environment, and after such a drive, were voted universally to deserve the best that had been said of them. Venomous beasts there were none, but venomous insects in plenty ; flies with bites as poisonous as a Saturday Reviewer's pen ; sand-ticks which had an eye for the bare leg above the stocking, and were expert in reaching it ; other creatures which could make themselves disagreeable after their kind, which I had never heard of and now forget ; but we were all happy and in the best of spirits, and vermin of all kinds in this world prefer the sick in mind and body and leave the healthy alone. We did very well ; Mr. Gillies allowed us half-an-hour for our cigars ; we were then packed upon our coach again, and were carried back as we had come. I was glad to have visited the place. It was something to have seen the biggest trees in the world, and to be able, in California, to affect disdain of the Yosemite, and, among tree-ferns, and lyre-birds, and eucalyptus, to be able to feel that we were in no strange land, among strange ways and strange faces. It was the old country still, with its old habits and old forms of enjoyment.

On the way home we turned aside to see a native settlement—a native school, &c.—very hopeless, but the best that could be done for a dying race. The poor creatures were clothed, but not in their right minds, if minds they had ever possessed. The faces of the children were hardly superior to those of apes, and showed less life and vigour. The men threw boomerangs and lances for us, but could not do it well. The manliness of the wild state had gone out of them, and nothing had come in its place or could come. One old fellow had been a chief in the district when Mr. Castella first came to settle there. It was pathetic to see the affection which they still felt for each other in their changed relations.

Another pleasant evening followed at the vineyard, a sound sleep, and I suppose more greengages in the morning. Then, after breakfast, the visit to St. Hubert's was over. The memory of the place, its master and his family, and the party assembled there, are a bright spot in the recollection of my travels. I liked Mr. Castella well, and was sorry to reflect that I should never see him more.

The heat was still extreme. The air glowed as over a fur
nace. There was not breeze enough to move a thistledown,
and the sun shone copper-coloured through the brown haze.
In the train on the way to Melbourne we observed an unusual
look in the sky ; a cloud hung over the horizon of a dirty
white colour, more like wood smoke than natural mist, and
becoming more and more like smoke as we came nearer to it.
It was in the direction of Mount Macedon, and seemed to
extend over the whole range of hills of which Mount Macedon
was the centre. At length it became obvious that many miles
of forest in that quarter, and apparently at that particular
spot, must be in flames. Sir Henry was painfully anxious.
An aide-de-camp waiting at the Melbourne station informed
us that our fears were well founded. The whole district was
burning. The Governor's cottage and Sir George Verdon's
house were safe so far ; but fires of this kind, and in such
weather, spread with extreme rapidity. Lady Loch with the
children were still on the spot. Sir Henry flew on with a
special engine. The danger on these occasions is always great
and may be terrible. He would have had us go with him ;
but we feared we could be of little service—we knew that we
should be assuredly in the way, and we decided to remain
ourselves at a club in the city of which we had been made
honorary members.

CHAPTER X.

Colonial clubs—Melbourne—Political talk—Anxieties about England—Federation—Carlyle's opinions—Democracy and national character—Melbourne
society—General aspects—Probable future of the Colony.

CLUBS in the Colonies answer the double purpose of the club
proper and the private hotel, where members, and strangers
for whom a member will become responsible, can not only
have the use of the public rooms, but can reside altogether.
The arrangement is convenient for the members themselves,
many of whom live at a distance, and come occasionally to the

K

city on business. It is particularly agreeable to visitors, who, if the club is a good one, are introduced at once to the best society in the place. We had already many friends there. At the Melbourne Club we made many more, and as we were soon relieved of our anxiety about Mount Macedon and its occupants, our time was usefully spent there. The fire had been most destructive. The excessive heat and the long drought had brought the undergrowth into the condition of tinder. The flames had spread as if the woods had been sprinkled with petroleum. Eight miles of forest, which we had left a week before in its summer beauty, were now a blackened waste. The mountains behind the cottage had been as a cone of dry fuel, and had been in a blaze to the very summit. Sir George Verdon's place had been saved by his own forethought ; a large area had been cleared of bush between the house and the rest of the mountains, which the fire had been unable to cross. It had descended to within fifty yards of the cottage. It had then stopped—partly from exhaustion, partly through the energy of the neighbours who had exerted themselves manfully and loyally. The danger was over ; the scene of ruin, with the flames still bursting out in distant parts of the woods, was so remarkable that Sir Henry sent again to beg us to go up and witness it. E—— went ; I preferred to retain unspoiled the image of that moonlight night, and remained where I was. The outbursting of the fierce irrational forces of nature has to me something painful and horrible, as if we lived surrounded by caged wild beasts, who might at any moment break their bars and tear us to pieces. Such indeed our condition is in this world, and it is well for us when only forests are set blazing, and not the distracted heads of human beings, like those French communists of whom I had been talking with my host at St. Hubert's. But if we cannot escape such things, I have no curiosity to be a spectator of them.

With the gentlemen whom I met at the club I had much interesting talk about colonial politics—federation, the relation of the colonies with the empire, &c., the results of which I shall sum up further on. There was anxiety about England too. When English interests were in peril, I found the Australians, not cool and indifferent, but *ipsis Anglicis Angliciores*, as if at the circumference the patriotic spirit was more alive than at the centre. There was a general sense that our affairs were being strangely mismanaged. The relations of large objects to one another can be observed better at a distance than close at hand, when we see nothing clearly except what is immediately next to us. New Guinea was half-forgotten in our adventures in Egypt, and men asked me, and asked themselves, what, in the name of wonder, we were about. It began to be perceived, too, that the disease was in the constitution. The fault was not in individual ministers, but in the parliamentary system, which placed the ministers at the mercy of any accidental vote in the House of Commons, laid them open to be persecuted by questions, harassed by independent resolutions of irresponsible members, and thus incapacitated them from following any rational policy, and drove them from insanity to insanity. There lay the secret of the mischief. The remedy it was less easy to suggest; but it was felt even there that a remedy of some kind would have to be found, if the empire was not to drift upon the rocks. One individual, indeed, did fall in for an exceptional share of blame. The second morning of our stay at the Club came the news of the fall of Khartoum and Gordon's death.

Upon the king—all falls upon the king.

With singular unanimity the colonists laid the guilt of this particular catastrophe at the door of the Liberal leader. They did not love him before, and had been at a loss to understand the influence which he had so long exercised. His mighty popularity they thought must now at least be at an end. It could not survive a wound so deadly in his country's reputation. They were deceived, it seems, yet perhaps they were only forming an opinion prematurely which hereafter will be the verdict of mankind. He, after all, is personally responsible, more than any other single man, for the helpless condition into which the executive administration of the English empire seems to have fallen.

It was suspected, by those whose distrust of this famous statesman was the deepest, that he might argue that now Gordon was dead the object of the campaign was over, and that orders might be sent to evacuate the Soudan. But the enthusiastic Victorians could not believe this even of him. A disgrace so flagrant was incredible. One gentleman suggested that Lord Wolseley would refuse to obey—as if we were arriving at a new passing of the Rubicon, and a new Cæsar; as if parliamentary government was a detested idol, which was cast out of its shrine, and worshipped no more; as if the tide of the sacred river, long running in the direction of anarchy, had passed its flood, and was now turning once more. There was no doubt that things were amiss in England somewhere, and I told them how Carlyle had thought about it all. In Carlyle's opinion the English nation was enchanted just now—under a spell which for the last fifty years had bewitched us. According to him, England's business, if she understood it, was to gather her colonies close to her, and spread her people where they could breathe again, and send the stream of life back into her loaded veins. Instead of doing this, she had been feeding herself on cant and fine phrases, and delusive promises of unexampled prosperity. The prosperity, if it came—which it wouldn't, and wouldn't stay if it did—meant only that our country was to be the world's great workhouse, our green fields soiled with soot from steam-engines—the fair old England, the 'gem set in the silver sea,' was to be overrun with mushroom factory towns, our flowery lanes turned into brick lanes, our church spires into smoky chimneys. We were to be a nation of slaves—slaves of all the world, slaves to mechanical drudgery and cozening trade, and deluded into a dream that all this was the glory of freedom, while we were worse off than the blacks of Louisiana. It was another England that Carlyle looked forward to—an England with the soul in her awake once more—no longer a small island, but an ocean empire, where her millions and tens of millions would be spread over their broad inheritance, each leading wholesome and happy lives on their own fields, and by their own firesides, hardened into men by the sun of Australia or the frosts of Canada—free human beings in fact, and not in idle name, not miserable bondsmen any more. All this was well received, though, of course, translated into the practical, with the metaphorical parts of it toned down. The Victorians were willing to provide for as many of our people as would come over to them in the ordinary way, but they did not want an inundation of paupers. England's manufacturing industries were the great sources of her present strength and wealth. England could not cease to be a manufacturing country. England had coal and iron, and must make calicoes and ironwork. They had land and gold, and would buy them of us. The colonies were the mother country's best customers, and bought five times more of our goods, in proportion to their population, than any other people bought, &c.

Very good doctrine as far as it went, but the great question of all seemed to be no more thought of in Australia than at home. They and we talk of our 'greatness.' Do we clearly know in what a nation's greatness consists? Whether it be great or little depends entirely on the sort of men and women that it is producing. A sound nation is a nation that is composed of sound human beings, healthy in body, strong of limb, true in word and deed—brave, sober, temperate, chaste, to whom morals are of more importance than wealth or knowledge —where duty is first and the rights of man are second—where, in short, men grow up and live and work, having in them what our ancestors called the 'fear of God.' It is to form a character of this kind that human beings are sent into this world, and those nations who succeed in doing it are those who have made their mark in history. They are Nature's real freemen, and give to man's existence on this planet its real interest and value. Therefore all wise statesmen look first, in the ordering of their national affairs, to the effect which is being produced on character; and institutions, callings, occupations, habits, and methods of life are measured and estimated first, and beyond every other consideration, by this test. The *commonwealth* is the *common health*, the common wellness. No nation can prosper long which attaches to its *wealth* any other meaning; yet, as Aristotle observed long ago, in democracies this is always forgotten. They do not deny it in words, but they assume that, political liberty once secured, all else that is good will follow of itself. Virtue is a matter of course. Make men politically equal and they cannot fail to be virtuous. Of virtue ὁπόσον οὖν will do. So Aristotle observed it was in the Greek democracies, and this was the reason why they were always short-lived. Virtue is obligation; obligation is binding; and men who choose to be free in the modern sense do not like to be bound. They are emancipated from human authority. They do not re-impose the chains upon their own limbs. Each of them thenceforth attends to his own interests. That is, he gets as much money as he can and as much pleasure as the money will buy for him ; and when he has lost the habits which he has inherited from an older and severer training and is brought to the moral level which corresponds to his new state of liberty, the soul dies out of him ; he forgets that he ever had a soul.

Hitherto this has been the history of every democratic experiment in this world. Democracies are the blossoming of the aloe, the sudden squandering of the vital force which has accumulated in the long years when it was contented to be healthy and did not aspire after a vain display. The aloe is glorious for a single season. It progresses as it never progressed before. It admires its own excellence, looks back with pity on its earlier and humbler condition, which it attributes only to the unjust restraints in which it was held. It conceives that it has discovered the true secret of being 'beautiful for ever,' and in the midst of the discovery it dies.

But enough of this. The principal men in Melbourne are of exceptional quality. They are the survivors of the generation of adventurers who went out thither forty years ago, on the first discovery of the gold fields—those who succeeded and made their fortunes while others failed. They are thus a picked class, the seeming *fittest*, who had the greatest force, the greatest keenness, the greatest perseverance. These are not the highest qualities of all, but they are sufficient to give the possessors of them a superiority in the race, and to make them interesting people to meet and talk to. Having large properties, and therefore much to lose, they are conservative in politics. Indeed, of native, aggressive radicalism there is very little in Victoria. There is no need of it where everyone has enough to live on. I lunched on Sunday at the house of one of these great millionaires in a fashionable suburb. House, entertainment, servants, &c., were all on the superb scale, just like what one would find in London or New York. Mr. Langton, who had been with us at St. Hubert's, lived in the same neighbourhood. We spent an evening afterwards with him and a party of literary friends, exchanging splendour for simplicity, and the shrewd talk of a prosperous man of the world for aesthetic and intellectual conversation. Both were well enough in their way, though the last was most to my taste, Mr. Langton himself being a very superior man. But again, I felt how entirely English it all was. There is not in Melbourne, there is not anywhere in Australia, the slightest symptom of a separate provincial originality either formed or forming. In thought and manners, as in speech and pronunciation, they are pure English and nothing else. There is more provincialism far in Exeter or York than in Melbourne or Sydney. We went home to our club in the evening by a crowded omnibus, and could have believed ourselves back in Piccadilly, the dress, look, and movements of the other occupants being so exactly the same.

We had now been a month in Victoria—a month into which had been crowded the experience of an ordinary year. I was now to go on to Sydney. We had been treated with old-fashioned English hospitality at Melbourne, and when the mayor invited us to a farewell entertainment at the town-hall, I was able to make some acknowledgment of the kindness to us of Governor, ministers, and people. So handsome they had all been, that I said I fancied that at bottom I must be a person of some importance, and that when I was in London again I should be like Cinderella going home from the ball. If the account which I am able to give of them all should further, even in an infinitesimal degree, a clearer understanding in my

own country of what they are and what they are doing, I shall
be content for myself to sweep the ashes again, and I will ask
no fairy godmother for any further present. The speaking on
their part was warm and manly. The impression which then,
and throughout, I formed of Victoria and the Victorians, I will
shortly sum up before taking my final leave of them.

The Colony, and Melbourne as its capital, have evidently
a brilliant future before them. They cannot miss it. The resources of the country—pastoral, agricultural, and mineral—
are practically unbounded. The people, so clever and energetic,
will not fail to develop them ; and if the Premier was over-
sanguine (as I think he was) in believing that Australia would
grow as rapidly as America has grown, and would grow to
equal dimensions, there is no doubt at all that, if they have no
misadventure and are not interfered with from outside, in
fifty years there will be an Australian nation, of which the
Victorian will be a leading branch, able to hold its own and to
take its place among the leading Powers of the world. The
political condition is not, I think, entirely satisfactory. In
Victoria there are no privileged classes, no inherited institutions which require to be modified to suit the change of times.
Where all are, or may be, comfortably off, there is no dissatis-
faction with the distribution of property, and, therefore, there
is no natural division of parties, which constitutes the principle of parliamentary government. Parties in the colonies
are artificial, and therefore unnatural and demoralising. It
would be far better if the heads of the departments could be
selected with reference simply to ability and character, and were
relieved, as they are in the United States, from responsibility
to the legislature. Politics in democracies tend always to
intrigue or faction, but the peril is intensified where there is
unreality in the very form of the constitution. The good
sense of the colonists has prevented so far any serious harm.
But they have passed through one dangerous crisis ; at any
moment they may fall into another ; and parliamentary
government, it is likely, will prove but a temporary expedient
adopted in imitation of English institutions, but incapable of
permanence.

Almost every leading man is professedly loyal to the connection with England, and the people generally, I think, are really and at heart loyal. Any speaker who advocated separation at a public meeting would be hooted down. But they are impulsive, susceptible, easily offended, and the language which I heard and read during the New Guinea excitement made me fear that if our relations are left as undefined as they are, and separation is allowed to be spoken of as a policy which may be legitimately entertained, they may be capable some day or other of rash acts which may be irreparable. One thing is certain—Victoria will not part with the liberties which it now possesses. It is not represented in the English Parliament, and will never, therefore, directly or indirectly, return under the authority of the English Parliament. But they acknowledge a duty to the mother country as they understand it. It used to be pretended that if England fell into a war which might threaten the Colonial port towns, they would decline to share its burdens or its dangers. This will never be. The Colonies will not desert us in time of trial, and if they leave us it will be for other reasons. They will never leave us at all, I think, if they are treated respectfully and considerately ; but they complain that the Downing Street despatches are flavoured still with the old indifference, and are haughty and ungracious. The broad evidence which they have lately given of their true disposition will for the future, perhaps, improve the tone. The English people must see to it if they desire a federal empire ; our rulers will obey their masters.

Society in Melbourne is like society in Birmingham or Liverpool. There is no aristocracy, and there are not the manners of an idle class. The 'upper classes' are the successful men of business and practical intelligence, who make large fortunes and spend them handsomely. There is no extravagance that I saw. In some things the tone is rather puritanical; as, for instance, cabs and carriages are made to walk in passing a church on Sundays during service time. They allow no rude or inconsiderate forgetfulness of public convenience. Carriages, carts, vehicles of all kinds have to walk at crowded crossing-places. If the Melbourne buildings are heterogeneous, you sco something to admire in the management of the traffic. There is an idle set at the lower end of the scale : noisy, riotous scamps, who are impertinent to peaceful passengers, and make rows at theatres, a coarse-type version of the old Mohawks— they call them *larrikins*. The young men who are to inherit fortunes are said also to leave something to be desired. To be brought up with nothing to do, with means of enjoying every form of pleasure without the trouble of working for it, with a high station so far as wealth can confer a high station, and to have no duties attached to it, is not a promising equipment ; but so long as a young man's first duty is considered to be the making of money, and the money is already made, what can be expected ? It is the same everywhere at present among nations called civilised, and is one of the ugliest aspects of our condition. But the Victorian youth have the old energy. They are fine shots, bold fearless riders ; in yachting, rowing, cricket-playing, athletics of all kinds, they have the national capacity and are as good as we are. There is an exuberance of force, and in a federated Oceana higher occupation would be found for them in the army and navy and the public service.

On the whole, considering that they have been nursed in sunshine, and have never known adversity, the merit of the Victorian colonists is very great. They have worked miracles in clearing and cultivating their land. In forty years—they take their name from the Queen and are only coeval with her reign—they have done the work of centuries. They are proud of themselves, and perhaps assert their consequence too loudly; but their country speaks for them, and they have fair ground for elation. In one point they differ from us—I know not whether to their advantage. Froissart says of the English that they take their pleasures sadly. A ' sad wise man ' was an old English phrase. With so fair a climate and with life so easy the Victorians cannot be sad, and it is pleasant to see a people who know so well how to enjoy themselves. But men and nations require in reserve a certain sternness, and if anything truly great is ever to come out of them this lesson will in time be hammered into them. For the present they are well off and ought to be thankful. They complain of want of sympathy ; I should say that no subjects of Her Majesty just now are less in need of it. Praise and appreciation are their fair due, and we will not quarrel with them if they insist on being respected as they deserve.

CHAPTER XI.

The train to Sydney—Aspect of the country—Sir Henry Parkes—The Australian Club—The public gardens—The Soudan contingent—Feeling of the Colony about it—An Opposition minority—Mr. Dalley—Introduction to him—Day on Sydney Harbour—The flag-ship—Sir James Martin—Admiral Tryon—The colonial navy—Sir Alfred Stephen—Sunday at Sydney—Growth of the town—Excursions in the neighbourhood—Paramatta river—Temperament of the Australians.

TRAVELLING in Australia was made an inexpensive process to us—we had free passes over all the lines in Victoria, and free passes were sent us from New South Wales on the mere report that we were going thither. We left Melbourne on February 11 by the night train to Sydney. They had been very good to us there. I had found true friends, and I was sorry to think that I should probably never see them again. The line passes through the highlands where the rivers rise that run inland to the Murrumbidgee. The heat had been followed by violent rain ; and near the frontier of New South Wales an embankment and bridge had been carried away by a flood at the moment when the train from Melbourne was coming up. I read in a newspaper that the pointsman on the bridge had seen the earth giving way, and had seen the lights of the approaching engine. His own cottage, with his wife and children sleeping in it, stood in a situation where it would certainly be overwhelmed, and instant warning could alone save the lives of his family. If he advanced along the rail to stop the engine the cottage would be lost, with all in it. The choice was hard, and nature proved the strongest. The wife and children were saved, the train fell into the boiling abyss. The broken lines had been repaired. The river had fallen back into its channel, and we passed the spot unconsciously without a sight of the ruins. We reached the frontier of New South Wales at Albany at midnight. We were now in another province, among other men, other principles, and other political theories. Victoria is democratic, progressive, and eager for colonial federation. New South Wales has the same form of government; is progressive, too, in its more deliberate manner; but it is Conservative, old-fashioned in favour of Imperial federation, and opposed to Colonial federation, which it fears, as likely to lead—little as the Victorians mean it—to eventual separation and independence. There are differences of tariff too, and a certain rivalry between the two colonies. New South Wales is the elder brother, and expects a deference which it does not always meet with. We were asleep when we crossed the border. A special carriage had been reserved for us, not lined with blue satin, but comfortable enough to make us unconscious of ornamental differences.

In the morning we became aware of a change in the aspect of the country. We were in the high bush, with an occasional clearing, but the land was generally uninclosed and unoccupied; we were among mountains, or what in Australia pass for mountains—from two to three thousand feet above the sea—a wooded plateau broken into ridges, with glimpses occasionally into deeply cut valleys below. Victoria had been brown and heat-scorched. Here trees and grass were greener and fresher from the rain. Of animal life there was little visible : not many sheep or cattle ; of rabbits, none ; of kangaroos, none. There were a few magpies, a few parrots, so pretty with their bright colours that one wished for more. A pair of laughing jackasses expressed their opinion of us as we went by—only a pair ; and this was nearly all. After breakfast the country improved : farms and homesteads began to show, with inclosed fields and gardens ; villages had grown up about the stations ; boys appeared on the platforms with baskets of grapes and newspapers. From the latter, New South Wales appeared to be wholly occupied with the Soudan business, the death of Gordon, and the discredit of our poor country at home. It seemed to be assumed that we should now rouse ourselves and make an effort to recover our honour, and in this day of our trouble the Australians wished to be allowed to stand at our side. We learnt that the Ministry at Sydney had offered to send a contingent to Suakin at the Colony's expense. The offer had been despatched and the answer was anxiously expected. This was a new feature in colonial history, confirming to me all the impressions which I had formed of the colonists' true disposition. It was an interesting but an anxious event, and I could perceive that much would turn on what the answer was. A refusal would be especially pleasing to those who wished ill to the English connection.

In the forenoon we ran down from the hills to the plains, which we had seen from our window stretching blue and hazy to the horizon. Ten miles from Sydney the detached cottages became thicker, villages smartened themselves into suburbs. The city spread inland to meet us, and we had been many minutes running between houses before we arrived at the station. Sydney proper—the old Sydney of the first settlement—stands on a long neck of land at the mouth of the Paramatta river, between two deep creeks which form its harbour—that is, its inner harbour, where its docks and wharfs are. Port Jackson, the harbour proper, from which these are mere inlets, is the largest and grandest in the world. A passage about a mile wide has been cut by the ocean between the wall of sandstone cliffs which stretch along the south-west Australian shores. The two headlands stand out as gigantic piers, and the tide from without, and the freshwater flood from within, have formed an inlet shaped like a starfish, with a great central basin, and long arms and estuaries which pierce the land in all directions, and wind like veins between lofty sandstone banks. The rock is grey or red. Worn by the rains and tides of a thousand human generations, it projects in overhanging shelves, or breaks off into the water and lies there in fallen masses.

The valleys thus formed, and widening and broadening with age, are clothed universally with the primeval forest of eucalyptus, and dark Australian pine—the eucalyptus in its most protean forms, and staining its foliage in the most varied colours, the red cliffs standing out between the branches, or split and rent where the roots have driven a way into their crevices. In some of these land-locked reaches, except for the sunshine and the pure blue of the water, I could have fancied myself among the yews and arbutuses of Killarney. The harbour is on an average, I believe, about nine fathoms deep. The few shoals are marked, and vessels of the largest size lie in any part of it in perfect security. Sydney itself is about seven miles from the open sea. The entire circuit, I was told, if you follow the shore round all the winding inlets from bluff to bluff, is 200 miles. There is little tide, and therefore no unsightly mud-banks are uncovered at low water. It has the aspect and character of a perfect inland lake, save for the sea monsters—the unnumbered sharks which glide to and fro beneath the treacherous surface.

There is no originality as yet in railway stations. The station at Sydney is, like all other stations, merely convenient and hideous. We were met there by Sir Henry Parkes, ex-premier, for the present retired from public life, but probably not to remain so. He had kindly written to me when I was at Melbourne with offers of hospitality. I found him a tall, fine, hale-looking man of seventy, warm and generous in manner, and most anxious to be of use to us. The Governor, Lord Augustus Loftus, was absent in the mountains. He had left a letter for me, expressing his regret that he could not receive us at Government House, but giving us a warm invitation to pay him a visit at his country residence. E—— was to leave us to stay with his friend, Admiral Tryon, on board the 'Nelson,' in the harbour. Sir Henry Parkes, with true colonial hospitality, proposed that we should be guests of his own, or that, if we preferred to remain in Sydney—for he himself lived a great many miles out of it—we should take up our abode with a friend of his, the editor of the leading Sydney paper. The editor himself, and his handsome, bright-looking wife, who had accompanied Sir Henry to the station, heartily endorsed this invitation. In Sir Henry we should have had a host who was intimately acquainted with the internal affairs of the colony. In the house of the editor we

should have met influential and interesting gentlemen connected with the press or with politics. But for many reasons
I wished to be independent. The question of the hour was
the despatch of the colonial contingent to Suakin, and Sir
Henry had already given a voice in opposition to the Government offer. The general sentiment of the Colony was loudly
favourable, but there was a minority, which might perhaps
become a majority, who held it unnecessary, uncalled-for, and
unconstitutional, and of these Sir Henry was the leading
representative. I desired to observe impartially the movements of opinion, and I hesitated to put myself directly in the
hands of anyone who was taking a decided part. He had anticipated that this might be my feeling, and as an alternative
had found lodgings for us, if we pleased to engage them, in
Macquarie Street, the Park Lane of Sydney. The lodgings
seemed all that could be wished, but on inquiring further I
found that for our sitting-room and two bedrooms I should
have to pay the modest price of 15*l.* a week. Modest price it
essentially was, though at the first mention startling. Wages
in Sydney are twice what they are at home; and most other
things are in the same proportion. What in England costs
sixpence, in Sydney costs a shilling; money is twice as easily
earned, and the result to residents is the same in the long run.
I, however, had not come thither to earn wages double or
single, and 15*l.* a week was beyond me. We had been offered
rooms at the Australian Club; Macquarie Street overlooked
the gardens and the harbour, and the prospect from it was
exquisite; the Australian Club was in the heart of the city;
but the charges there were moderate, the bedrooms said to be
comfortable, and the living as good as could be desired. It was
close to the Bank, the public offices, and the commercial port;
the gardens were within a short walk; the Club was clearly
the place, and to this we decided to go. Sir Henry accompanied me in a cab to the door, showing me the park, and
Woolner's great statue of Cook on the way. He then left
me, not choosing to go in, as he might meet excited politicians
there. My son brought down the portmanteaus in a cab, for
which he had to pay five shillings. We settled in, and found

our quarters as satisfactory as we had been led to expect. There was not the splendour of Melbourne, but there was equal comfort, and from the cards and invitations which were instantly showered upon us we found that the disposition of the inhabitants was as warm, though it differed in form. In Victoria they wished to show us their colony ; in New South Wales they offered us admission into their society. They are not behind in energy and enterprise ; in essentials, New South Wales is as ' go-ahead ' as the sister community ; but it has been longer settled, and they go about their work more quietly. Four generations have passed since Sydney became a city, and the colonists there have contracted from the climate something of the character of a Southern race. Few collections of human beings on this planet have so much to enjoy, and so little to suffer ; and they seem to feel it, and in the midst of business to take their ease and enjoy themselves.

Among the other cards there was a note from the admiral, asking us to dine the next day on board the 'Nelson.' The deck of an English man-of-war, wherever she may be, is English soil. When you stand on those planks you are an English subject, and nothing else, under English law and authority. Colonial jurisdiction reaches to the ship's side, but goes no further. The colonists were loyal fellow-subjects and were that moment giving a distinguished proof of it ; but Oceana is not yet a political reality ; it would be pleasant to feel entirely at home, if but for a few hours ; and the account of the admiral which we had heard from E——, made me glad of an opportunity of becoming acquainted with him.

On the first evening we were left to ourselves. I walked up in the twilight to the esplanade at the gate of the public garden, and I think I have never in my life gazed on a scene so entirely beautiful. It was not for the trees and flowers. They were lovely, and anywhere in Europe would be celebrated as a wonder. But there was not the science, there was not the elaborate variety, which I had admired at Ballarat. Sydney is many degrees hotter. Tropical plants which there require glass to shelter them, at Sydney breathe luxuriantly

SYDNEY GARDENS

the free air of heaven ; but the roses and lilies of the tempo-
rate zone, which are the fairest flowers that blow, grow feebly
there, or will not grow at all. It is the situation which gives
to the Sydney garden so exquisite a charm. The ground
slopes from the town to the sea with inclining lawns, flower-
beds, and the endless variety of the tropical flora. Tall Norfolk Island pines tower up dark into the air, and grand walks
wind for miles among continually varying landscapes, which
are framed by the openings in the foliage of the perfumed
shrubs. Within the compass of the garden the sea forms two
deep bays, one of which is reserved for the ships of the squadron. Five vessels lay at anchor there, their spars black
against the evening sky, and the long pennants drooping at the
masthead ; the 'Nelson' sitting like a queen in the midst of
them, the admiral's white flag hanging over the stern. Steam-
launches were gliding at half power over the glassy waters,
which were pink with the reflection of the sunset. Boats
were bringing off officers and men who had been at leave on
shore ; the old order, form, and discipline in the new land of
liberty—the shield behind which alone the vaunted liberty is
possible. Behind the anchorage were rocky islands, with the
deserted ruins of ancient batteries, now useless and superseded
by ampler fortifications inside the bluffs. Merchant ships
lay scattered over the outer harbour, and a yacht or two lay
drifting with idle sails. Crowded steam ferry-boats were
carrying the workmen home from the city to distant villages.
On wooded upland or promontory shone the white palaces of
the Sydney merchants, and beyond again were the green hills,
softened by distance and the growing dusk into purple, which
encircle the great inlet of Port Jackson.

As a mere picture it was the loveliest that I had ever
looked upon. The bay at Rio, I am told, is equally fine, and
indeed finer, being overhung by mountains. There are no
mountains at Sydney. The Blue Range is far off on the land
side, and makes no part of the harbour scenery. But one
does not always wish for grandeur. Sydney has the perfection of soft beauty, and one desires no more. At Rio, moreover, if the English flag is seen, it flies as a stranger. At

L

Sydney there are the associations of home—we are among
our own people, in a land which our fathers had won for us.

I stood admiring till twilight had become night. The
stars grew visible and the great bats, the flying squirrels, came
out to hunt the foolish moths. I could take in the scene only
as a whole. The details of it I studied afterwards. The air
was sultrier even than at St. Hubert's ; greater heat had not
been known, even at Sydney, for several years. I returned to
my club and to bed, to find, alas ! that I was not yet in Paradise ; or if I was, it was Paradise after the Fall.

Dead-tired, I slept till morning—safe, as I fondly believed,
behind mosquito-curtains. I awoke bitten over hands and
face as a young author is bitten by the critics on his first
appearance in print. The mosquito of Sydney is the most
venomous of his whole detested race. Where he has fastened
his fangs and poured in his poison, there rise lumps and blotches
which irritate to madness. The blotch opens into a sore, and
I was left with a wound on the back of my right hand which
did not heal for a month. Happily, again like the critic, he
chiefly torments the new-comers. I was inoculated that night
and suffered no more afterwards. Perhaps the blood is in
some way affected and the venom finds an antidote.

One forgets, however, even mosquito-bites among entirely
new sensations. The club reading-room after breakfast was
full of gentlemen in eager and anxious conversation on the
auxiliary force. Was it right to have made the offer, and
would the offer be accepted ? The prevailing tone was of
hope and warm approval. New South Wales had been accused
of coldness to the Australian federation scheme, and of indifference to the German aggression in New Guinea. The
true heart of the colony had now an opportunity of showing
what it really was. If the proposal was coldly refused, as
some thought it would be, then indeed it would be a fresh
instance of the indifference with which the colonies were
regarded. It would be a sign that the Separatist policy was
to be persevered in at home, and an impulse would be given to
the Separatist policy in their own country to which, in that
case, they might have reluctantly to yield. But they hoped

better things. The people of England would not cast away a hand so freely held out to them. It might draw the nation together instead of dividing it, and prove a turning-point in the relation between the colonies and the mother country.

There was not unanimity, however. There were some, and these not at all fools and not disloyal, who maintained that the answer would certainly be negative, and that they were exposing themselves gratuitously to an affront. If even it were accepted, the offer ought not to have been made so precipitately, when the Colonial Parliament was not sitting, and the constitutional sanction could neither be asked nor obtained. Mr. Dalley, who had taken upon himself to speak for the Colony, was not even Prime Minister. He was the Attorney-General and acting-Premier only in the absence of his chief, Mr. Stuart. On the general merits of the question there was no occasion for Australia to thrust herself unasked into England's foreign complications. If the great Powers combined to injure England there would be a claim on them to which, of course, they would respond ; but this Egyptian affair was a war of England's own seeking, and for them to mix themselves up with it would be at once gratuitous and useless, and an unjustifiable burden upon the colonial resources. England had withdrawn her troops from the colonies, and had charged them with the cost of their own defence. If they wanted soldiers she had warned them that they must provide soldiers for themselves. An English fleet was still in their waters, but they had been encouraged and were expected to fit out ships of their own, and had already formed an imperfect squadron. They had been even forced to accept a difference in their flag. It was absurd, under these circumstances, to strip themselves of the scanty force which they possessed, to leave themselves without sufficient trained men to serve their batteries, and to invite attack from the rest of the world in case the war spread, which it was exceedingly likely to do. England's conduct in the Egyptian business had left her without a friend in Europe. Already rumours were heard of differences on the Afghan frontier with Russia, and the Russian fleet in the Amoor was a dangerous neighbour.

So long as they kept aloof from these complications, foreign nations might respect their neutrality. England had ostentatiously told them that she wanted nothing of them except that they should spare her further trouble. To put themselves forward unasked was to challenge attack, and was Quixotic and absurd. They might wake up some morning to find the Russian ironclads at the Bluff, and Sydney at their mercy, and Sir Henry Parkes had said plainly that a minister who went into such an enterprise without leave of Parliament, on his own responsibility, would deserve to be impeached.

The answer from Lord Derby had been delayed. Something was said to be wrong with the telegraph on the Persian frontier. Strange to think that communication between London and an island at the Antipodes should be carried on through ancient Parthia and across the rivers of Ecbatana and Babylon! It was not to be denied that there was force in Parkes's arguments. England's own attitude to the colonies, so far as it had been defined by the leading Liberal statesmen, had incited and provoked them to dissociate themselves from her. Had the answer of England when it arrived been hesitating, or had it been long in coming, reflection would have given weight to the objections. The impulse would have died away and no more would have been heard about the matter. But the wires were replaced quickly, and brought a warm and grateful assent. The Agent-General in London sent word that the offer of the Colony had been welcomed with universal appreciation by the whole English nation, and the corresponding enthusiasm was irresistible. To be allowed to share in the perils and glories of the battle-field, as part of a British army, was regarded at once as a distinction of which Australia might be proud and as a guarantee of their future position as British subjects. The help which they were now giving might be slight, but Australia in a few years would number ten millions of men, and this small body was an earnest of what they might do hereafter. If ever England herself was threatened, or if there was another mutiny in India, they would risk life, fortune—all they had—as willingly as they were sending their present contingent. It was a practical demonstration in favour of Imperial unity.

Volunteers crowded to enrol their names. Patriotic citizens gave contributions of money on a scale which showed that little need be feared for the taxpayer. Archbishop Moran, the Catholic Primate, gave a hundred pounds, as an example and instruction to the Irish ; others, the wealthy ones, gave a thousand. The rush of feeling was curious and interesting to witness. The only question with me was if it would last. The ancient Scythians discussed critical national affairs first drunk and then sober. Excited emotion is followed by a cold fit, and it is desirable to postpone a final decision till the cold fit has come. If the force went and was cut to pieces, if it was kept in garrison and not exposed in the field, if it suffered from sickness or from any one of the innumerable misadventures to which troops on active service are liable, the sense of glory might turn to discontent, the tide would change, and worse might follow than if the enterprise had never been ventured. The opposition was not silenced ; I listened for a quarter of an hour to an orator haranguing a crowd in the public park. He spoke well, and I was glad that I had not to answer him. 'What was this war in the Soudan ?' he said ; 'who were these poor Arabs, and why were we killing them ? By our own confession they were brave men who were fighting for the liberty of their country. Why had we invaded them ? Did we want to take their country from them ? If it was necessary for our own safety there would be some excuse, but we had ostentatiously declared that after conquering them we intended to withdraw. Neither we nor anyone could tell what we wanted. We were shooting down human beings in tens of thousands, whose courage we ourselves admired. They had done us no wrong, and no object could be suggested save that the English Government had a difficulty in keeping their party contented in Parliament. Was this a cause in which far-off Australia should seek a part uncalled-for, or lend her sanction to an enormous crime ? Let her keep at home and mind her own business, and not add, without better occasion, to the burdens of her people.'

The crowd listened, and here and there, especially when the speaker dwelt upon the right of all people to manage their own affairs, there were murmurs of approval; but the immense majority were indifferent or hostile. The man, in fact, was speaking beside the mark. The New South Wales colonists cared nothing about the Soudan. They were making a demonstration in favour of national identity. Many causes combined to induce them to welcome the opportunity of being of use. There was a genuine feeling for Gordon. There was a genuine indignation against Mr. Gladstone's Government. Gordon was theirs as well as ours. He was the last of the race of heroes who had won for England her proud position among the nations; he had been left to neglect and death, and the national glory was sullied. There was a desire, too, to show those who had scorned the colonists, and regarded them as a useless burden on the Imperial resources, that they were as English as the English at home. We might refuse them a share in our successes. We could not and should not refuse them a share in our trials. 'You do not want us,' they seemed to say, 'but we are part of you, bone of your bone; we refuse to be dissociated from you.' It was an appeal to the English people against the English political philosophers; an answer which would at last be listened to against the advocates of separation. If it failed to convince Mr. Goldwin Smith and his disciples, it would deprive them of further support from the body of the nation. It would have a further effect which would be felt all the world over. In their estimate of the strength, present and future, of Great Britain, the great Powers had left the colonies unconsidered. In that quarter, at least, the effect of Mr. Goldwin Smith's theories was well understood. Other nations would grow. England, if it shut itself within its own limits, could not grow, or would grow only to her own destruction. They would increase and she would decrease, and they despised her accordingly. They had taken the political economists as the exponents of the national sentiment. They had assumed that if war came the colonies would immediately fall off. In this spontaneous act of the Australians the great Powers would see that they would have to reckon not with a small island whose relative consequence was decreasing daily, but with a mighty empire with a capacity for unbounded expansion, her naval fortunes duly supported in the four quarters of the globe, a new England growing daily in population and in wealth with incredible speed, and all parts of it combined in a passion of patriotism, with the natural cord of affinity to which the strongest political confederacy was as a rope of straw. A contingent of 700 men was nothing in itself, but it was a specimen from an inexhaustible mine. To India too a lesson would be read, if any there were dreaming of another mutiny. It would be seen that the British rulers of India had a fresh reservoir of strength within striking distance.

This sudden display of feeling had been recognised by the remarkable man who at the moment was at the helm in New South Wales, and being himself an earnest believer in Oceana, he saw an opportunity before him of bringing that splendid vision a step nearer to reality. Mr. Dalley knew as well as his opponents that he was running a risk. But for a great object great risks must be run. No great thing has ever been done in this world by a man who is afraid of responsibility. The present moment was his own. For the time, at least, he had the opinion of the Colony at his back. It might have been better perhaps to have deliberated longer—safer for him to have called the Parliament together. But there was no time for either. The thing, if done at all, must be done immediately. The colony was in a fever of military preparation; all available stores were laid hands upon. The steamers in the harbour were secured with the most splendid indifference to expense. In the temper which men were in, five or six times the force could have been raised with equal ease if the occasion had required. Was the despatch of the Contingent a mere ridiculous outburst of vanity and sentiment? Was it a wise and generous act, good in itself, and promising to lead in future to greater good? This was the question which all men were asking one another on the morning after

our arrival in Sydney, and our visit could not have fallen at a
more interesting time. A gentleman at the club, Mr. Augustus
Morris (I mention his name that I may thank him for many
acts of politeness), was a friend of Mr. Dalley and volunteered
after breakfast to introduce me to him. I was shy of intruding upon a man who was engaged in so large an affair and
whose time was precious. Mr. Morris, however, undertook
that Mr. Dalley would be glad to see me, and that my call
upon him would not be regarded with impatience. The Government offices—a large and handsome range of buildings overlooking the Commercial harbour—were but a few steps distant.
It was still extremely hot. We found the acting-Premier
in a spacious lofty room, the windows all open, himself at his
table in his shirt-sleeves ; secretaries about him busy writing ;
officers, civil and military, waiting instructions, and the
Premier himself, the coolest-looking object in the apartment,
giving out his instructions with an easy unembarrassed
manner, as if organising expeditions had been the occupation
of his life. Several minutes passed before he could attend to
us, and I used them in looking closely at a man who was
making, perhaps, an epoch in Colonial history. Mr. Dalley
was a short, thickset man of fifty or thereabouts, with strong
neck, large head, a clear steady eye, and firmly shaped mouth
and chin. The face was good-humoured, open, and generous.
When he laughed it was heartily, without a trait of malice.
The directions which I heard him giving were quiet but
distinct, no words wasted, but the thing meant clearly said.
He was evidently a strong man, but perhaps generally an in-
dolent one, who might not think it worth while to exert himself except on extraordinary occasions. In fact, he had not
so far cared to take a leading part in Colonial politics. He
was a successful lawyer. He was Attorney-General, but pro-
fessionally too he had not been covetous of extensive business.
He was a Roman Catholic, but a Catholic of the high cultivated and liberal type of which Cardinal Newman is the chief
living representative. He had read largely, was a fine Italian
scholar, a collector of pictures, an architect—in short, a man
at all points, in whom the accident of his leader's ill-health

had, at a critical moment, placed the direction of the affairs of
the Colony. An anecdote—a very touching one—was mentioned to me of his private life, which I hope that he will
pardon me for mentioning. I was looking at a singularly
pretty house overhanging the water, picturesque in itself and
beautifully situated. 'That was Dalley's,' a friend observed
to me. 'He built it ; his wife died there, and he could never
bear to enter it afterwards. It was sold, and he now lives,
with his only child, at the other end of the harbour. He never
thought of marrying again, and he never will.'

This was the man whose leisure we were waiting for. As
soon as he was able to speak to us, he was most kind and
cordial, but of leisure he had very little. He said a few words
to me about the expedition, and seemed pleased with such
answers as I could give ; but a dozen fresh people were waiting for his orders. 'You see how I am situated,' he said ; 'I
cannot talk to you now, but I shall have other opportunities.
We must make your stay at Sydney as pleasant as we can.
What can we do for you this morning ?' Mr. Morris suggested
something. 'Yes, that will be the best,' he said ; 'we will send
you round the harbour.' He called a servant, bade him order
the Government steam-launch to be ready at the stairs in a
quarter of an hour, and then dismissed us, to go on with his
work. There, I thought to myself, is a man whom it is worth
while to have come all this way to see.

Mr. Morris kept us in charge. The launch duly appeared
with the British flag at the stern—a long, fast, handsome boat,
the stern-seats comfortably, but not luxuriously, fitted, and an
awning spread over them. A large basket of delicious black
grapes was provided, as a corrective of the heat, and away we
steamed eight or ten knots an hour, and making a breeze out
of our own speed, to explore the recesses of the loveliest of all
salt-water lakes. There are a few spots marked with white as
we look back over the story of our lives—with me chiefly
landscapes of wood and water, or interviews with some superior
man. This day stands among the brightest in my memory on
both accounts, for I had seen Mr. Dalley, and next I saw Port
Jackson. We shot under the stern of the 'Nelson,' ran

through the squadron, and skirted the shores of the public
gardens, as beautiful from the sea as the sea was beautiful
from them. We wound round the shallow bays, under the
windows of palaces like Aladdin's.   I inquired who might be
the owner of one of these which was of exceptional magnificence.   Mr. Tooth, I was told, brother of the Mr. Tooth theo-
logically famous some years ago in London, the family talent
being many-sided and achieving distinction in more lines than
one.   The fine houses grew scarcer as we increased our distance
from Sydney.   The primitive forest was less invaded save by
an occasional sea-mark or memorial column.   Yachts and
fishing-boats were round us.   Sydney is a great place for
yachting, in the still water and yet ample sea-room.   The
ship-channel narrows two miles within the Heads, and becomes
intricate among hidden rocks and shoals.   The passage between
them has been selected as the point of defence, and we saw on
either side among the hills the escarpments of modern batteries,
on which, I believe, a few guns of heavy calibre are already
mounted, and others are to follow.   Turning in and out along
the coast line we doubled the distance which we had to travel
over.   After an hour of fast-going we came in sight of the
Heads, and exchanged the lakelike stillness of the inland
water for the ocean swell that rolled in between them.   The
sandstone cliffs now became more rugged from the fretting of
the waves, projecting in overhanging shelves where the softer
stone was eaten out below them.   Trunks of dead trees stood
bare and desolate among the fallen blocks.   Had our launch
been less 'tender,' we could have looked outside and perhaps
caught a shark or two by trailing a baited line ; but she was
already lurching heavily as we crossed the mouth and were
broadside to the swell.   We got into shelter again in a long
deep inlet at the head of which was a beach of white sand and
a number of good-looking cottages and houses, one of which
belonged to Mr. Morris himself ; another and a larger on an
eminence was the second house of Mr. Dalley, which he had
again erected on his own design.   Mr. Morris gave us luncheon,
and afterwards we walked up to look at it, the owner being,
as we knew, absent.   It was a castle half finished ; built in

pieces, a room completed here, a turret there, with the intervals to be filled up at leisure. The exterior of the mansion was picturesque in its way, or promised to become so. The interior jarred a little on my bigoted Protestantism, for the walls of the living-rooms were covered either with fresco paintings or pictures and engravings, all of a neo-Catholic complexion. The view from the terrace was curious as well as magnificent, for we could see across the sandy ridge at the head of the inlet into the open ocean. The distance was scarcely a quarter of a mile from sea to sea, and a second entrance into the harbour is very nearly formed there.

Taking again to our launch we entered what might have been the mouth of a river, but is merely a deep estuary with long narrow reaches running for many miles between shores which became higher and bolder as we went on. Inlet opened out of inlet as with the fiords in Norway. The primeval eucalyptus forest was here undisturbed in its original condition ; the trees, some enormous, with distorted and fantastic stems, the foliage so luxuriant and so many-coloured that no painter could dare to imitate it. Sometimes we were in utter solitude ; sometimes we came suddenly on waterside hotel or boarding-house to which the Sydney people went for change of air.

A cottage boldly placed behind a high crag hanging over the sea and half-concealed among rocks and trees, was the home of one of the professors of Sydney University. Then again we passed a group of tents where students were out on a reading party ; while between hollows in the hills we caught sight of the masts and spars of a ship lying at anchor in a bay, which by water might be a dozen miles from us and over the land might be a mile or less.

Mr. Morris was the best of guides ; naturally, however, he had much to ask about our affairs at home. The morning's telegraph had brought news of General Earle's death, and Frederick Burnaby's, with many other officers'. What was to come of all that ? Then again about the great Upas-tree policy ? I could only tell him that this last had resulted so far in Ireland being put into a strait waistcoat, while the

English influence there had been ruined. Crimes had lessened, some people thought as a consequence of the concessions to Irish ideas, others thought from the waistcoat only ; but I would have preferred not to talk about so dreary a subject. We turned home after seeing about half of the wonders of the harbour, leaving the rest to another day.

In the evening there was a dinner on board the 'Nelson,' where we found E—— again. The admiral is in person a giant, but, unlike most giants, a man of marked ability, a first-rate sailor, an accomplished and prudent administrator, a diplomat, dignified, courteous, cultivated, a gentleman in the finest sense of the word. His flag-captain—Captain Lake, whom I had met in England—dined with us, and several other officers. Among the guests was the Chief Justice, Sir James Martin, a stout, round-faced, remarkable old man, with the fine classical training which belonged to the last generation of distinguished lawyers, and well read in the best modern literature. Sir James has filled successively all the highest posts in the Colony, and all with eminent success. He was a brilliant talker, and I sat with him alone after coffee, in the stern gallery, hearing his opinions on many interesting subjects : Greek and Roman literature, modern poetry, modern philosophy, and then naturally modern democracy with its causes and tendencies. Again, as at Melbourne, I perceived that in respect of intellectual eminence the mother-country has no advantage over the colonies. If Sir James Martin had been Chief Justice of England, he would have passed as among the most distinguished occupants of that high position ; and I should say that the Australian colonies, in proportion to their population, have more eminent men than we have. The English race, wherever it is planted, is of the same natural texture, but the development depends on the conditions of life and the intellectual atmosphere. England in the sixteenth century contained greater statesmen, greater poets, greater seamen, and probably greater lawyers, than she has produced at any time since, because the nation was in full health, and was occupied with great subjects. The mental occupations of the Australian colonists are probably much of the same sort as ours. But they breathe a freer air. The material race of life is less severe, and they are less harassed with vulgar anxieties. If intellect is the eye of the mind, and, like the eye, is good or bad as the images which it forms of things correctly represent the truth of the things themselves, I should not wonder if the few elect among them had more of this quality than we have.

Sir James Martin, though one of the chief persons in a progressive and democratic community, did not seem to believe that either progress or democracy was about to work any miracles in the alteration of human character. They had to be accepted like all other facts, when brought on by the nature of things, but were not therefore either to be particularly rejoiced over, or particularly hated. On the whole, democracy worked like galvanism in disintegrating the existing conditions of human society; but human society occasionally fell into a state when disintegration could not be helped. Constitutional government in the colonies was full of anomalies. It might have been better if, instead of leaving the colonists to govern themselves, we had been careful to send out efficient governors, who would have attended to colonial opinion, and ruled firmly, with no consideration of anything but each colony's good. A monarchy, when there was security that the monarch himself should be a wise man, was the best of all forms of government. But as things stood at present, this was out of the question. As long as the colonies were under the authority of Downing Street, and Downing Street was under the authority of the British Parliament, it was impossible that the affairs of the colonies would receive anything like fair and impartial consideration, or that the persons selected to conduct their affairs would always be the wisest that could be found. The policy which would be adopted would be measured, not with a view to the good of the colony, but to party advantage at home. In fact, a country under a parliament could govern itself more or less ill, but could not govern other countries, and the system had to end. All causes of disagreement between the mother-country and its dependencies were now removed; nothing but good-will need exist between them, and the closer union on another basis, which so many practical men regard as a dream, Sir James seemed to look at as the natural outgrowth of our present relations. He not only had formed considerable hopes that confederation would be brought about, but he anticipated that it might turn to the spiritual advantage of the whole of us, and help to disenchant us of the empty wind and nonsense to which we were at present given over. So long as ' progress,' et cætera, was mere talk, it was contemptible, but might be borne with ; but issuing now as it was doing in Soudan massacres, Irish anarchy, and a second Ireland growing in South Africa, it deserved the hatred and indignation of all serious men. The celebrated person whom we have chosen as our chief leader and representative in this adventure is no favourite in Australia. He and his amazing popularity were mere subjects of astonishment to Sir James, as they are, so far as my travels extend, wherever the British language is spoken. Leaders of another type would rule in a United Oceana.

It was interesting to me to remember where I was sitting. It was democracy which had brought about these ugly features —democracy, which had invaded all other departments of the State, but had stopped short at the man-of-war. On the fleet the noisiest demagogue of us knew that our salvation depended; and as the fleet required to be a fact which would stand hard blows, there at least the old order and the old principles of authority were allowed to remain. A ship of war administered on elective and representative principles would not be a dangerous combatant. There would perhaps be a corresponding improvement if a nation was administered as a ship of war. Such England once was. Such, perhaps, she will one day be again, when she has delivered herself from a condition in which a majority in an election or in a House of Commons division is exulted over as a victory over a domestic enemy, and national honour, national integrity, even national interest are second to the triumph of party.

The admiral spoke to me afterwards about a matter of which I have already said something : the navy or navies of the colonies. Indirect overtures seemed to have been made to him for some change in the arrangements now existing. He could not himself entertain these overtures, but they had been referred to the Admiralty at home, and the matter itself was a considerable one. The Russian scare was not yet at the acute stage, but the appearance of things was threatening. If war came, Australia would be exposed to serious danger. The colonists were anxious, and the state of the defences both on land and sea was not at all satisfactory. The admiral will have given his own views to the home authorities. I can myself only explain the bearings of the situation as I learnt them from general conversation. The Colonial Governments, when started on their own account, were expected to provide themselves with armed vessels adequate to their own defence, which in time of war were to be under the command of the admiral of the station. They were to be themselves responsible for the equipment and maintenance of these vessels in a condition fit for service, and they have done, perhaps, all that it was in their power to do. We have ourselves given them the nucleus of a navy, in ships which we could afford to part with. They have been furnished with trained officers from home. Whether they have built or bought ships of their own I do not know. But let them do what they will, they have enormous difficulties to contend with. In countries where the executive is weak, where wages are high, and the demand for labour so constant, where every man is accustomed to be his own master, and unrestrained liberty is a special privilege of their present mode of existence' it is almost impossible to keep efficient crews together and maintain the necessary discipline. The naval department is extremely expensive in proportion to the results which it can achieve, and although the spirit of the colonists can be relied upon at any moment of emergency, a squadron fit to go to sea cannot be extemporised in a hurry. The Colonial Legislature cannot be expected to spend very large sums annually on a service which in time of peace has no duties to discharge. The consequence is that the ships, however good in themselves, are not and cannot be kept in readiness for immediate action. In these days warnings are short. A serious danger, it is morally certain, would find every one of our great colonies unprepared to meet it, and the duty of defending the colonial ports—a duty which could not be declined—would fall, after all, on the mother-country. The colonists are generous enough to feel that the mother-country is thus not treated fairly. It is a state of things which cannot and must not continue, and this being so, the same suggestion had been made (I believe by responsible persons) to the admiral which had been mentioned to me at Adelaide and Melbourne, that the colonies—the Australian colonies at any rate—should make an estimate of the present cost of their ships, and pay it as a subsidy to the British Admiralty, on condition that an effective squadron or squadrons should be kept always in Australian waters.

In addition to the immediate object in view, the security of Sydney and Melbourne, a joint interest in the fleet would be a long step—so long that another would hardly be needed—towards Imperial Confederation. The cords that hold Oceana together may be slight in appearance if they are woven of seaman's hemp, but no hemp is better spun than the Admiralty ropes with the red thread at their heart. The union with Australia would be at once a visible fact, and that in a form which would leave no opening for interference with colonial autonomy. The misgiving in New South Wales was that the Imperial Government, being committed to the doctrinal theory of colonial independence, would refuse to listen to the proposal. I do not know whether the subject has yet been brought officially before either the Admiralty or the Colonial Office, or how many of the colonies, or whether any, have put their wishes into formal shape. The advances, of course, must come from them. The expression of a desire on our part for such an arrangement would be construed into a design for levying a revenue on them, and would be met at once by suspicion and jealousy. The act must be their own, if it is to take effect at all. We have given them free control of their own affairs, and it is not for us to ask for part of it again. But, in my own poor opinion, if the Australian colonies do of their own free accord propose such conditions, the ministry responsible for rejecting them will leave a sinister record of themselves in English history.

Many gentlemen were good enough to call on me in the next few days ; one of them, Sir Alfred Stephen, Deputy-Governor of the Colony, and near kinsman of our own distinguished Sir James. Any Stephen could not fail to be interesting. I was out when he came to the club, but I returned his visit at the earliest moment. I found a bright-eyed, humorous old man, whose intellect, though he was over eighty, advanced years had not yet begun to touch, and whose body they had touched but lightly ; for eye and check kept their colour, and the step was still elastic and the voice keen and clear. I could trace no resemblance in the actual features to our English Stephens, yet, with the knowledge of the relationship, I fancied a likeness of expression, and certainly in mind and temper there was very great likeness indeed. Sir Alfred was not given to sentimental views of things. On the bench he was famous for the straightforward view which he took of rogues. 'The law is far too indulgent to such people,' he said. Yet there was no harshness about him, or needless severity. He had the family perception of the ridiculous and humorous side of things, and was full of pity for all who deserved it, and for a great many more that didn't. His talk with me was most amusing, chiefly on his old English recollections. He had been brought up in the 'Clapham sect,' and had known their chief notabilities. He had himself once boxed Sam Wilberforce's ears for impudence. He remembered old Wilberforce one day talking intolerable nonsense, and a great-uncle of his who was unable to bear it breaking a couple of eggs on old Wilberforce's head. He had thought much on serious subjects. Most men's minds petrify by middle age, and are incapable of new impressions. Sir Alfred's mind had remained fluid. He had held by the Clapham theory of things till he found the bottom break out of it. He disliked especially the irreverent acquaintance with the intentions of Providence to which conventionally religious people pretend. His reputation in the colony is of the very highest, and it is a reputation which no one envies and is cheerfully conceded. If you ask Sydney people who their greatest man is, nine out of ten of them will say Stephen. He has been at the head of his own

M

profession for half his life; he has filled the highest offices in the Colony, and has been universally honoured and respected. The family will not die out in New South Wales. He has several sons, all of whom are making their way, and some are already distinguished. He was himself a beautiful old man, whom it was a delight to have seen. Unhappily it was but once, and only for an hour, as he was called off on business to Melbourne, and thought as little of the journey of four hundred miles as if he had been starting on his first circuit.

Afterwards, in New Zealand, I fell in with a brother of Sir Alfred's, Mr. Milner Stephen, also a very noticeable person. In him the hereditary spiritual tendencies had drifted into technical spiritualism. He professed, and evidently believed himself, to have acquired the apostolic power of working miracles. He was willing to cure you of any disorder whatever by some simple methods, which he was ready also to teach you to exercise if you cared to learn them—not, of course, gratuitously. I suppose he thought that those who ministered at the altar must live by the altar. I did not see any instance of his power, but his look and manner were lively and clever.

Admiral Tryon was most hospitable. The 'Nelson' was always open to us for dinner, luncheon, and on Sunday for service. She is not an ironclad. If she goes into action, shot and shell will find free passage through her; but she is a magnificent ship of immense beam, and a fit symbol of England's naval greatness. Sunday afternoons were holidays. On board, the seamen were off duty and lay about, reading or otherwise amusing themselves. On shore there was the same disposition as at home to walk or lounge in the parks and gardens. It is a good opportunity for seeing the Sydney people at their average best. On Sunday, in the public park, I saw a number of black groups, gathered as with us round persons who were addressing them. I went from group to group, to hear what was going on. It was Battersea or Hyde Park over again. At one was a temperance orator, clamorous for local option; at another a 'nigger,' eloquent on the way of salvation; at a third a Wesleyan minister or school teacher declaiming on the same subject. The crowd listened respectfully, but languidly, brightening up, however, when the addresses were exchanged for one of Sankey's hymns. One thing struck me especially, both here and at Melbourne, that there was no provincialism, either formed or tending to form. One county in England differs from another county. Devonshire has one voice and manner, and Yorkshire another voice and manner. The Devonshire man and the Yorkshire man can scarcely understand each other when they are eager and fall into dialect. The Australians speak all pure English as it is taught in schools. There are no local distinctions among themselves. There is no general tone, like the American, that my ear could detect. I could not tell whether to be pleased or not at this. On the one side it showed how English they yet were ; on the other, it indicated that they were still in the imitative stage. Original force and vigour always tend to make a form for themselves, after their own likeness.

Though I care less for places than for people, I made excursions in the neighbourhood of Sydney and drove over the city itself. I saw the villas on the bay, with their fairylike gardens. Invitations were kindly sent to me to stay in various houses. The 'glory of hospitality,' which Camden speaks of as in his time decaying in England, has revived among the colonists. They are proud of their country and like to show it off, and they welcome anyone who comes to them from the old home. I had many persons to see, however, and much to do, and the club remained my headquarters. Sydney is antique for Australia ; it is nearly a hundred years old, with the foundations of it laid in a penal settlement. The convict traces have long disappeared, but you can see, in the narrow and winding streets in the business quarter, that it is not a modern town, which has been built mechanically and laid out upon a plan, but that it has grown in the old English fashion. There are handsome streets, with grand fronts and arcades, and there are lanes and alleys as in London, with dull, unsightly premises, where nevertheless active business is going on. Trees are planted wherever there is room for them, and there is ample breathing ground in the parks. After various fortunes trade is now developing with extreme rapidity, and the ambition of the inhabitants is growing along with it. The tonnage of the vessels which now annually enter and leave the port of Sydney exceeds the tonnage of the Thames in the first year of our present Queen. As in London, the city proper on the edge of the harbour is given up to warehouses, commercial chambers and offices, banks and public buildings. In the daytime it is thronged. In the evening the hive empties itself, and merchants, clerks, and workmen stream away by railway or ferry to their suburban houses. Property rises fast in value, and the 'unearned increment' is in no danger from Socialistic politicians. Capital frightened away by recent experiments from England and Ireland is flowing fast into these countries, and house property in Sydney is being sought after for investment. I examined various blocks of buildings which had been purchased recently for a friend of my own, which yield him now six per cent. after all expenses have been deducted, and must inevitably grow more and more valuable. The houses of the wealthy and moderately wealthy classes are solid and well-looking. The working people, who in late years have flocked into the place in such numbers, are accommodated in more makeshift fashion. Whole villages have sprung up lately in the environs, made of mere boards and corrugated iron, slatternly sheds rather than human habitations, and without the plantations and flowers about them which had been universal in Victoria. But this is per-haps a temporary accident which a few more years will mend.

We went out one day to Paramatta, the original seat of the Government when Sydney was no more than a landing-place. It is a strange mixture of old and new—walls and gables of English manor-houses of the type of the last century, with big gateways and oak avenues, the oaks the largest that I had seen in Australia ; the spot still shown where an over-rash governor, driving four-in-hand, upset his carriage and killed his lady. Antiquarian interests of this kind stand side by side with painted and gilded modern streets, telling of money-making and what is called enterprise.

The Paramatta river is navigable as far as the town. The site was chosen for the ' Residence,' I suppose, for the same reason which, Thucydides says, led the Greeks to build their cities up creeks and inlets—to be safe from visits from privateers. Buccaneers are gone ; the successors of Kidd and Blackman now work in stealthier ways. Paramatta has sunk into a suburb of Sydney, and the river is now chiefly famous as the scene of the champion boat-races. We had gone out by rail ; we returned in a steamer. The stream at the head of the tideway is about the breadth of the Thames at Richmond, and of a dirty brown colour, like most of the Australian rivers, from the alluvial soil which they bring down. The banks were at first low and swampy, fringed with some kind of willow, with high wooded hills behind, which as we descended came nearer to the river, and at last on one side touched it, rising picturesquely out of the water which opened into a wide estuary. The scene was pretty enough. Cranes and other waders stalked about the mud-flats. Cottages appeared on the slopes with orchards and vineyards. We stopped at some platform every mile, where brightly dressed women and children came on board, with grapes and fruit for the Sydney market. On long wooded peninsulas large houses began to show among the trees, some of them rising to the dignity of 'places,' or even palaces ; the utterly wild and the utterly civilised brought close together, fancy pleasure-grounds adjoining the primitive jungle. The Sydney people are much given to picnics. In one of the wildest spots we came on two steamer-loads of young gentlemen and ladies who had landed, and were scattered about in pairs, the pink parasols and green and blue dresses shining among the rocks and bushes, the artificial flowers of modern society dropped strangely into the primeval forest.

All human beings have their deficiencies. The deficiency of the Sydney colonists is one which they share at present with a large part of the civilised world—that they have no severe intellectual interests. They aim at little except what money will buy ; and to make money and buy enjoyment with it is the be-all and the end-all of their existence. They are courteous and polite, as well to one another as to strangers, in a degree not common in democracies. They are energetic in bringing out the material wealth of the soil. They have churches and schools and a university, and they talk and think much of education, &c. They study sanitary questions, and work hard to improve the health of their city, and to keep their bay unpolluted. They are tunnelling out a gigantic sewer through several miles of rock and clay, to carry the refuse of the town to the open ocean. But it is only to conquer the enemies of material comfort, that their own lives may be bright and pleasant. ' Woe to those that are at ease in Zion !' the prophet cried. Was this the language of a true seer ? or the complaint of a sour dyspeptic, who grudged to others the enjoyment denied to himself ? It is hard to quarrel with men who only wish to be innocently happy. And out of this very wish there is growing a taste for art which in time may come to something considerable. They have a picture gallery of considerable merit. Mr. Montefiore (a relation of Sir Moses) took me to see it. There are many good water-colour sketches of Australian scenery by Sydney artists, one or two fair oil landscapes, with an admirable collection of engravings and casts from the finest classical works. I especially admired a set of drawings which showed real genius. I inquired for the hand which had executed them, and I learnt, to my surprise, that it was Mr. Montefiore's own. He had been modestly silent about his own accomplishments, and only my accidental question had led him to speak of him-self. Yet with the exception of two or three leading lawyers and the more eminent statesmen, there were no persons that I met with who showed much concern about the deeper spiritual problems, in the resolution of which alone man's life rises into greatness. They have had one poet—Gordon—something too much of the Guy Livingstone type, an inferior Byron, a wild rider, desperate, dissipated, but with gleams of a most noble nature shining through the turbid atmosphere. He, poor fellow, hungering after what Australia could not give him— what perhaps no country on earth at present could give him— had nothing to do but to shoot himself, which he accordingly did. Our stepmother Nature grudges to individuals and to nations too unbroken prosperity. She has a whip for the

backs of most of us, and insists on our learning lessons which
nothing but suffering will teach. Left wholly to themselves
to work out their own destiny, the Australian colonies might
have to fight for their liberties against invaders, or, as most
other mutually independent communities living side by side
have done, might fall out among themselves. Ambitious men
would force their way to the front, aspire to dictatorship, or
covet their neighbours' territories. Nations are but enlarged
schoolboys. The smallest trifle will bring about a quarrel between rival adjoining states, as long as it is undecided which
of them is the strongest. It has always been so from the
Greek democracies to the Italian republics or the Spanish
states in modern South America. Or, again, they would have
their war of classes, their internal revolutions, their dreams of
a millennium to be brought about by political convulsions.
These are Nature's methods of disciplining human character
and bringing us to know that life is not all a holiday. Out of
such struggles great men have risen and great nations, and, so
far as we know, greatness cannot be purchased at any lower
price. For the English colonies there is no such school yet
opened, nor while they remain attached to us on the present
terms can such a school ever be opened.

Fortunati nimium sua si bona nôrint.

We must ourselves be a broken power before a stranger
can invade Australia or New Zealand. Revolutions and internal wars are not permitted to them as long as they are
British dependencies. They have no foreign policy, no diplo-
matists, no intercourse with the political circles in other parts
of the world, to call out their intellect or extend their interests beyond their own shores. For the immortal part of
them, concern for which in other ages has raised peasants into
heroes and students into saints—as to this they are no better
off than the rest of us. Religion has become a matter of
opinion, a thing about which nothing certain can be known,
and on which, therefore, it is idle and unbecoming to be
dogmatic or violent. Individuals have their personal convictions, strong enough and sincere enough to make their lives

holy and beautiful ; but Church and creed have ceased to be
factors in the commonwealth. The laws by which we regulate
the conduct of our affairs are learnt from earthly experience,
and would be equally necessary and equally expedient if we
were consciously and avowedly without notions of religion at
all. A faith for which men were ready to sacrifice life and
fortune was powerful to fill their existence, and give dignity
to any position and any occupation. Our beliefs no longer
exercise such an all-absorbing, all-pervading influence. The
serious side of our nature requires other objects both for con-
templation and for action, if it is not to rust in us unused ;
and in this respect, and for the present, we have the colonists
at advantage ; we have our national concerns to look after,
and our national risks to run, and therefore our thoughts and
anxieties are enlarged. They have none of these interests ;
their situation does not allow it. They will have good lawyers
among them, good doctors, good men of science, engineers,
merchants, manufacturers, as the Romans had in the decline
of the Empire. But of the heroic type of man, of whom
poets will sing and after ages be anxious to read, there will not
be so many, when the generation is gone which was born and
bred in the old world. Such men are not wanted, and would
have no work cut out for them. Happy, it is often said, the
country which has no history. Growing nations may pass
their childhood in obscurity and amusement, but the neutral
condition cannot last for ever. They must emerge out of it
in some way, or they might as well never have existed. The
rising Australians are ' promising young men.' If they mean
to be more, they must either be independent, or must be
citizens of Oceana.

Meanwhile party followed party, and we had more invitations than we could accept. One evening we dined with Sir
Wigram Allen, the late Speaker in the House of Assembly, a
man of vast wealth, one of the millionaires of Sydney. His
house, three miles out of town, was like the largest and most
splendid of the Putney or Roehampton villas. There was a
large gathering of distinguished people, legal and political
magnates ; ladies dressed as well, perhaps as expensively, as

the ladies of New York, some of them witty, all pretty, and one or two more than pretty. The *cuisine* would have done credit to the Palais Royal. The conversation was smart, a species of an intellectual lawn tennis which the colonists play well. There were as many attendants as you would find in a great house at home, with the only difference that they wore no livery. Liveries might, indeed, as well be dropped everywhere. They are a relic of feudalism, when the vassal wore his lord's colours. In democratic communities, where there are no vassals, and a lord's coronet is often a fool's cap, they are exotics which can be dispensed with ; and, indeed, no *man* with a respect for himself, and with no further connection with his master than a contract to do certain services hanging at so loose an end that he may be hired one month and dismissed the next, ought to submit to be dressed like a parrot. In Australia, any way, they have parrots enough in the woods, and do not introduce them into their households. Sir Henry Parkes was among the guests, and the editor of the Sydney paper to whom he had before introduced me. I found the latter a man of superior education, correct in all his thoughts, right-minded even to the extent of rigidity, but wanting in lightness, and taking all subjects on their solemn side. The person whom I liked best was Lady Allen's father, a beautiful old clergyman of eighty-two, who told me that he had read all my books, that he disapproved deeply of much that he had found in them, but that he had formed, notwithstanding, a sort of regard for the writer. He followed me into the hall when we went away, and gave me his blessing. Few gifts have ever been bestowed on me in this world which I have valued more. Sir Wigram Allen, I regret to see, is since dead ; the life and spirits which were flowing over so freely that night, all now quenched and silent ! He could not have had a better friend near him at the moment of departure than that venerable old man.

Another evening we dined with the Chief Justice. Mr. Dalley was present, and several distinguished members of the Sydney bench and bar. There were no ladies. Lawyers are always good company. They have large experience of life' and endless entertaining anecdotes. They are mainly occupied with the questionable side of human nature, but on the whole take a genial view of it. In the hardest stone, in the muddiest clay, there are often veins of gold. The lawyer neither hates men nor particularly loves them, but takes them as they are and understands them. Priests in Catholic countries who receive many confessions acquire a similar tolerance. You cannot hear acknowledgments of immoralities day after day from the most unexpected quarters and fall into convulsions of distress over them. A fervent convert once told me that the Church was the only body which understood how to treat sin therapeutically.

The more I saw of Sir James Martin the more I esteemed and admired him. His face is full of humour. His manner is bright and rapid. He has been a great official, but the *man* is more. If there was an interchange, as there ought to be, between the mother-country and the colonies, in the promotion and employment of their eminent men, Sir James would be as well known and as much valued in London as he now is in Now South Wales.

Mr. Dalley was preoccupied and talked but little. His conversation is usually careless and brilliant. That evening, to my regret, he sat silent. The anxieties of the Suakin expedition were apparently weighing upon him, and it was quite right that they should. He was doing a considerable thing, with far-reaching consequences for good or evil. No one could say which it would be. Mr. Dalley was risking his position and his reputation for what he conceived to be the good of his country ; and we live in days when to run risks for anything except our own advantage is far from common, and when ventured is still more rarely understood. Political critics who are not conscious of such impulses in themselves are impatient of the pretence of them in others. They suspect always that behind the alleged patriotic motive there lies a sinister personal motive. We interpret other people's natures by what we know of our own ; and public men, if they would be safe, must keep to the common level and venture nothing which cannot be interpreted by the average selfishness. The expedition went, and has returned. So far as its immediate object went it accomplished nothing, for it arrived only in time to see the war abandoned. If in its higher aspect, as an exhibition of the affectionate feeling of the Australians to the mother-country, it continues to be remembered and appreciated in England, it has accomplished an end in comparison with which the war was nothing, and it may prove the seed of innumerable benefits. If, on the other hand, there comes of it only polite words of meaningless applause, and then oblivion, Mr. Dalley's patriotism will have spent itself in vain.

CHAPTER XII.

Visit to Moss Vale—Lord Augustus Loftus—Position of a Governor in New South Wales—Lady Augustus—Chinese servants—English newspapers—Dinner-party conversations—A brave and true bishop—Sydney Harbour once more—Conversation with Mr. Dalley on Imperial Federation—Objections to proposed schemes—The Navy—The English flag.

LATE hours, fine cookery, and agreeable society are very pleasant, but less wholesome than one could wish them to be. The town became insufferably hot. My mosquito-bites refused to heal, and some change was desirable. The Governor, who had already asked me to visit him in his highland quarters, graciously renewed his invitation. His aide-de-camp assured me that it was meant in earnest, and that Lord Augustus Loftus would be disappointed if we left the country without seeing him, so we agreed to go.

Moss Vale, the summer residence of the Governor of New South Wales, is a hundred miles from Sydney. Why it is called Vale I do not know, for it stands on the brow of an eminence two thousand feet above the sea. It corresponds to Mount Macedon in Victoria, save that, instead of being in the midst of forests, it is surrounded with rolling grassy uplands, thickly sprinkled with trees, sheep, and cattle-farms, &c., and long ago taken up and appropriated. The house has been lately purchased by the colony for the Governor's use.

It is small, considering the dignity of its destination, and is unfinished within and without. Like all other country places in Australia, it is well protected by plantations. Pines and fruit-trees grow with great rapidity, and when an Australian means to build a house, his first step is to sow acorns and fir-cones. To those who were fond of riding, the situation of Moss Vale was perfect, as the green turf stretched out into infinity. Otherwise in the locality itself there was little to interest. The change of climate was delightful. It was like passing from the tropics to the temperate zone. But Lord Augustus himself was the chief attraction. The railway brought us within five miles of the place, and we found a carriage waiting there to take us on. I had known a brother of Lord Augustus long ago; himself I had never fallen in with. I found him sitting under the trees at the door of a tent, which served as a retreat in hot weather; a most gracious, courtier-like old gentleman, nearer perhaps to seventy than sixty. He had been employed from early youth in the diplomatic service. He had been ambassador at St. Peters-burg, at Vienna, at Berlin. He had been intimate with the three great emperors. He had been in daily intercourse with Bismarck, Gortschakoff, Andrassy. His occupation had been with the higher politics of Europe, and his private life had been passed in the most accomplished, wittiest, and worldliest society to be met with at present on the globe. It was a strange fate which sent such a man in his old days to preside over a constitutional colony, in the midst of men whose aims, interests, and ways of thinking must have been absolutely un-known to him; members, all of them, of the great British middle class, with whom, neither on the Continent nor at home, he was ever likely to have been thrown. Those who have lived in Courts have learned to breathe the air of Courts, and their lungs are fitted for no other. Lord Augustus in New South Wales might easily have been as ill off as Ovid found himself in Thrace.

But a trained and sensible man is not long at a loss, what-ever be the situation in which he finds himself. Lord Augustus accepted his destiny and loyally conformed to it. He had not, perhaps, found his work particularly congenial. But with his knowledge of men he could not fail to discern the essential worth of the politicians by whom he was surrounded; and a far feebler imagination would have been struck with the work which the English race was carrying through in the Colony. At the time when he was sent out, the theory was still in fashion among leading statesmen that the connection with the Colonies was wearing out and was soon to be severed; and so long as the impression prevailed, a far-off settlement could not be looked upon as an organic part of England. Lord Augustus might regret a policy which outside the circle of the Economic Radicals appeared as unwise as it was ungracious. It was a policy which he was not required to promote actively either by word or deed. His duty was to be guided by his constitutional advisers, and no one had complained that he had transgressed the lines laid down for him. But the position was not an exciting one; the change from the cabinets of Ministers who were deciding the fate of nations to the local interests of a remote dependency was almost ridiculous; and if New South Wales and the other Australian provinces were so near to their final separation from us, if they were held to be of so little value that their departure from the parent nest would be rather a relief than a loss, the Governor could be no more than a spectator of the development of a community in which he had but a transitory concern.

Of late, however, there had been a revulsion of feeling at home. The attachment of the Colonies had been proof against the hints and exhortations to take themselves away. The anti-colonial policy had been confined after all to a school of doctrinaires, and the English people became acquainted with the evil intentions of these gentlemen only to repudiate them with indignation. A candidate for Parliament had found that to win or keep his seat he must stand up for Imperial unity, and the discovery had worked a wholesome revolution in the views of many aspiring Liberals. Mr. Dalley's action in the despatch of the contingent, and the recognition which it had met with, had improved the chances still further, and

Lord Augustus had begun to take a deeper interest in the fortunes of his temporary subjects. He could now talk about Australia eagerly and hopefully. He had studied its history, he knew its resources ; he could estimate the probable future of the Australian colonies themselves, and perceive the enormous and indefinite strength which they must add eventually to the British Empire if they remained a part of it. He understood—none could understand better—how the influence of England was no longer what it had been in European politics. If England was 'effaced' as the saying went, it was because she was effacing herself. Germans, Russians, Americans were adding yearly to their numbers, and they had boundless territory in which millions could mature into wholesome manhood. England might add to her numbers, but to her an increasing population was not strength but weakness. England was already full to overflowing, and by taking thought could add no acre to the area which nature had assigned to her ; she had her colonies, and in her colonies she had soil, air, climate, all she needed to eclipse every rival that envied her ; but she was flinging them away in disdainful negligence, or alienating them as she had alienated Ireland, and the fate before her was to dwindle away into a second Holland. These were the anticipations which Lord Augustus had seen growing in the minds of the keen-eyed continental statesmen, and now it seemed as if they might be disappointed after all. Mr. Dalley's action might prove the first active step towards the reversal of a policy which had it continued a few years longer would have undone us for ever.

It was pleasant to talk the subject over with an old diplomat, who, like Ulysses, 'had been in many cities and known the thoughts of many men.' These experienced old stagers see farther and wider than English parliamentary politicians, for it is the very nature of 'party' that party leaders shall never see things as they really are, but only as they affect for the moment the interests of one section of the community. They are as men who, having two eyes given them by nature, deliberately extinguish one. There is the point of view from the 'right' and the point of view from the 'left,' and from each, from the nature and necessity of the case, only half the truth can be seen. A wise man keeps both his eyes, belongs to no party, and can see things as they are.

The share in the official duties which fell to Lady Augustus was, perhaps, heavier than her husband's. He, as a man of the world, could accommodate himself to any circumstances and any persons, and as soon as colonial politics put on a grander character he could find pleasure and honour in being associated with their expanding aims. On her fell the obligation of giving balls and dinners, of entertaining the miscellaneous multitude which constitutes Sydney society; and there are some women, and those perhaps of finest quality, to whom the presiding in public ceremonies of this kind, in any sphere and among any kind of guests, is naturally uncongenial. Lady Augustus was (and is) a woman whose intellectual powers have been cultivated into unusual excellence. The finest pictures in the drawing-room at Government House were her work. There was one especially which I saw—a group of seamen on a raft in the ocean catching sight of a distant sail, which—so admirable it was, both in conception and execution—would have made a sensation in the Royal Academy Exhibition. But she had lived in another world. In her youth she must have been strikingly handsome. Now she had sons grown to manhood, and out in the world in various professions. She had delicate health, and it was late in life for her to take up with a new round of interests. She was admired and respected in the Colony, but her stately manners alarmed more than they attracted, and I could easily believe when I was told of it that she was not generally popular. The few who could see through the reserve into the nature which lay below would delight in being admitted into intimacy with her. But *vice-queens* (and the Governor is a *quasi-sovereign*) cannot have intimates. They are expected to be universally gracious—and universal graciousness is perhaps only possible to the insincere, or the commonplace, or to the supremely great and fortunate.

In her own house and to her private guests Lady Augustus

was a most charming hostess. In her charge I was driven round the neighbourhood, saw interesting stations, farms, country houses, and country neighbours ; but her own conversation was always the best part of the entertainment. One morning at breakfast she amused us with an account of a young Chinaman who was employed in the garden. In New South Wales there would soon be as many Chinese as there are in San Francisco, if they were encouraged to settle there. They are quiet, patient, industrious, never give any trouble, and if the prejudices against them could only be got over, would be useful in a thousand ways. But one never knows exactly what is inside a Chinaman. His face has no change of expression. He smiles at you always ' with the smile that is childlike and bland ' ; and remembering 'Ah Sin' and the packs of cards concealed in his sleeve, one fears always that the 'Heathen Chinee' is the true account of him, and that he has no immortal soul at all. Be this as it may, however, he is the best of servants, especially in garden work, for which he has an inborn genius. There were several Chinese employed in the garden at Moss Vale. One of them, a lad of twenty, was an especial favourite. The lady told us that morning that this particular youth had announced that he must leave. She had inquired the reason. Were his wages too small ? was he dissatisfied with his work ? &c. He was dissatisfied with nothing. The reason was merely that his uncle had arrived in the colony. He must be with his uncle. If his uncle could be taken into the Governor's service he would stay ; if not he must go. We all laughed. It seemed so odd to us that a Chinaman should have an uncle, or, if he had, should know it and be proud of him. But why was it odd ? or what was there to laugh at ? On thinking it over, I concluded that it was an admission that a Chinaman was a human being. Dogs and horses have sires and dams, but they have no ' uncles.' An uncle is a peculiarly human relationship. And the heathen Chinee had thus unconsciously proved that he had a soul, and was a man and a brother—a man and a brother—in spite of the Yankees who admit the nigger to be their fellow-citizen, but will not admit the Chinaman.

In my travels I avoided newspapers, English newspapers especially, wishing to trouble myself as little as possible with the Old World, that I might keep myself free to observe the New. I forgot my rule at Moss Vale so far as to take up a stray number of the 'Pall Mall Gazette,' and I had to throw it down in disgust. I found that —— and —— had been accusing Carlyle in the American journals of 'worship of rank and wealth,' and that —— had spoken of myself as the 'slip-shod Nemesis'—modern synonym, I suppose, for the halting Furies—who had laid bare his weakness. Such men judge after their kind. These are of the same race, as Carlyle always said they were, with those who cried, 'Not this man, but Barabbas.' The judgment which they pass is but the measure of their own intelligence. I was vexed for a moment, but I recalled what I had said to myself from the beginning. In writing the biography of a great man you are to tell the truth so far as you know it. You are not to trouble yourself with the impression which you may produce on the rank and file of immediate readers. You are to consider the wise, and in the long run the opinion of the wise will be the opinion of the multitude. Carlyle was the noblest and truest man that I ever met in this world. His peculiarities were an essential part of him, and if I was to draw any portrait of him at all, I was bound to draw a faithful portrait. His character is not likely to please his average contemporaries, of whom he himself had so poor an estimate. Had I made him pleasing to such as they are, I should have drawn nothing which in any trait could resemble the original. How could they feel less than dislike for a man who at each step trod on their vanity and never concealed his contempt for them? He can wait for the certain future, when he will be seen soaring as far beyond them all as the eagle soars beyond the owl and the buzzard—or, rather, he will alone be seen, and they and their works will be forgotten.

The earth, we are told, is a single great magnet. Thought, like electricity, penetrates everywhere, and as Paris and London are so are the Antipodes. On our return to Sydney we had more dinners. At one of these, my immediate neighbour, a

N

considerable person, asked me 'confidentially' if I believed in a future state. I do not know why he should have been shy in putting such a question. There is none of greater moment to all of us, none on which we have a better right to seek such advice as we can find; and shyness and reticence are no evidence of the completeness of our conviction, but rather of the opposite. We dare not look into one another's minds for fear of what we should find there. A bishop lately arrived in one of these colonies, a very honest man, was requested, during a late drought, to issue a circular prayer for rain. He replied that an average sufficiency of rain fell every year, and that he declined to petition God to work a miracle until the colonists had done all that lay in themselves to preserve it by constructing reservoirs. If the Church authorities throughout the world had been as brave and sincere in their language as the prelate of whom I speak, the world would have been more ready to accept their judgment when they told us what we ought to believe. I regretted that I had not seen this good bishop. Dr. Barry, too, the new bishop of New South Wales, was absent in Tasmania at the time of my visit. From him also, so far as I could gather from report, all good may be expected. Hereafter, it is to be hoped there may be less occasion for these confidential interrogatories.

The harbour continued our chief attraction. The Government had left their steam-launch at our disposition whenever we pleased to use it. The water was the coolest place which we could find; and to skim over it with a self-created breeze and a basket of grapes at our side, was the most delicious method of passing the day. We made one more circuit of the wooded inlets, penetrating beyond the furthest points which we had visited before. E—— was with us this time, bringing his sketch-book with him. We rested at midday in a secluded reach of the deepest of the estuaries. The strata, which had been tilted vertically, turned the shores into broken walls. The water ran deep to the edge, and we found a spot where the launch could lie safely beside a natural causeway overlaid with oysters. The red sandstone rock rose steep above our heads. Huge fallen masses fringed the sides of the inlet, their shadows mixing with the forms and colours of the trees which lay inverted on the transparent water. Enormous eucalypti, which had struck their roots between the clefts in the stones, towered up into the air, or spread outwards their long branches, shielding us from the sun. Here we had luncheon—one of those luncheons which linger on in memory, set in landscapes of lake or river-side or mountain glen; where food becomes poetical, and is no longer vulgar nutriment ; and old friends, now 'gone to the majority,' show their pleasant faces to us as figures in a dream. Instead of wine we had our grape-basket—great bunches like those which Virgil's country-men gathered wild to mix with the water of Achelous. E—— made a water-colour drawing of the place, to remember it by in years to come. In the foreground stood the blighted stem of a gigantic gum-tree which had tried to fall and had been arrested half-way in its descent by a buttress of rock. There it was, leaning out at a steep angle over the water, lifeless, leafless, the trunk twisted into the shape of some monstrous writhing saurian, the naked branches clear against the sky as if blasted by lightning. E—— dared to draw the ghostlike thing, and succeeded actually in catching the form, and some-thing of the emotion belonging to it. I, in a humbler way, contented myself with the landscape, and flinched from such a horrid object.

Our time in Sydney was now running out, and, indeed, the time which we could give to Australia. We had been nearly two months there. I was sorry to miss Van Diemen's Land, which they say is the most like England of all our possessions in those seas—an England with a gentler climate. We had been pressed to visit Queensland ; but my object had been to learn the thoughts and views of such reflecting persons as could best forecast the future, and for the rest to look rather at what the colonists themselves were doing than at new countries as nature had made them. I had therefore given all my leisure to the two leading states, where energy and enterprise had accomplished the most.

Before we left I had a second and extremely interesting talk with Mr. Dalley, the substance of which, or at least

parts of it, I saw afterwards fairly well reported in one of the
Sydney papers, and for this reason, and because I think Mr.
Dalley wished that his opinions should be known in England,
I transcribe from my note-book the principal things which he
said to me.

The main subject was the much talked of ' Federation '
of the colonies and the mother-country. Could the colonies
and Great Britain coalesce in a political union ? and if so how
and into what kind of union ? The next chapter will contain
the conclusions which I drew about it from miscellaneous conversations, not with Mr. Dalley only but with all kinds of
persons. The views of Mr. Dalley himself, as the most remarkable of all the Australian statesmen that I met with,
must have a place by themselves. ' Oceana ' to him was no
unreal union. It was an object of distinct and practical hope.
He desired himself to see us all united—not in heart, not in
sentiment, not in loyalty and British feeling ; for that we, or
at least those colonies, were already—but one in so completed
a confederacy that separation should no longer be mentioned
among us even as a crotchet of an English public office. He
did not despair of such a consummation, though he was well
aware of the difficulties in the way. He thought that if the
British people really wished for it, if no unwise experiments
were tried prematurely, and if no attempt were made to force
any one of the colonies into a course for which it was unprepared, time and the natural tendencies of things would accomplish what had been called impossible.

Of the detailed schemes already suggested Mr. Dalley had
no good opinion.

1. The confederation of the Australian colonies among
themselves was supposed in England to be a step towards a
larger union. It had been pressed upon them by high authorities at home ; Victoria was eager for it—and where Victoria
led the other provinces would be inclined to follow. New
South Wales, however, the eldest of the South Sea communities, was opposed to it for many reasons, most of all because
he believed it would not tend in any way to promote Imperial
federation, but rather would have an opposite effect. The

Colonial Office might wish to escape trouble, and probably adhered in secret to the old policy, which was to make Australia independent. New South Wales objected, and he trusted that the Imperial Government would respect their opposition and understand the motives of it. A confederation of the Australian colonies, through and in an Imperial federation, Mr. Dalley would welcome and would promote with all his strength. A separate local federation he had opposed, and would oppose to the end.

2. Some English advocates of Imperial federation had conceived that there could be no unity without a central council or parliament in which the several colonies could be represented, and had suggested that a convenient body could be formed immediately out of the colonial agents-general. To this proposal Mr. Dalley had many and, as it seemed to me, well-grounded objections. The agents-general were originally little more than colonial consuls, engaged exclusively with commercial business or financial. As the colonies grew in importance, the functions of these gentlemen had necessarily extended and had assumed political consequence. It was right, and indeed inevitable, that they should so extend. The persons chosen for these offices were generally men who had grown old in the colonial service, who had been distinguished in the various legislatures, had held office, and were of weight and consequence. They were thus fit and proper advisers of the Colonial Office, each for the colony by which he was accredited. They might properly be sworn members of the Privy Council—a step which the Crown itself could take without consulting either the British or the Colonial Parliaments. But this was something entirely different from erecting them into a responsible and deliberate assembly. In the first place, Mr. Dalley said, the functions of such an assembly would have to be defined, and the longer this question was considered the less easily would the answer to it be found. In the second place, the agents-general were not representatives of the colonies ; they held their offices at the will of the party who happened to be in power. They were not now recalled or changed at each change of Government, because their present

duties were not of a kind which required alteration ; but they could no longer retain this political neutral character if so great a change was made in their position. Each new Administration would be tempted to appoint a new agent-general, at great inconvenience to the colony. Even then he would not and could not represent the colony as a whole, and there would be instant jealousy if he attempted to act in any such capacity. Supposing these objections overcome, and a council of agents-general brought together directly elected for the purpose, such a council from its very nature would have to debate and decide questions on which the colonies would have separate and perhaps opposite interests. The interest of one was not always the interest of another ; when there were differences of opinion the majority would determine ; and why was New South Wales to submit to be outvoted by agents from Jamaica or Canada or the Cape, in matters of which New South Wales herself might claim to be the only competent judge ? The only possible result would be confusion and quarrels. The scheme would break down on the very first occasion when there was serious division of opinion. The interference of Downing Street itself, even as it was now constituted, would be less intolerable than the authoritative rule of a council composed of agents-general collected from all parts of the empire.

Other projects of an analogous kind—projects for a great Imperial Parliament to supersede the present, &c., Mr. Dalley dismissed as still more unworthy of serious consideration. Such a parliament as that would have to grow, if ever it was to exist at all, out of the exigencies of future occasions. Organic institutions could not be manufactured to order by closet speculators ; they developed of themselves.

But if Imperial deliberative assemblies were not to be thought of, there was something of immeasurably greater importance which might be thought of, and Mr. Dalley referred to the subject of the Colonial Navy. Oceana, the great empire of which Great Britain was the stem, and the colonies the branches, was the creation of the naval enterprise of England. She had spread her race over the globe, and had

planted them where they were now flourishing, because she
had been supreme upon the seas. The fleet was the instrument
of her power and the symbol of her unity. British ships of
war were the safeguard of colonial liberty, and the natural
chain which held the scattered communities together. The
fleet, therefore, ought to be one. Division was weakness,
and the old story of the bundle of sticks had here its proper
application. Let there be one navy, Mr. Dalley said, under
the rule of a single Admiralty—a navy in which the colonies
should be as much interested as the mother-country, which
should be theirs as well as hers, and on which they might all
rely in time of danger. Let there be no more colonial ships
under a separate authority, unlikely to be found efficient if
their services were needed on a sudden, and liable to be mis-
chievously misused if maintained continuously in a condition fit
for sea. Let each great colony or group of colonies have its
own squadron, which should bear its name, should be always
present in their waters, and be supported out of its own resources, while it remained at the same time an integral part of
the one navy of Oceana. So the empire would be invulnerable
on its own element, and, invulnerable there, might laugh at
the ill-will of the nations of the earth combined. It would be
linked together by a bond to which the most ingenious parliamentary union would be as packthread. Each member of
the vast community would be left free to manage its internal
affairs as might seem best to itself, and, secure in being admitted into partnership with the most splendid empire which
the earth had ever seen, it would as little think of separating,
as the hand would think of separating from the body.

This was the scheme for Imperial confederation put before
me by the minister whose action in sending the contingent to
the Soudan has been so much admired and applauded. Each
colony was to estimate what its naval defence would cost if it
were left to its own resources, and to offer this as a subsidy to
the expenses of the Imperial fleet. Money would be but a
slight difficulty, and would be a less and less difficulty as their
wealth increased.

'Only,' he said, and with some emphasis, 'we must have

OCEANA

the English flag again '—and on this one subject Mr. Dalley
seemed to speak with bitterness. The Australians do not like
a bar sinister over their scutcheon, as if they were bastards
and not legitimate ; and surely of all ill-considered measures
in our dealings with the colonies, the dignity of forcing upon
them a difference in the flag was the very worst. No affront
was, of course, intended. The alteration originated, I believe,
in some officialism unintelligible to the ordinary mind, and
was taken up and insisted on as part of the Separatist policy.
By our poor kindred it has been taken as an intimation,
flaunted perpetually in their faces, that we look on them as
our inferiors and not as our equals. Those who are talking and
writing so eagerly now about a confederated empire should
insist at once, and without delay, that when any colony
expresses a desire to fly over its ships and forts the old flag of
England, neither childish pedantry nor treacherous secret
designs to break the empire into fragments shall be allowed to
interfere with a patriotic and honourable purpose.

CHAPTER XIII.

Alternative prospects of the Australian colonies—Theory of the value of
colonies in the last century—Modern desire for union—Proposed schemes—
Representation—Proposal for Colonial Peers—Federal Parliament impossible—Organised emigration—Danger of hasty measures—Distribution of
honours—Advantages and disadvantages of party government in colonies—
Last words on South Africa.

WE had now seen all that our limits of time would allow
us of Australia and the Australians. New South Wales
and Victoria are vast territories, and ours had been but a
glimpse of a small part of them ; but a stay indefinitely
prolonged could have taught me no more than I already
knew of the opinions of those who were guiding the destinies
of Australia, and of the alternative possibilities of the
future. If those colonies remain attached to the mother-
country, a great and prosperous destiny seems, in human pro-

bability, assured to them. If fate and official want of wisdom divide us asunder, these colonies will also, I suppose, form eventually a great nation, or several nations, but they will have to pass through the fire of affliction. Trials await them of many kinds, as certain as the disorders of childhood, some made by fate, some by human wilfulness. Nations cannot mature, any more than each individual of us, without having their school lessons drilled into them by painful processes. ἐν πάθει μαθεῖν is the law of human progress, from the growth of the schoolboy to the growth of the largest community. The Australians, being of English blood, will probably pass successfully through their various apprenticeships. It is possible, on the other hand, that they may repeat the experience of the Spanish colonies in America, and have a long period before them of war and revolution. Human nature is very uniform, and the Spaniards in the sixteenth century were as advanced a race as we. They had degenerated before their colonies were cast adrift, and British communities may hope reasonably for a better future than befell any Spanish settlement which achieved its independence. But dangers of some kind there must be, and the Australian colonists will not expose themselves unnecessarily to the accidents inseparable from isolation. Their nationality at present is English, and if they leave us it will be by the action of Great Britain herself, not by any action of their own. To the question what political measures should be taken to preserve the union, they would answer generally, no measures at all save in a better organisation of the navy. Let well alone. The ties which hold us together are daily strengthening of themselves. The trade of England with the colonies grows far more rapidly than with any other parts of the world. Intercourse is increasing. Melbourne and Sydney are as easy of access now as New York was fifty years ago. Steam and telegraph have made an end of distance. The English in the colonies and the English at home will not fall out if the officials in Downing Street do not set them by the ears. If the officials persist, there will be the remedy of the unwilling duellists who turned their pistols on the seconds that had made the quarrel.

In the present state of public feeling, the danger is rather from premature experiments on the part of those who are anxious to see the union assume a more defined form. I will therefore add a few more words to what was said by Mr. Dalley, on the different schemes which have been put forward, and mention the opinions which I heard expressed about them.

The colonial theory in favour in England in the last century, was that the colonies existed only by favour of the mother-country; that the mother-country was entitled to impose upon them such conditions as it pleased, in return for her protection. The value of the colonies was as a market for British manufactures. We arranged the terms of the market as seemed most to our own advantage. We allowed them to trade only with ourselves, and in such articles as we chose to prescribe. They were dissatisfied, and when we proceeded further to try to raise a direct revenue from them, they resisted. The cry rose which remains the first article of modern political faith—'No taxation without representation.' The American States demanded to be allowed to send representatives to the English Parliament. Had the demand been conceded, Franklin and Washington would have been satisfied; and thenceforth no 'colonial question,' in the sense in which we now speak of it, would ever have existed. The colonies would have been represented in proportion to their wealth and population; the empire would have grown homogeneously, and British subjects in all parts of the world would have had equal political rights. For a time at least this would have answered the demands of the Americans. No one can say what would eventually have happened; but a precedent would have been set for all subsequent arrangements, which could have been easily followed or modified as occasion required. The authorities at home were stubborn; they despised the colonies too much to acquiesce in a reasonable demand. The Sibyl tore the pages from her book, and the American provinces were lost. We have boasted loudly that we will not repeat the same mistake—that we will never try to coerce a British colony into remaining with us against its will. But

the spirit has continued absolutely unaltered; the contempt
has been the same; we have opened our trade with the rest of
the world; and the sole value of the colonies being still supposed to lie in their being consumers of English goods, it has
been imagined that they would consume as much whether
dependent or independent, and that therefore it was a matter
of indifference whether their connection with us was sustained
or broken. We could have saved America by admitting its
representatives. We have never so much as thought whether
we might not give representation to Canada and Australia.
It might have been done fifty years ago. The opportunity has
been lost now and cannot return. The colonies have their
several legislatures, are accustomed to be completely masters
of their internal affairs, and will not part with privileges which
have become precious to them. Great Britain will not allow
colonial representatives to vote her taxes or her trade policy,
unless the colonies will allow the Parliament so constituted to
revise their tariff and tax them in return. As things now
stand, no member for Sydney or Melbourne or Ottawa or
Montreal can ever sit in the British House of Commons. It
has been suggested that the agents-general might have official
seats, and might speak but not vote; but a position of impotence and inferiority would irritate more than it would con-
ciliate. There is no instance on record of a successful experiment of this kind; and the fatal objection still holds that the
agents-general cannot represent the colonies because they are
not elected to represent them; and the system on which they
are appointed cannot be changed, to confer merely on them the
ineffectual privilege of being present at debates where their
voices will have no power.

If the colonies cannot be represented even in such equivocal fashion in the House of Commons, it has been thought
that in another place there might not be the same difficulty;
that into a reformed House of Lords, or even into that House
as it exists at present, colonial statesmen might be admitted
as life-peers. Distinguished political services would thus
receive an appropriate recognition, and the Upper House
might gain an increased Imperial consequence which now

hardly attaches to it. I have myself often imagined that such an experiment might at least be tried. My experience in Cape affairs taught me how inestimable would be the advantage if each of our self-governed dependencies could have someone who could speak on their affairs publicly and with a less equivocal authority than would belong to them as non-voting members of the Lower House. Agents-general communicate only with the Colonial Office, and the public are left in ignorance whether their advice has been accepted or passed over. The despatches of Governors may be published in blue-books, but their private letters are not published. The world generally does not read blue-books, and only hears what they contain from party fights in Parliament. This or that person may have private knowledge, and may write to the newspapers or make a speech on a platform; but he is only an individual, and may be suspected of having objects of his own. If we had among us men who could speak in the name and with the authority of the general sense of a colony, the public would listen, and the expensive mistakes which are now so frequent would not be permitted. The public trusts its representatives and the cabinets formed out of them far too implicitly. It knows—it cannot but know—that the constituencies do not choose men to represent them because they are wise. The constituencies choose them for other reasons, and ought not therefore to expect to find them wise. If there had been anyone in England who could have told us the truth about South Africa from a position which would have commanded attention, the Orange River would have remained where it was fixed by treaty as the frontier of the colony; the Diamond Fields would never have been torn from the Orange Free State; the Transvaal would not have been annexed, on the plea that the Dutch desired it. Sir Bartle Frere would have made no wars against the Caffres and Zulus; the shadow of Majuba Hill would not have withered our military laurels. The country would not have been deluded into a belief that when Sir Charles Warren had conquered Bechuanaland the Cape ministry would relieve us of the cost of ruling it. These freaks of our rulers—the earliest of them but fifteen years old,

the last in progress at this moment—have cost several millions
of pounds and tens of thousands of human lives. Honour
does not go for much in these days, but honour has been lost
too. And all these blunders would have been avoided, and
the Cape Colony would now have been a peaceable and prosperous community, had the true condition of things been
known. The English public rarely goes wrong when the facts
are fairly put before it. The weighty voice of a single well-
informed person, who could speak with authority, would
have echoed over the country, and ministers would have been
forbidden to indulge themselves in these ambitious but costly
levities.

The House of Lords seemed to offer the required opportunity, and admission thither promised to bring the colonies
into political relations with us in a form to which the least
objection could be taken. I am obliged to say, however, that
I did not find in Australia a single person who would seriously
attend to the mention of such a thing. In the first place, they
said men could not be found for such a purpose in whom the
colonists would place continuous confidence. The Peers I
spoke of would have to be appointed for life, or at least for a
period of several years. The growth of colonies is so rapid,
and the change of circumstances so frequent, that a man who
might be trusted wholly one year would be half-trusted the
next, and the third would not be trusted at all. Being absent
he would lose touch of popular feeling. There would be a
demand for his recall, and if this could not be, he would be
disowned, and his influence gone. Again, how were they to
be elected? Like creates like, and a popular vote could not
make a peer. Crown appointments through the Governors
would please no one; if made by the Ministry of the day,
they would displease the Opposition, who, when their turn of
power came, would claim to nominate others, and as ministries
change fast, colonial peers would multiply inconveniently.
Thirdly, the choice would be limited to men of wealth and
leisure, with a reputation for character and intelligence, and
the number of persons combining the necessary qualifications
could be counted on the fingers of one hand. Lastly, and

conclusively, the colonists are democratic. They are pleased to see our noble lords who come visiting among them, but they do not wish to see such high dignities naturalised among themselves, even in the most diluted form. In short, they treated the suggestion as ridiculous, and ridicule is fatal. There will be no colonial life-peers till the House of Lords has undergone a process like the aged Greek king; till it has been taken to pieces, dissected, and reconstructed by some revolutionary Medea.

Another project has been suggested, I know not whether I need mention it. A new Parliament, a Federal Parliament, composed of representatives for all parts of the empire, is to sit side by side with the existing Parliament and relieve it of the charge of foreign and colonial policy. The ministry will have to be chosen from this new Parliament. On it will fall the decision of all questions of peace or war. Therefore it will have the overruling voice in the taxation which its acts may make necessary. The House of Commons is now omnipotent. No man, or body of men, has been known yet to relinquish voluntarily powers of which he was in present possession. Who is to persuade the House of Commons to abdicate half its functions, and construct a superior authority which would reduce it to the level of a municipal board? What force short of revolution and soldiers' bayonets could bring them to it? Of all the amateur propositions hitherto brought forward, this of a Federal Parliament is the most chimerical and absurd.

Is there then nothing which can be done? Must we drift on at the mercy of man or the mercy of circumstances, drift as we always do drift when we abandon the helm on the lee shore of disintegration? Everything may be done which it is fit and right to do if we know our bearings, if we know the ocean currents, and the capabilities of the ship which carries us. But we must look at the facts as they are, not as in our imaginative enthusiasm, or equally imaginary alarms, we may wish or fear them to be. What, then, are the facts, and what is our object? We say that we desire the colonies to be united to the empire. They are united already, united by the bond of nature. The inhabitants of Victoria and New South Wales are as completely subjects of the Queen of Great Britain as any of ourselves; they are as proud of their sovereign, they are as heartily loyal, they as little dream of throwing off their allegiance. Nay, perhaps they have more part in David than those who are nearer to the throne. Their attachment is enhanced by the emotional enchantment of distance. Well then, let this identity be recognised in all communications which are exchanged with them. They complain of the coldness of tone and almost estrangement with which they have been hitherto addressed : and the complaint is not without reason. When they make impetuous demands upon us, when they require us, as in the case of New Guinea, to challenge one of the great Powers of Europe on account of injuries which to us seem visionary, we may be right and wise in declining; but we might so decline as to show them that we understand their feelings, respect their ambition, regard even their impatience as a sign that they are zealous for the greatness of Oceana. Kind words cost nothing, and kind words would be precious to these far-off relations of ours, for they would show that the heart of England was with them.

Again, they are passionately attached to their sovereign. The Queen is present with them through the Governor; and the Governor might and should be worthy always of the dignity of the great person whom he represents. I am well aware that for these high offices we select occasionally men of capacity and character. No fitter President could have been found for Victoria in all the British dominions than Sir Henry Loch. But it is notorious that, at least in past times, other considerations have influenced our selection. Minor political services, social rank, the desire to 'provide' for this gentleman or that, have been sufficient recommendations for the vice-royalties of our grandest dependencies, when men of tried ability and high administrative experience, who have been so unhappy as to displease the Colonial Office, have been allowed to fall out of the service. The indirect influence which a really able and trained Englishman who has moved in a larger sphere can exercise in a constitutional colony is necessarily immense. His duty is to abide by the advice of his ministers; but his ministers and the colonial public will pay the voluntary respect to his judgment which his wider education and mental superiority command. He will lead without commanding. The presence among them of first-rate men is a compliment which the colonies appreciate as an evidence of the estimation in which they are held ; just as when some mere man of rank, or some hack of party is sent among them, they resent it as a sign of disrespect. If we value the attachment of the colonies, we are bound to furnish them with the fittest chiefs whom we can provide ; and there will be no difficulty when the situation of governor of a great colony is recognised as of the importance which really attaches to it.

This is one thing which we can do. If it is done already we have so far discharged our duty and must continue to discharge it.

Again, the colonies need immigrants, and the right sort of immigrants. Immigration from Europe has raised America in half a century to the first rank among the nations of the world. Four-fifths of the English and Scotch and Irish who annually leave our shores to find new homes become citizens of the United States. Can no effort be made in connection with the Colonial Governments to direct at least part of this fertilising stream into our own dominions ? Can we afford to spend tens of millions upon Russian wars, Egyptian wars, Caffre and Zulu wars, and can we afford nothing, can we not afford so much as attention, in order to save the British nationality of so many hundreds of thousands of our fellow-citizens ? With some care and some fraction of the enormous sums which we fling away so lavishly, we could be weaving threads to bind the colonies stronger than the web which Maimuna spun round the arms of Thalaba. Some years ago a colonial premier spoke to me on this subject. I said that thousands of boys and girls would now annually be leaving our Board schools with a rudimentary education, who had no parents, no friends, no prospects. I asked him if his colony would take some of them, fetch them out, and apprentice them, till they were twenty-one, to colonial farmers and artisans—the colony to be responsible for their good treatment, and to bear the expenses, in consideration for the services of these boys and girls while under age. I conceived that it would be a means of providing the colony with the most valuable recruits that could be found for it, while to the children themselves, if they behaved well, it would assure a happy future. My friend answered that we could do nothing, absolutely nothing, which would be received more warmly and gratefully by his colony. He promised everything—co-operation, supervision, any securities and guarantees that we liked to ask. I laid the matter before the home authorities. After a few weeks I received a reply, covering a quire of foolscap paper, proving to the satisfaction of the writer that nothing of the sort could or ought to be tried. Miss Rye and other generous women have proved that it can be done, and have provided hundreds of destitute children with homes in Canada. Government officials can only answer—Impossible.

For other measures we must wait for the occasion. Interfederation of the Australian States, or free trade, or a Zollverein, or any other project may, and perhaps will, be raised as a hustings cry in England. But those who really desire the union of Oceana will avoid, as far as possible, all such idle suggestions. The colonists are doing our work; they are, or some of them are, the most vigorous members of our whole empire. If they contribute nothing directly to the Imperial treasury, they pay their own internal expenses. They are opening their soil to as many of our people as they can attract; they are finding employment for our capital; they are feeding our trade; they are accumulating wealth, which, in fact, is national wealth; they have shown that in a supposed time of danger they are eager to share our burdens; they are doing all which we have a right to expect of them; each year their resources increase, and, as they become conscious of their importance, they will seek and, perhaps, will claim a more intimate connection with the Imperial administration. But as long as they are contented to be as they are, while they are ready to encounter such risks as may befall them on the present terms, we may well leave them to be themselves the judges of what is good for them. All advances towards a closer political connection must come from their side. Let each colony, if it feels uneasy anywhere, make its wishes known, and let each desire be considered as it rises on its own merits. General comprehensive schemes will almost certainly fail; they will fail assuredly if suggested from England. We have not deserved the entire confidence of our colonies; all that we have ever done, or tried to do, in connection has been in relation to some interests of our own, and fine professions of generous views will only seem suspicious. Anything which they consider would be for their good, unless it be itself unreasonable, ought to be done; but we had better wait for them to ask it. Even as concerns the fleet and the flag, the advances must be made by them.

But we are ourselves the distributors of our own honours, and of the high places in our own professions. I do not see why eminent colonial judges should not, if they wish it, be transferred from their bench to ours. Service at a colonial bar might be as sufficient a qualification as service in the law courts at home. The Order of St. Michael and St. George was created especially to decorate colonists; but why make a distinction? The Garter, we know, is never given for merit, and therefore they would not aspire to so supreme a dignity; but why not admit them to the Bath? Intellect and worth, wherever found, ought to circulate freely through all the arteries of the empire. We should place their old men in the Privy Council; we should invite their young men into the army and navy and Indian service; and promotion should know no difference between English, Scots, Canadians, Australians, and South Africans. Every single colonist in the service of the nation would be a fibre of the great roots which hold us all together. These things are easy, and when facilities are wanting we can create them, without disturbing existing arrangements. It may be said that all this field is already open. If a young Australian lawyer will come to England as Copley came, he, like Copley, may sit upon the woolsack. Yes, but it will be by ceasing to be an Australian; and the provincial character which may fitly lose itself in the Imperial greatness of 'Oceana' ought not to be merged in the constitution of Great Britain—at least till Great Britain has come frankly to admit the equality of the colonies with herself.

For the rest, ample as is the freedom which the self-governed colonies now possess, I would give them more if they desire it. We have bestowed on them parliamentary institutions formed after our own model. But it does not follow that this particular form of government is the best for all times and all countries. The British constitution, with its two parties alternately taking the helm, has grown out of our national circumstances. It has been a contrivance for conducting peacefully the transition from the feudal England of the Plantagenets to the England of liberty and equality. For better and worse it has answered that purpose, and may for a time continue to answer it. But beyond the England of equality there may be further changes. Nothing in this world reaches its final shape till it dies; and England is not dead. There are already signs that even at home parties have lost their original outlines, that they are degenerating into factions, and forget the interests of the empire in their mutual animosities. In the colonies there are no natural parties at all; they have to be created artificially; and it is likely that, if left to themselves, Canadians and Australians would have preferred a government on the model of the American, where a president is chosen directly by the people for a period of years. In the president rests the supreme executive authority. He chooses his own ministers; he is responsible to the nation and not to Congress; his cabinet is not liable to be displaced by factious combinations, and for his term of office he is able to follow some consistent and rational policy. In the colonies governments have hitherto been changed with inconvenient rapidity. It is possible that, weary of intrigues and jobs and other phenomena of the British method, this or that colony may conclude that the American is preferable, that its affairs would be more wisely and more economically conducted if it, too, might elect its own chief, deliver him from the hands of the legislative Philistines, and give him power independent of them. Such a power as this the colonies of course would never give to a governor appointed by England. A chief minister elected directly by the people would be the people's minister and not the governor's, as in fiction he is still supposed to be, and the governor would in that case become a superfluity. Yet, if there was a serious wish in any colony to make such a change, I should be sorry to see it resisted. A president elected by the people would be as much a representative of his sovereign as a governor appointed by an English minister. There would be no change of nationality unless the people demanded a change, and if they did demand it an official nominee from Downing Street would not long remain an obstacle. You do not alienate men by allowing them opportunities of improving their condition, and a slack chain is less easily broken than a tight one.

In concluding this chapter, I will add a few more words about South Africa ; that country being a most signal example of all the faults in the past methods of colonial management, and therefore a favourable specimen of the treatment most to be avoided. South Africa is self-governed, and it is not self-governed. In precipitate haste, without forethought or common consideration, a constitution was forced upon the Cape Colony. Natal was and is a Crown Colony. The Transvaal and the Orange Free State are independent republics. Yet the four states are so interconnected that measures adopted in one affect all the others, while the governor of the Cape Colony, to increase the confusion, holds a further office of High Commissioner and protector of the native tribes. From this complexity of jurisdiction, there has been sometimes an occasion, and always a pretext, for interference from home. We have relinquished the right to govern the Cape Colony ourselves ; we have made it impossible for the colonists to govern with the necessary independence ; and thus the unlucky country has been the prey of well-intentioned philanthropists, of colonial secretaries ambitious of distinguishing themselves, and of internal factions fed by the hope of English support. So things must continue, and South Africa will become a second Ireland unless we choose between one of two courses, for no third is possible. We cannot control the interior States as long as the Cape Colony is out of our hands and refuses its support. Therefore we must either revoke the constitution so prematurely bestowed, or we must, *bonâ fide*, leave South Africa to govern itself, as Australia and Canada govern themselves, do away with the High Commissionership, and cease to meddle· in any way. The first course might answer, but it cannot be adopted; the colonists will not willingly part with their liberties, and the state of parties at home forbids the thought of high-handed measures. The alternative implies the surrender of the native policy to the colonists. The success of the Dutch in the Free States—a small minority of whites in the midst of twenty times their number of warlike blacks— proves that a *modus vivendi* can be found under which the two races can live side by side, and the white man can acquire his natural ascendency. But if we withdraw, it will be the Dutch method which will be adopted all over the country, and not the English. I should not myself object to this. The Dutch method, in the long run, is the more merciful of the two. We have killed hundreds of natives where the Dutch have killed tens. But the Dutch, who are the majority, would be virtually masters of South Africa. They look on themselves as the lawful owners, and on us as intruders. The connection on such terms would perhaps be found galling on both sides, and further changes might come in view. Even to the Dutch the English connection has many advantages. It may not yet be too late to recover their confidence, and even their loyalty. But past experience forbids any sanguine hope that prejudices on both sides so deeply rooted will easily be overcome, while the problem is further complicated by the naval station, which we cannot afford to part with. The possession of Simon's Bay, at the extreme south point of Africa, is indispensable to us. It commands the ocean route to India, which at any time may become our only one. Whoever holds Simon's Bay holds at his mercy our entire sailing commerce with the East. A handful of privateers with their headquarters there might capture or destroy every trading vessel passing outside it ; and to hold the Cape peninsula and to let the rest of the country go is declared to be impossible by the political and military authorities. Therefore it may be said that we have so twisted and entangled our South African affairs that the knots now can neither be cut nor untied. Want of wisdom has brought it about. We must hope for more wisdom; but where is more wisdom to come from, and how is it to find its way into our public offices?

CHAPTER XIV.

Sail for New Zealand—The 'City of Sydney'—Chinese stewards—An Irish priest—Miscellaneous passengers—The American captain and his crew—The North Cape—Climate and soil of New Zealand—Auckland—Sleeping volcanoes—Mount Eden—Bishop Selwyn's church and residence—Work and wages—The Northern Club—Hospitalities—Harbour works—Tendency to crowd into towns—Industries—A Senior Wrangler—Sir George Grey—Plans for sight-seeing.

ON February 26 we left Australia for New Zealand in an American steamer of between three and four thousand tons. She was going on to San Francisco, touching at Auckland on the way, and was called the 'City of Sydney.' We were able to take our tickets through to London across the American continent, either to proceed at once or to stay on the route as we pleased. Our plan was to remain in New Zealand for a month, and to follow in the next monthly vessel belonging to the same line. The telegrams from England were becoming warlike. E—— who had meant to extend his tour, determined to return with us, at least as far as the Sandwich Islands. English travellers, officers on leave, militia captains, colonels, &c., were streaming homewards from all quarters, like flights of rooks to their roosting-trees at evening, expecting that their services might be required.

In the 'City of Sydney' we were under the 'stars and stripes,' a flag always welcome to Englishmen when they cannot have their own. She was a handsome ship to look at, smart and well-appointed. Her captain was a man of thirty, gentlemanlike, but with the cool indifferent manners of his countrymen. We regretted our old 'Australasian'—we could not hope for such quarters as we had found there ; her we left at Sydney, taking on board the Soudan contingent. But we had been well off all along, and we took our chance with no great alarm. As we steamed out of the harbour we were attended by a large launch crowded with ladies and gentlemen who were cheering and waving handkerchiefs. Evidently we had someone on board who was a special favourite, and we distinguished the object of these attentions in a young Irish priest who was starting for home.

I and my son had a state-room on deck to ourselves, very pleasantly situated, with a gallery outside, between us and the sea, so that we could keep our windows open in all weathers. The cabin-boys, under-stewards, &c., were Chinese, the first with whom we had come in contact in a domestic capacity— little brown fellows in flowing dresses of blue calico with gilt buttons or clasps, a soft smile on their faces, and their pigtails coiled in a knob upon their heads, to be let down when in full dress at dinner-time. Noiselessly the little creatures moved about in slippered feet, and were infinitely obliging and engaging. Though it was out of feeding hours when we went on board, and the ship's rules were strict, they brought us luncheon to our cabin. So far as waiting attentions would secure our comfort we felt at ease at once. My difficulty was that there were many of them running about, and I could not distinguish one from another. The shepherd knows his sheep, and I suppose that to Chinamen the separate personalities are as easily recognised as ours. To me they seemed only what Schopenhauer says that all individual existences are : 'accidental illustrations of a single idea under the conditions of space and time.'

The cook of the 'Australasian' had spoilt us for average passenger steamer fare. The saloon was crowded ; we had to scramble for seats at the table. The dinner, when it came, was served American fashion : a multitude of small, ill-dressed dishes huddled round one's plate. We grumbled, perhaps audibly. But if their food is not poisonous, sensible people remember nothing about it five minutes after it is done with. We were in fine health and spirits. The evening on deck was delightful, the sea like a mirror, the air tropically soft, the twilight sliding into night, and the stars shining out calm and soft and clear. I made acquaintance with the young priest. His coat was threadbare, his cheeks were lean, his eyes were eager and dreamy. We talked much, and at first chiefly on theology. I observed in him what I have seen in many Catholics lately, since it has become their *rôle* to fall in with modern ideas—a profession of respect for the rights of conscience. Every man, he said, was bound to act according to his own honestly entertained convictions. For a Protestant to become a Catholic, unless he was converted at heart to the truth of Catholic doctrines, would be a mortal sin. To constrain the conscience by temporal pains and penalties was wicked. It would follow, though he did not say so, that a Catholic whose faith in the Church became shaken, might lawfully—indeed must—become a Protestant. What Liberal could desire more ?

A lady convert to Romanism once told me that she had 'gone over' out of prudence. Protestants admitted that Catholics might be saved. Catholics insisted that out of the Church there was no salvation possible, therefore the safest place was with them. I suppose, according to my young friend's view of the matter, this was a sin. I could not share his opinion that it was right for average people to go by their own judgment in so serious a matter as religion. Average men are too ignorant to be capable of forming a judgment on such subjects. I found myself, rather to my amusement, arguing with a priest in defence of authority. I asked him whether an officer who was not satisfied about the justice of any particular war ought to refuse to fight and to abandon the profession of his life. He saw no difficulty in deciding that the officer would be bound to throw up his commission. I might have asked him whether he held Luther to have been right in leaving the Church when he came to the conclusion that the Church was teaching lies. But I did not wish to be captious ; I thought him an innocent and interesting person, and rather liked him. On further acquaintance I found that he was not a priest only but a patriot, and that he was going back to Ireland, not on business of his order, but to witness, and perhaps assist at, the resurrection of his country. Patriotism was hereditary with him: he was the great-nephew of Father John, who commanded the Wexford insurgents at Vinegar Hill. He had written a book, said to be popular, on the rising of 1798, and was about to write another. He did not wish to separate Ireland from England. Restore to Ireland the constitution of 1782, he said, and all would be well. Englishmen and Irishmen, Protestants and Catholics, lambs and lions, would lie down together, and the new era would begin. No one seems to remember that the constitution of 1782 was Protestant ascendency—the Upas tree in fullest leaf. Catholics had not so much as votes at the elections for Grattan's Irish Parliament, and obtained them only on England's insistence. They might have waited till Doomsday in the afternoon before the Irish gentry would have deliberately committed suicide by opening the doors to them. I seemed now to understand the sudden zeal for toleration. If Irish Emancipation was to be anything save a signal for civil war, the strife of creeds must cease, and the Protestant North must be conciliated to the Catholic South. The idea was not new ; the original leaders in 1798, Wolfe Tone, Hamilton Rowan, &c., were not Catholics. The chief of the Irish Parliamentary party, Ireland's present ' uncrowned king,' is not a Catholic. In the obliteration of religious party lines lies the hope of every rational Irishman who desires the repeal of the Act of Union. They have the sense to see that to revive the principles of 1641, and retaliate on Protestant ascendency by Catholic despotism, would make an end of them and their cause—this time for ever. I believe myself that, with or without toleration, the revival of an Irish nationality is equally a dream. No cause ever prospered which was initiated by dynamite explosions and murders and repudiated contracts. The modern movement must come at last, as all similar movements have come in times past, to broken heads. Nationalities are not to be made by Parliamentary oratory flavoured by assassination. Yet there was something interesting and even pathetic to me in the conversation of this new victim of the old illusion.

It was late summer, answering to the end of our August. In the latitude of 35° the temperature of the sea-water was 76°, the air was motionless, the Pacific, on which we were now entering, unruffled by the smallest wave ; but even under these conditions we could sleep soundly and peacefully. The absolutely pure atmosphere flows over deck and through cabin in the soft breeze which is due to the vessel's motion. In the morning, I was just conscious of some object flitting about my berth. When I roused myself I found my faithful 'Johnnie' had arranged clothes and washing things with the silence and neatness of a Brownie. There was a spacious deck-house dignified by the name of the Social Hall, where the passengers collected before breakfast, and which was all day their favourite lounge. When I entered there was a miscellaneous crowd there of all sorts and nations. 'Sir,' said one of them rising, and addressing himself to me in a loud voice, 'St. Paul says, Corinthians ii. 7.' He stopped. I waited to hear what St. Paul had said, but nothing came, so I bowed. He then began again to all of us, 'St. Paul, in Ephesians v.' But he advanced no further, and sat down, looking round him with importance. There were many colonists on board of a type somewhat different from those that I had hitherto met. They were good people, but a little consequential, and presuming that I wanted information, were eager to bestow it upon me. 'I, sir,' said one, 'was for three years in Her Majesty's service. I was second manager of Her Majesty's Kangaroo Department ; I was Director-General of such and such a company ; I was treasurer of this or that colonial society. You desire to understand the colonies. Without wishing to boast, I can assure you that you will find no one better able to instruct you than myself,' &c. 'Excuse me, sir,' said another, 'but I cannot regard you as a stranger. I have read your estimable writings, sir. Permit me to introduce myself, I am Mr. T——,' and he produced his card. There were several more of the same kind. To myself they were most agreeable, for they were always amusing one way or another, and they conveyed to me the average opinion of successful colonists who had made money and represented colonial sentiment. What they had to tell me was to the same effect precisely as what I had heard before. Recent newspapers had brought out Lord Grey's letters recommending the constitution of the agents-general into a Committee of the Privy Council. They all laughed at it. Privy Councillors we might make them, if we cared to give and they to accept the title of Right Honourable ; but to entrust them as a corporate body with political power was what no colonist would hear of. They agreed with me in wishing to have someone to speak for them to the public at large, independent of the Colonial Office ; the people were now sovereign, and it was always better to deal with principals than with subordinates ; but they repudiated, as everyone else had done, the notion of colonial representative Peers. A colonist might be created a Peer, like anyone else. There were Knights and Baronets already, and the ladies of their families were supposed to like it. A peerage or two would be no great innovation, provided it were understood to mean nothing. But peers evidently were held cheap among them, and Tennyson, it was supposed, must have been losing his wits when he consented to receive so ambiguous an elevation.

The American captain was good company when one got over the brusqueness of his manner. He told me a singular thing. I had been looking at his crew, and had been puzzled to make out what they were, or how he had picked them up. ' I make a rule,' he said, ' when I engage my men for a voyage, to take no English, no Scotch, no Irish, no Americans. There is no getting along with them. They go a-shore in harbour, get drunk, get into prison, give me nothing but trouble. It is the same with them all, my people and yours equally.' ' Then whom do you take ?' I asked in astonishment. ' I take Danes,' he answered ; ' I take Norwegians, Germans, Swedes ; all of these I can trust. They are sober, they make no row, are never in the hands of the police. They save their wages, are always quiet and respectable, and I know that I can depend on them. The firemen, ship's servants, &c., are Chinamen ; I can trust them too.' I recollect a Portuguese nigger at the island of St. Vincent once showing me, with a grin, an iron-grated cage, and telling me it was specially reserved for

English sailors. At the time I thought him a malicious lying rascal—one never knows about these things.

The second day out the captain promoted us to his own table in the saloon, where the fare was slightly improved. The weather continued perfectly fine ; the colour of the water appeared to me—perhaps it was fancy—a little different in the Pacific from what it is in the South Atlantic and Indian Ocean. Always the colour of sea-water is due to the radiation of the light of the sky upwards, either from the bottom when it is shallow, or when out of soundings from organic particles floating in solution like motes in the air. Elsewhere the deep ocean is violet-tinted : Homer's ἰοειδής. Between Australia and New Zealand it was sapphire, occasionally thickening into turquoise.

A library is always part of the stock of a modern ocean steamer. There are religious books—some people read nothing else—there are books of travels for those who want to be entertained without feeling that they are wasting their time. The great proportion are novels, generally, but not always, well-selected. I observed one, by —— ——, and being curious to see what manner of man he might be who had been sitting in judgment on Carlyle, I looked through it. The story was of a High Church rector, who seduced his church organist, fell in love with his friend's wife, then, to make all right, went in violently for religion, and ended in turning Papist. It seemed to me to be the worst book I had ever read ; but perhaps I was prejudiced. I took the taste out with Charles Reade's 'Peg Woffington.' I liked this well enough, but it is a play, and not a novel ; all the situations are dramatic, and, with a few verbal changes, it could be brought on the stage. After all I had to fall back on my own supply, Homer and Horace, Pindar and Sophocles. These are the immortal lights in the intellectual sky, and shine on unaffected by the wrecks of empires or the changes of creeds. In them you find human nature, the same yesterday, to-day, and for ever. These great ones are beyond the power of Fate, and no intellectual revolution can shake them from their thrones. I have sometimes thought that the human race has passed its spiritual zenith, and will never more bring forth kings such as they.

The distance from Sydney to Auckland is eleven hundred miles—a five days' passage, for we took things leisurely and economised coal. The time went pleasantly, and we did not find it too long. In the afternoon of March 2 we passed the North Cape of New Zealand, and the hill to which the Maori chiefs were carried, dying, that they might take their departure from it into the unknown world. We saw nothing to explain the custom, save that the northern point of the island might be supposed to be nearest the sun ; otherwise, it is like other Land's Ends—a high, stern, barren, sea-and-wind-swept promontory. Auckland is on the east side of the island. After doubling the point we turned south, and ran for a hundred miles along the shore. The sea swarms with fish, but there were no fishermen looking for them, and singularly few sea-gulls—I cannot tell why, as there is such abundant food for them. There being a telegraph wire to Auckland, we should find news five days later than the last which we had heard. We were all anxious. What had happened in Egypt, what on the Afghan frontier, what in Ireland, what at home ? The expectation was that the Ministry would have fallen, and I may say that all through my travels I did not meet a single person to whom that news at least would not have been welcome hearing. But we were now close upon a new and an intensely interesting country, and I believe I was thinking more about this than about House of Commons division-lists.

New Zealand is composed of two long islands lying north and south, with a narrow strait between them, and a further small island of no consequence at the south extremity. The extreme length of the three is 1,100 miles, with an average breadth of 140. The climate ranges from that of Naples in the Bay of Islands, to that of Scotland at Foveaux Strait. There is abundant rainfall ; there are great rivers, mountains, volcanoes, a soil luxuriantly rich, a splendid clothing of magnificent forest. So far as the natural features of a country tend to produce a fine race of men, New Zealand has the advantage of Australia. Australia, too, has hills and rivers,

whose head still ached.   After a winding walk of half a mile,
we came again on the river, which was rushing deep and swift
through reeds and Ti-tree.   A rickety canoe was waiting there,
in which we crossed, climbed up a bank, and stretched before
us we saw the White Terrace in all its strangeness ; a crystal
staircase, glittering and stainless as if it were ice, spreading
out like an open fan from a point above us on the hillside, and
projecting at the bottom into a lake, where it was perhaps two
hundred yards wide.   The summit was concealed behind the
volumes of steam rising out of the boiling fountain, from
which the siliceous stream proceeded.   The stairs were about
twenty in number, the height of each being six or seven feet.
The floors dividing them were horizontal, as if laid out with a
spirit-level.   They were of uneven breadth ; twenty, thirty,
fifty feet, or even more ; each step down being always perpendicular, and all forming arcs of a circle of which the crater
was the centre.   On reaching the lake the silica flowed away
into the water, where it lay in a sheet half-submerged, like ice
at the beginning of a thaw.   There was nothing in the fall of
the ground to account for the regularity of shape.   A crater
has been opened through the rock a hundred and twenty feet
above the lake.   The water, which comes up boiling from
below, is charged as heavily as it will bear with silicic acid.
The silica crystallises as it is exposed to the air.   The water
continues to flow over the hardened surface, continually adding
a fresh coating to the deposits already laid down; and, for
reasons which men of science can no doubt supply, the crystals
take the form which I have described.   The process is a rapid
one ; a piece of newspaper left behind by a recent visitor was
already stiff as the starched collar of a shirt.   Tourists ambitious of immortality had pencilled their names and the date
of their visit on the white surface over which the stream was
running.   Some of these inscriptions were six and seven years
old, yet the strokes were as fresh as on the day they were
made, being protected by the film of glass which was instantly
drawn over them.

    The thickness of the crust is, I believe, unascertained, the
Maories objecting to scientific examination of their treasure.

THE WHITE TERRACE, NEW ZEALAND

It struck me, however, that this singular cascade must have been of recent, indeed measurably recent, origin. In the middle of the terrace were the remains of a Ti-tree bush, which was standing where a small patch of soil was still uncovered. Part of this, where the silica had not reached the roots, was in leaf and alive. The rest had been similarly alive within a year or two, for it had not yet rotted, but had died as the crust rose round it. Clearly nothing could grow through the crust, and the bush was a living evidence of the rate at which it was forming. It appeared to me that this particular staircase was not perhaps a hundred years old, but that terraces like it had successively been formed all along the hillside as the crater opened now at one spot and now at another. Wherever the rock showed elsewhere through the soil it was of the same material as that which I saw growing. If the supply of silicic acid was stopped the surface would dry and crack. Ti-trees would then spring up over it. The crystal steps would crumble into less regular outlines, and in a century or two the fairy-like wonder which we were gazing at would be indistinguishable from the adjoining slopes. We walked, or rather waded, upwards to the boiling pool; it was not in this that we were to be bathed. It was about sixty feet across, and was of unknown depth. The heat was too intense to allow us to approach the edge, and we could see little, from the dense clouds of steam which lay upon it. We were more fortunate afterwards at the crater of the second terrace.

The crystallisation is icelike, and the phenomenon, except for the alternate horizontal and vertical arrangement of the deposited silica, is like what would be seen in any Northern region when a severe frost suddenly seizes hold of a waterfall before snow has fallen and buried it.

A fixed number of minutes is allotted for each of the 'sights.' Kate was peremptory with E—— and myself. Miss Marileha had charge of my son. 'Come along, boy!' I heard her say to him. We were dragged off the White Terrace in spite of ourselves, but soon forgot it in the many and various wonders which were waiting for us. Columns of steam were rising all round us. We had already heard, near at hand, a noise like the blast-pipe of some enormous steam-engine. Climbing up a rocky path through the bush, we came on a black gaping chasm, the craggy sides of which we could just distinguish through the vapour. Water was boiling furiously at the bottom, and it was as if a legion of imprisoned devils were roaring to be let out. 'Devils' hole' they called the place, and the name suited well with it. Behind a rock a few yards distant we found a large open pool, boiling also so violently that great volumes of water heaved and rolled and spouted, as if in a gigantic saucepan standing over a furnace. It was full of sulphur. Heat, noise, and smell were alike intolerable. To look at the thing, and then escape from it, was all that we could do, and we were glad to be led away out of sight and hearing. Again a climb, and we were on an open level plateau, two acres or so in extent, smoking rocks all round it, and, scattered over its surface, a number of pale brown mud-heaps, exactly like African anthills. Each of these was the cone of some sulphurous geyser. Some were quiet, some were active. Suspicious bubbles of steam spurted out under our feet as we trod, and we were warned to be careful where we went. Here we found a photographer, who had bought permission from the Maori, at work with his instruments, and Marileha was made to stand for her likeness on the top of one of the mud piles. We did not envy him his occupation, for the whole place smelt of brimstone and of the near neighbourhood of the Nether Pit. Our own attention was directed specially to a hole filled with mud of a peculiar kind, much relished by the natives, and eaten by them as porridge. To us, who had been curious about their food, this dirty mess was interesting. It did not, however, solve the problem. Mud could hardly be as nutritious as they professed to find it, though it may have had medicinal virtues to assist the digestion of cray-fish.

The lake into which the Terrace descended lay close below us. It was green and hot (the temperature near 100°), patched over with beds of rank reed and rush, which were forced into unnatural luxuriance. After leaving the mud-heaps we went down to the waterside, where we found our luncheon laid out in an open-air saloon, with a smooth floor of silica, and natural slabs of silica ranged round the sides as benches. Steam-fountains were playing in half-a-dozen places. The floor was hot—a mere skin between us and Cocytus. The slabs were hot, just to the point of being agreeable to sit upon. This spot was a favourite winter resort of the Maori—their palaver-ing hall, where they had their constitutional debates, their store-room, their kitchen, and their dining-room. Here they had their innocent meals on dried fish and fruit, here also their less innocent on dried slices of their enemies. At present it seemed to be made over to visitors like ourselves. The ground was littered with broken bottles, emptied tins, and scraps of sandwich papers. We contributed our share to the general mess. Kate was out of spirits, with her head-ache ; we did what we could to cheer her, and partially succeeded. The scene was one to be remembered, and we wished to preserve some likeness of it. The Maori prohibit sketching, unless, as with the photographer, permission has been exorbitantly paid for. Choosing to be ignorant of the rule, E—— sat himself down and took out his drawing-book. Two or three natives who had joined us howled and gesticu-lated, but as they could speak no English and Kate did not interfere, E—— affected ignorance of what they meant, and calmly finished his pencil outline.

We were now to be ferried across the lake. The canoe had been brought up—a scooped-out tree-trunk, as long as a racing eight-oar, and about as narrow. It was leaky, and so low in the water that the lightest ripple washed over the gunwale. The bottom, however, was littered with fresh-gathered fern, which for the present was dry, and we were directed to lie down upon it. Marilcha stood in the bow, wielding her paddle, with her elf locks rolling wildly down her back. The hot waves lapped in and splashed us. The lake was weird and evil-looking. Here Kate had earned her medal. Some gentleman, unused to boats, had lost his balance, or his courage, and had fallen overboard. Kate had dived after him as he sank, and fished him up again.

The Pink Terrace, the object of our voyage, opened out

before us on the opposite shore. It was formed on the same lines as the other, save that it was narrower, and was flushed with pale-rose colour. Oxide of iron is said to be the cause, but there is probably something besides. The water has not, I believe, been completely analysed. Miss Mari used her paddle like a mistress. She carried us over with no worse misfortune than a light splashing, and landed us at the Terrace-foot. It was here, if anywhere, that the ablutions were to take place. To my great relief I found that a native youth was waiting with the towels, and that we were to be spared the ladies' assistance. They—Kate and Mari—withdrew to wallow, rhinoceros-like, in a mud pool of their own. The youth took charge of us and led us up the shining stairs. The crystals were even more beautiful than those which we had seen, falling like clusters of rosy icicles, or hanging in festoons like creepers trailing from a rail. At the foot of each cascade the water lay in pools of ultra-marine, their exquisite colour being due in part, I suppose, to the light of the sky refracted upwards from the bottom. In the deepest of these we were to bathe. The temperature was 94° or 95°. The water lay inviting in its crystal basin. E—— declined the adventure. I and A. hung our clothes on a Ti-bush and followed our Maori, who had already plunged in, being unencumbered, except with a blanket, to show us the way. His black head and copper shoulders were so animal-like that I did not entirely admire his company ; but he was a man and a brother, and I knew that he must be clean, at any rate, poor fellow ! from perpetual washing. The water was deep enough to swim in comfortably, though not over our heads. We lay on our backs and floated for ten minutes in exquisite enjoyment, and the alkali, or the flint, or the perfect purity of the element, seemed to saturate our systems. I, for one, when I was dressed again, could have fancied myself back in the old days when I did not know that I had a body, and could run up hill as lightly as down. The bath over, we pursued our way. The marvel of the Terrace was still before us, reserved to the last like the finish in a pheasant battue. The crater at the White Terrace

THE PINK TERRACE, NEW ZEALAND

had been boiling ; the steam rushing out from it had filled the
air with cloud ; and the scorching heat had kept us at a distance. Here the temperature was twenty degrees lower ;
there was still vapour hovering over the surface, but it was
lighter and more transparent, and a soft breeze now and then
blew it completely aside. We could stand on the brim and
gaze as through an opening in the earth into an azure infinity
beyond. Down and down, and fainter and softer as they re-
ceded, the white crystals projected from the rocky walls over
the abyss, till they seemed to dissolve not into darkness but
into light. The hue of the water was something which I had
never seen, and shall never again see on this side of eternity.
Not the violet, not the hare-bell, nearest in its tint to heaven
of all nature's flowers ; not turquoise, not sapphire, not the
unfathomable æther itself could convey to one who had not
looked on it a sense of that supernatural loveliness. Comparison could only soil such inimitable purity. The only colour I
ever saw in sky or on earth in the least resembling the aspect
of this extraordinary pool was the flame of burning sulphur.
Here was a bath, if mortal flesh could have borne to dive into
it ! Had it been in Norway, we should have seen far down
the floating Lorelei, inviting us to plunge and leave life and
all belonging to it for such a home and such companionship.
It was a bath for the gods and not for man. Artemis and her
nymphs should have been swimming there, and we Actæons
daring our fate to gaze on them.

This was the end of our adventure—a unique experience.
There was nothing more to see, and any more vulgar wonders
would have now been too tame to interest us. Kate and Mari
had finished their ablutions and returned to the canoe. They
called to us to come. We washed out our canvas shoes with
the lake water, as, if left to dry as they were, they would have
stiffened into flint. We lay again upon our fern leaves.
Marileha resumed her paddle, and, singing Maori songs—the
vowel sounds drawn out in wild and plaintive melody—she
rowed us down the lake, and down the river to Tarawara.
Flights of ducks rose noisily out of the reed-beds. Cormorants
wheeled above our heads. Great water-hens, with crimson

crests and steadfast eyes, stared at us as we went by. The stream, when we struck into it, ran deep and swift and serpentine, low hidden between flags and bushes. It was scarcely as broad as our canoe was long, and if we had touched the bank anywhere we should have been overturned. Spurts of steam shot out at us from holes in the banks. By this time it seemed natural that they should be there as part of the constitution of things. Miss Mari's dog swam panting behind us, and whining to his mistress to take him up, which she wouldn't do. In a few minutes we were at the spot where we had landed in the morning. Our five Maories woke out of their blankets and took their oars again, and in two more hours we were ourselves crawling up the same path from the Lake boat-house to Wairoa, on which we had watched the returning party of the preceding day. There were fine festivities in the village that evening, our four pounds being all converted into whisky. We did not stay to witness them, but drove back at once to Ohinemutu, the blue lake looking more mysterious than ever in the autumnal twilight, and the shadows in the forest deeper and grander. An hour later it would have been all ablaze with fire-flies, but we were hurrying home to be in time for dinner, and missed so appropriate a close for our generally witch-like expedition.

CHAPTER XVII.

Ohinemutu again—Visitors—A Maori village—An old woman and her portrait —Mokoia island—The inhabitants—Maori degeneracy—Return to Auckland—Rumours of war with Russia—Wars of the future—Probable change in their character

Tue time of our stay at Ohinemutu depended on Sir George Grey. He had held out hopes of showing us the Maori monarch. He was to let us know whether he could come up, and when. We found no letter from him as we expected, and E——, who wished to see the utmost possible in the four weeks allowed us, was a little impatient. However, we settled to remain a day or two longer. We had not half-seen the immediate neighbourhood. I for myself could be very happy, poking about among the springs and the native huts, and doing amateur geology and botany. The river of tourists was flowing full as ever. There had been thirty-five new arrivals at our single hotel during our brief absence. They were mainly Australians on an excursion trip, and I found that I had already met several of them at Melbourne or Sydney. The natives, when observed more at leisure, were not so absolutely inactive. There is a small fish in the lake like white-bait, which multiplies preternaturally in the tepid water, especially as there is nothing there to eat it. The men net these fish in millions, spread them out on mats in the sun to dry them, and infect seriously, for the time being, the sweetness of the atmosphere. I was anxious to see a little more of the people, and, if I could, at some spot where they were not, as in Ohinemutu, artificially maintained in idleness.

There was a second village on the lake a few miles off, and one afternoon we walked along the shore to look at it. We found distinct improvement. There was less money going about, either from visitors or the Government, and consequently more signs of industry. The soil was almost black, so rich it was. A few acres of it were spade cultivated, much like an English allotment garden, and were covered with patches of potatoes, maize, and tobacco.

The cabins are of the purely primitive type—four mud walls, two gables, a roof of poles leaning against each other at a high angle and filled in with reed and turf. Essentially they are exactly the same as the mud cabins in Ireland, but they are cleaner, neater, and better kept. Round each is a stout Ti-tree fence, through which the pigs, at any rate, are not allowed free entrance. As in Ireland, however, it was the wrong sex that was doing the hardest work. The men lay about on the ground, or looking on while the women were digging. We saw more than one young mother, with a child slung in a pouched shawl at her back as if she were an inverted marsupial, hoeing maize and turning up potatoes, while the husband sat smoking his pipe as composedly as if he had been bred in Connemara. Natives in a declining moral condition show the same symptoms, whatever be the colour of the skin. We felt a little uncomfortable in trespassing on their private grounds. They are proud in their way, and do not approve of liberties being taken with them, and as we could command no word of Maori, and they understood no English, we could neither ask leave, nor even begin an acquaintance. They were perfectly quiet however, and let us walk by without seeming to notice us. We ought to have done the same, but, alas! we didn't. On our way back we passed a cottage with creepers growing over the roof, a patch of garden, and a clump of bushes closing it in and sheltering it. Before the door an ancient Maori dame, black-haired, black-eyed, but with a skin wrinkled by the suns of many summers, was engaged in drying some fish. She was a hard-looking old savage, bare-headed, bare-armed, and bare-legged, with a short brown petticoat and a handkerchief crossed over her neck. The scene was characteristic ; E—— wished for a recollection of it and produced his sketch-book. Now the natives object strongly to being drawn—either themselves or their houses. Partly they look on it as enchantment, partly as a taking away something of theirs for which their leave is required, and a bargain arranged beforehand. E—— had forgotten his experience at the Terraces, or had supposed it to be only one of the many forms of extortion there. He sat himself down in the fern, about half a dozen yards from where the old woman was at work, lighted a cigar, and began to draw. She looked up uneasily, glanced first at E—— and then called to some of her own people, who were digging potatoes not very far off. Either they did not hear her or did not understand what was the matter. They took no notice and she turned again to her fish. But she was evidently restive. Presently she raised herself to her full height, turned direct to E—— and then to us, and gave a long howl. E—— sat on, puffing his cigar, glancing at her movements with increasing interest and transferring them to his paper. She howled again, and as he showed no sign of moving she made a step towards him, flashing her eyes and gesticulating violently. The more angry she grew, the more picturesque

A SCENE AT OHINEMUTU, NEW ZEALAND

became her figure and the more deliberately E—— studied her.
She snatched up a stick and shook it at him. The arm and
stick were instantly introduced into the drawing. It was too
much ; she went for him like a fury, came so close that she
could have struck him, and had her arm raised to do it. With
the most entire imperturbability he did not move a muscle,
but smoked on and drew as calmly as if he had been drawing
a tree or a rock. Her features were convulsed with rage.
His indifference paralysed her, perhaps frightened her. There
is a mesmerism in absolute coolness which is too strong for
excited nerves. She dropped her stick, turned sullenly round,
and hid herself in her cabin. Poor old woman ! E——'s
composure was admirable, but I felt real sorrow for her.

I mentioned Mokoia, and our intention of paying a visit
to so romantic and historical a spot. The island lay four
miles off in front of our window ; and there was a sailing-
boat ready to take us over. We should see the bath in which
Hinemoia warmed herself after her long swim ; in a tree there
the bones were said to be still mouldering where they had been
thrown by Hangi after his dinner. Our hostess, who knew
the place, urged us not to leave Rotorua without seeing it,
and even volunteered her services as guide again. It was
very good of her, and she would have gone had she not been
called away to arbitrate in a land dispute. We had to be content with our own company, but the dangers and difficulties
were not great. Mokoia is a sleeping volcano which has been
thrown up in the middle of the water, or may have been raised
before there was a lake at all. The ridges on the top are
densely wooded and entirely unoccupied, but on the north side
is a long, low, level plain, a thousand acres or so in extent,
extremely fertile and well filled with people who have occupied it again since Hangi's raid. Once Mokoia was a
favourite missionary station, and the good people have left
pleasant traces of their presence there. We found in the
gardens peaches, figs, apples, pears, potatoes, maize, parsnips,
peas and beans ; and tobacco, green and growing. The missionaries were not always wise, but they meant well always,
did well often, and deserve to be more kindly remembered than
they are.

We landed close to the bath, saw the bushes under which Hinemoia had hid herself, and her lover's cabin where they lived happy ever after. The island was very pretty, rock, wood, water, and cultivation pleasantly combined. The missionaries are departed. There was no sign of chapel, church, or heathen temple. The people seemed to be altogether pagans but pagans of an innocent kind. In other respects, if I had been carried into Mokoia and awakened suddenly, I should have imagined myself in Mayo or Galway as they were forty years ago. There were the same cabins, the same children running about barefoot and half-naked, the same pigs, the same savage taste for brilliant colours, the women wearing madder-coloured petticoats ; the same distribution of employment between the sexes, the wife working in the fields, the man lying on his back and enjoying himself. The Mokoians were perhaps less ragged than the Irish used to be, otherwise Nature had created an identical organisation on the opposite side of the planet. Even the children had learnt to beg in the same note, the little wretches with hands thrust out and mouths open clamouring for halfpennies.

There were flights of gulls on the lake—drawn thither, I suppose, by the white fish. Otherwise I had seen few birds in the district, as indeed anywhere in New Zealand. Mokoia, however, was full of them. The English sparrow was there—where is he not ?—taking possession of everything, as if Nature had been thinking only of him when she made the world. There were native birds also, hiding in the foliage of the thick trees, with a deep cooing note, something like the Australian magpie's. These were chary of showing themselves. One that I caught sight of was like a blackcap, and of the size of a thrush.

It was hard to realise that this sunny, dreamy island had been the scene of such unspeakable horrors in the days of Bible Societies and Exeter Hall philanthropy. Men, still living, may remember Hangi,[1] who in his time was a London lion, much rejoiced over on platforms, and who showed the

---

[1] I tell Hangi's story merely from the traditions on the spot, which may require correction before they can be accepted as accurate.

fruits of his conversion in that spot in so singular a manner. We found a tree with a few bones in a cleft of it. The trunk bore the names of many visitors cut into its bark, and I presume, therefore, was the original one. The bones were probably what tradition said they were, and the owner of them had played a part in that tragedy, as killer, or killed, or both.

Mokoia would be a pretty possession for anyone who, like Sancho Panza, wished for an island all his own to occupy. Sir George Grey had thought of buying it, before he settled at Kawau. We made a sketch or two without being interfered with ; we ate our luncheon, and sailed home again.

We had been now a week at Ohinemutu. Sir George Grey had been detained at Auckland by other arrivals there, and had been unable to join us. Without him, it was useless to think of going into the country of the King, and this part of our scheme had to be abandoned. I was sorry ; for a sight of the natives who had kept their old customs, and had lived removed from European influence, might have modified the dreary impression which had been left upon me by those whom I had seen. The Maori warrior, before the English landed in New Zealand, was brave, honourable, and chivalrous ; like Achilles, he hated liars 'as the gates of Hell ;' firewater had not taught him the delights of getting drunk ; and the fragments which survive of his poetry touch all the notes of imaginative humanity—the lover's passion, the grief for the dead, the fierce delight of battle, the calm enjoyment of a sunlit landscape, or the sense of a spiritual presence in storm or earthquake, or the star-spangled midnight sky. The germ of every feeling is to be found there which has been developed in Europe into the finest literature and art ; and the Maori man and Maori woman, as we had seen them, did not seem to have derived much benefit from the introduction of ' the blessings of civilisation.' Their interest now is in animal sloth and animal indulgence, and they have no other ; the man as if he had nothing else left to work for or to care for ; the woman counting it an honour to bear a half-caste child. It is with the wild races of human beings as with wild animals, and birds, and trees, and plants. Those only will survive who can domesticate themselves into servants of the modern forms of social development. The lion and the leopard, the eagle and the hawk, every creature of earth or air, which is wildly free, dies off or disappears; the sheep, the ox, the horse, the ass accepts his bondage and thrives and multiplies. So it is with man. The negro submits to the conditions, becomes useful, and rises to a higher level. The Red Indian and the Maori pine away as in a cage, sink first into apathy and moral degradation, and then vanish.

I am told that the Catholic missionaries produce a more permanent effect on the Maori than the Protestants do. If one and the other could learn from the Mahometans to forbid drink and practically prevent it, they might both of them be precious instruments in saving a remnant of this curiously interesting people.

We returned to Auckland as we had come, sleeping a night on the way at Oxford, where I found the landlord still busy over his Artesian well. At the Club everybody was talking of the coming war with Russia. The reluctance with which Mr. Gladstone would embark in such an enterprise was well understood; but the Egyptian business was supposed to have shaken his popularity, and it was expected that he would now go with the stream, to keep himself and his party in office. I for my own part was incredulous. I could not believe that he would so soon forget what he had said and done seven years ago. Mad as people are when the war fever is upon them, I could not believe that England herself, in a mere panic, which in a few months she would be ashamed of, could insist on starting a conflict over a mere frontier dispute in Afghanistan, which would probably spread to Europe and set the world on fire. Yet we were living in impulsive days, and parliaments, led by irresponsible orators, might rush at problems which single statesmen would pause over. It was impossible to say that there could not be war, and a person like myself, who had never shared in the general alarm about the aggressive Muscovite, could only regret the desperate consequences which seemed too likely to follow.

I had always thought, and I still think, it improbable in

the highest degree that Russia should have designs upon
British India. She has work enough upon her hands elsewhere, and the object to be gained is incommensurate with
the risk. We have ourselves three times invaded Afghanistan, burnt the bazaar at Cabul, and killed a great many
thousand people to teach them to love us. Even now it is
doubtful if we could count upon their friendship, and, on the
mere ground of fairness, we were not in a position to declare
war against another power for doing as we had done ourselves
and drawing her frontier in that quarter as her military
necessities required. It was again uncertain to me whether,
if we had determined to fight, we were choosing a favourable
battlefield, so far away from our own resources. At the
commencement of our wars we were generally unsuccessful.
If the Afghans did not love us, as perhaps they didn't, and
were prepared to throw in their lot with the strongest side,
a reverse might decide them to be our enemies, and in the
event of a serious misfortune, such as befell us at the Khyber
Pass, the Native States might be disturbed in India itself.
Nor did I think that the irritation in England was based on
a well-considered knowledge of the real state of Russia.
We spoke of her at one time as a modern Macedonia,
dangerous, from her unceasing encroachments, to the liberties
of Europe; at another, as bankrupt in finance, as honeycombed
with disaffection, as so weak that Cobden, in a memorable
speech, talked of crumpling her up in his left hand. She
could not be all these things at once. If she was weak,
Europe need not be afraid of her. If she was strong, the
struggle might be serious and not to be lightly entered on. The
contempt and fear combined, which seemed to be the feelings
entertained by us, were rather indications of dislike to
Russia and anger at it, than signs of any sound insight
into her actual condition. Whatever might be the result of
a war with her, it would be likely to verify the saying that
'nothing was certain but the unforeseen.' The risk would be
out of all proportion to the advantage to be gained if we were
victorious.

These views I ventured now and then to express, but I

had to be cautious, for the patriotism of the colonists was inflammable as gunpowder. To bo against war was to be lukewarm to our country, and half-a-dozen regiments could have been raised with ease in New Zealand alone, to march to Herat. I did venture, however, to express a hope that, if there was to be war, Mr. Gladstone would leave the work to others, and would not crown the inconsistencies of his late career by adopting a policy which he had condemned in his rival with all the powers of his eloquence. Nay, I suggested also that, in these democratic days, a better expedient than national wars would by-and-by perhaps be accepted—as easy of application as it would be infinitely beneficial to the entire communities concerned. Ministers of different nations fall out from time to time about various questions. Things in themselves of no significance at all are made of importance by the fact of being insisted on. Despatches are exchanged, each unanswerable from its own point of view, and the object on each side is not to settle the quarrel but to put the other in the wrong. At last, when diplomacy has succeeded in tying the knot so tight that it cannot be disentangled, the persons who have conducted the negotiations come to their respective countrymen, and say : 'We have done our best, but you see how it is : the perfidious A. or perfidious B. is determined in his wicked courses. There is but one way out of it. You must fight.' Fighting, as it is now carried on between great nations, means the killing of hundreds of thousands of people, and the wasting of hundreds of millions of money ; and it seems to me that in nine cases out of ten this expenditure is not the least necessary. In nine cases out of ten it can make no sensible difference to the great body of the nation which way the matter is decided. No one will pretend, for instance, that any English labourer's family would be differently fed, differently clothed, or differently lodged if the eastern Russian frontier were drawn a few miles this way or that way. Therefore I think the people will by-and-by reply on such occasions to their rulers : 'It may be as you say, gentlemen. A. or B. may be very wicked, and this question, which you tell us is of consequence, cannot be settled without fighting. You under-

huge black bull, who was glaring at us not six yards off. Sir George was undisturbed. He seemed to know that none of these creatures would molest us. All living things of earth or air were on confidential terms with him. The great New Zealand pigeons, large as blackcock, fluttered among the leaves above our heads, spread their wings, and made a circuit to show their shining plumage, then settled again as calmly as they might have settled in Adam's garden before the Fall. It was very pretty—one so rarely sees the natural movements of wild birds. They know man only as their enemy, and when they get a sight of him they are anxious and alarmed. Sir George understood the habits of them all. He talked about natural history as easily as he talked of everything else—in a genial, soft, deferential tone, his blue eyes fixed half on his listener and half on vacancy, while he poured out information which must have cost him years of study. Singular man ! I could enter now into the feelings with which he was regarded in every part of the world where he had played a part. Even now, at the eleventh hour, I wish the Colonial Office would restore him to the Cape. It would cost him his life, but he would cheerfully sacrifice the few years that may be left to him, part with Kawau and the beauties which he has created there, to do his country one last service. In these walks we had an opportunity of seeing the undergrowth in the woods which we had admired at a distance on our drive to the lake. The ferns were the great ornament ; tree-ferns fifty feet high, with great fronds twenty-five feet long, feathering from the crest ; the fern-palm, with leaves yet longer, striking spirally from the stem, and stretching upwards in easy arches ; on the ground, besides the common varieties, a kidney fern, which was new to me—curious, if not otherwise remarkable ; and climbing fern, which crept over stick and stone, hanging in long festoons with pale green fronds—transparent, like the Killarney fern—the most perfectly lovely subject for imitation in wood-carving that I have ever met with. These grew everywhere, covering the whole surface ; only the majestic Kauri tolerated no approaches to his dignity. Under his branches all was bare and brown.

T

We made one delightful expedition into the interior. Starting, like Robinson Crusoe, in a boat for the extreme end of it, we picnicked in a rocky cove. Sir George then guided me up a steep hillside through a dense thicket of Ti-tree. We emerged on the brow, upon the open neck of a long peninsula which reached out into the ocean, with the remains, now overgrown, of a grassy track which once ran across the island, and ended at the house. It had been cut and cleared as a bridle-road, and Sir George used in past years to take his early ride there with a favourite niece. Strange that in these new countries one should already have to witness decay and alteration! Sir George has ceased to ride ; a little more and his island and he will be parted for ever.

> For age will rust the brightest blade,
> And time will break the stoutest bow ;
> Was never wight so starkly made
> But time and age will lay him low.

We turned from the path into the forest, forcing our way with difficulty through the thicket. Suddenly we came on a spot where three-quarters of an acre, or an acre, stood bare of any kind of undergrowth, but arched over by the interwoven branches of four or five gigantic Pokutukama trees, whose trunks stood as the columns of a natural hall or temple. The ground was dusty and hard, without trace of vegetation. The roots twisted and coiled over it like a nest of knotted pythons, while other pythons, the Rata parasites, wreathed themselves round the vast stems, twined up among the boughs, and disappeared among the leaves. It was like the horrid shade of some Druid's grove, and the history of it was as ghastly as its appearance. Here, at the beginning of this century, the Maori pirates of the island had held their festivals. To this place they had brought their prisoners; here they had slain them and hung their carcases on these branches to be cut and sliced for spit or caldron. Here, when their own turn came, they had made their last bloody stand against the axes of the invaders, and had been killed and devoured in turn. I could fancy that I saw the smoking fires, the hideous preparations, the dusky groups of savage warriors. I could hear the shrieks

A MAORI BANQUET HALL, NEW ZEALAND

of the victims echoing through the hollows of the forest. We ourselves picked up relics of the old scenes, stone knives and chisels and axeheads, forgotten when all was over and the island was left to desolation.

Sir George was a perfect host. He had his own occupations, and he left us often to amuse ourselves as we liked : E—— making sketches, and I attempting the like with unequal hand and at distant interval. The boats and boatmen were at our disposition. I, as an old sea-fisherman, was curious to see the varieties of fish to be found in these waters. The men promised to show me as many as I pleased; and one afternoon we sailed two or three miles away among the islands, brought up there, and sent out our lines. We had caught a bream or two, very like the bream of the Channel, when we found the lines torn out of our hands, and tackle broken to pieces by some monster of another kind. The men knew what they had to deal with; they produced lines like colour halyards, hooks such as you would hang a flitch of bacon on, mounted on a foot of chain which no tooth could cut. Half a mullet made the bait, and instantly that we had them overboard each of us was fast in a shark—not sharks of the largest size, but man-eaters—six or seven feet long and a foot in diameter. It was desperate work; we dragged the creatures by brute force alongside, where our friends stunned them with heavy clubs, hauled them in, and flung them under the thwarts. Two hours of it was as much as we were equal to; our hands were cut with the lines, and the carnage was sickening. In that time we had caught twenty-nine, running from forty to seventy pounds' weight. An archbishop, once killing a wasp with an eagerness which someone present thought unbecoming, defended himself by saying that it was part of the battle against sin. Sharks are as sinful as wasps and are natural enemies besides. Their livers are full of oil, and our afternoon's sport was worth three or four pounds to the men. But it was not a beautiful operation, and a single experience was enough.

There was a return match to this adventure where the sharks were near having an innings. I was still anxious to see more of the smaller fish, and another day, after luncheon, the sky threatening nothing but a calm, I and my son started, with a single hand, in a dingy about sixteen feet long, for a second trial. E——— would not go. There were only three of us, and three was as many as such a boat would conveniently hold. A soft breeze gently rippled the water; we sailed across an open channel, the only channel, unluckily for us, which was exposed to the ocean swell. We anchored again under the lee of some rocks which were covered at high tide. We worked away for an hour or two, finding no sharks, but finding little else. The afternoon was drawing on, and we were about to set our sail and return, when a singular-looking cloud formed up rapidly to seaward. It looked as if a shower were coming, and, as a puff of wind might come with it, we thought it better to stay where we were till it was over. The shower did not come, but the squall did, and instead of passing off as we expected, it grew into a gale, every moment blowing more fiercely. The two miles of water between us and our haven were a sheet of boiling foam; to row across was impossible. To try to cross close-hauled under sail, as from the wind's direction we should be obliged to do, would be certain destruction. Our cockle-shell would have filled and gone down with the first wave we met. When the tide rose there would be no shelter where we were lying. There was an island under our lee a quarter of a mile off, about an acre in extent, not more. The mainland was five miles off. We waited, hoping that a storm which had come so suddenly would drop as it had risen; but drop it would not, and the sea grew wilder and wilder, and it was now growing dusk. The boatman said that we had two courses before us: we might drop behind the little island, and lie there for the night. We could not land upon it; the waves were washing too heavily all round; but the rocks would keep off the wind, and the boat would ride safely, unless the wind changed. We had neither coats nor rugs, and the prospect of being rocked about all night in an open cradle in a storm was in itself unpleasant, while if the wind shifted there would be an end of us. The alternative was to run for the mainland. Though we could not cross the seas we might run before them. I asked if there was a harbour. There was no harbour, but there was a long sloping, sandy shore. Our boat drew but a few inches of water. The large waves would break some way out. If we escaped swamping in the outer line of breakers, we should then be in comparatively smooth water and would drive on till we could walk ashore.

There was a farmhouse where we could sleep, if we could succeed in getting on land at all. Between these two courses I was to choose and to choose quickly, for night was coming on. We could not stay where we were, and in twenty minutes the land would be invisible. I decided to run. We set the foresail, a mere rag ; our attendant, who was as cool as if he had been standing on Sir George's pier, sat forward to hold the sheet in his hands. I took the helm, fixed my eyes on the point which we were to make for, and we shot away over the crests of the boiling sea. The danger was that a following wave might strike our stern and fill us, but the boat was buoyant and flew through the foam. The waves in our wake looked ugly, curling over and rushing after us. My companions saw them. I had my work to attend to and looked straight forward. Nothing hurt us. The danger was not so great as it seemed so long as we managed our boat properly. It grew dark, but there were lights in the farmhouse window which served to steer by. Our hearts beat a little when we came up to the breakers, but there was no help for it. We could only go at them, and we dashed through on the bursting crest of a big roller.

In another minute we were running quietly through smooth and shallowing water. We took off shoes and stockings, stepped overboard, and dragged our boat ashore.

Two tall, athletic young men came down over the beach to help us. They had seen us coming, knew what must have happened, and guessed where we came from. To be friends of Sir George Grey was to be sure of help and hospitality at every house on the coast of the North Island. They told us that their mother would make us welcome : and thus what might have been a misadventure of a serious kind ended in giving me an opportunity of seeing a new side of English life in New Zealand.

The tide was low when we landed. The sands were set with oyster-shells, a good many of them placed edgeways. We were barefooted, and it was so dark that we could not see where we were stepping, so that I have a lively recollection of the three hundred yards which we had to walk before we reached the house.

It was a substantial wooden mansion, with big trees about it, a verandah and garden in front, and a large back-yard with various outhouses. Hills covered with forest rose darkly behind and on either side. I could see little more, as the light was almost gone, but in the morning, when I could look about me, I found that between these hills and reaching up to the farm station, there was a fair expanse of rich level land, part under the plough, part in meadow, with herds of cattle feeding on it. A river ran down through the middle of the valley, forming a lagoon before it reached the sea, the banks of which were littered with the skeletons of rotting trees.

Our conductor led us to the door, took us in, and introduced us. I could have fancied myself in a Boer's house in South Africa. The passage opened into a large central apartment with open roof and strong and solid rafters, which served as hall, kitchen, and dining-room. A large wood fire was burning in the grate, which had an oven and fire-plate attached to it. The walls shone with pots, pans, dishes, plates, all clean and shining. There was a settle, a sofa or two, some strong chairs, and a long table with a fixed seat at the end for the head of the family. Doors opened into bedrooms, which were chiefly on the ground floor. In front, where the verandah was, there were best rooms, reserved for company and state occasions, but the life of the establishment was in the hall-kitchen which we first entered. The owner was a matron of about sixty, a good-natured but energetic, authoritative woman, who had once been a servant, had married a Portuguese, and had been left a widow with three sons and two daughters. Something, a very little, had been secured to her as a provision. She had purchased a small farm at this place when land was more easy to be had than at present. She had thriven upon it, she had added to it, and had now 500 acres of her own—

the richest parts reclaimed and the rest in primitive forest. Her farm stock was worth 1,500*l.*, and she also owned houses in Auckland, besides money out at interest. Her eldest son had married and gone from her, and so had one daughter. She was now living alone with the remaining daughter and the two younger sons whom I had seen. She had no servant, and they did the entire work of the house and the farm between them. The young men cut the timber, ploughed, dug, fenced, and took care of the cattle. Mother and daughter kept all in order within doors, cooked the food, washed, made, and mended the clothes, &c., all in a notable way. As there were rooms to spare, and as any possible addition to the income was not to be neglected, summer lodgers from Auckland were occasionally taken in for sea-bathing. This was the explanation of a ladylike young woman whom we found there with two or three children, evidently not members of the family.

We all had supper together, consisting of tinned meat, bread, and tea—rough but good and wholesome. The sons and Sir George's man went out afterwards to see after the boat, which we had left moored on the sands. They returned after half-an-hour to say that the night was so dark that they could see nothing, and the wind and sea so furious that they could scarcely approach the beach. They had not found the boat nor any traces of it, and concluded that it had gone to pieces.

There was nothing for it but to go to bed and to sleep, which we succeeded in doing, the beds being as clean as care could make them. Our principal anxiety was for Sir George, who we knew must be alarmed, but we could not consider ourselves to blame. It had been a misfortune and nobody's fault. He would have seen the storm come on, and would conjecture what must have become of us. The tempest roared on through the night. Looking out in the morning, we saw a wild scene of driving sand and foam, but through it all, at any rate, we beheld our little boat riding safely where we had left her. The tide had risen. Buoyant as a cork, she had floated dry in breakers where a stouter vessel would have been swamped and wrecked.

We saw that we had means of getting home again when the weather would let us, and our worst care was removed. We breakfasted as we had supped, the whole party sitting round the table. The mother presided, decently saying grace. We walked afterwards round the farm, saw the cattle and crops, saw the young men cutting Ti-bush, and carting it to the sea to be shipped for Auckland. Two young ladies cantered up on their ponies from some adjoining station for a morning call. It was all very pretty—a quiet home of peaceful and successful industry, far pleasanter for one to look at than the high wages and hot-pressed pleasures of the large towns. One day there will be homesteads such as this all over New Zealand, when the municipalities can borrow no more and the labourers must disperse or starve.

At midday the wind lulled; the sea dropped; and we could take our leave. Our good landlady charged me and my son four shillings each for two suppers, two breakfasts, and two faultless beds. Sir George's boatman had been entertained as a friend, and for him nothing was to be paid at all. All the virtues seemed to thrive in that primitive establishment. The good people could hardly have been paid the cost of what we consumed. I was glad and proud to have made acquaintance with a family whom I counted as one of the healthiest that I had met with in all my travels. We started home, and our stout little barque rattled through the water and worked to windward as if proud of what she had gone through. Half-way back we were met by a steamer, which had gone into Kawau for shelter from the gale, and had been despatched by Sir George to look for us. He had been more uneasy than his consideration for us would allow him to acknowledge.

This was the last day of our visit. The week which we had passed at Kawau was one of the most interesting which I remember in my life, and our host certainly was one of the most remarkable men. It is sad to think that in all human likelihood I shall never see Sir George Grey again. When he goes the Maori and the poor whites in New Zealand will have lost their truest friend, and England will have lost a public servant, among the best that she ever had, whose worth she failed to understand.

In another week the 'Australia,' sister-ship to the 'City of Sydney,' would call for us at Auckland. My purpose was to return by San Francisco and the United States. Sir James Harrington had seen in prophecy the English race dispersed over the whole globe. The greatest of all its branches—in its own opinion no branch any longer, but the main trunk of the tree—was, of course, America ; and it would be interesting to contrast and compare what the 'plantations' of Harrington's time had grown into, and of which he was chiefly thinking when he wrote his 'Oceana,' with the 'Oceanic' planets which still revolve around the English primary. There was not time left for further distant expeditions. There were several able and superior men in Auckland whose opinions about many things I was anxious to learn. There was Professor Aldis and his wife, who were of the elect of cultivated man and woman-kind. So we arranged to remain at the club there till the steamer arrived. Everybody was good and hospitable to us, and tried to make our time pass pleasantly. The bishop showed us at leisure Selwyn's house and library ; the trees now surrounding the palace, which he had himself planted; the genius of him still traceable in the rooms and the bookcases and the furniture. Selwyn's appointment to New Zealand had been a notable thing in its day. Colonial bishops going among savages were less common than they are now. We had laughed over Sydney Smith's cold missionary on the sideboard, with which the chiefs were to entertain him. He was an athlete, and we had heard of him as swimming rivers with his chaplain when out on visitation, &c. He was the first, and much the best, of the muscular Christians, who at one time were to have been the saviours of society. His name was connected for ever with the history of English New Zealand, and we looked respectfully on the traces which remained of his presence.

Social duties fell on us of the usual kind. We dined with Auckland merchants, one of them with a mansion and esta-blishment on the scale of Sydney, and for his lady an artist of high accomplishments. Dinner-parties sadly resemble one another. Colonial society is too imitative of home manners, and would be livelier if it ventured on originality; but no strangers anywhere could have been received with more kindness or with more desire to do the best they could for us. The Aldises kept their word and called on us, and invited us to their home under Mount Eden. The situation of their residence, save for the purity of sky and air, reminded me of suburban houses in our own Black Country, for the roads and walks were made with cinder and slag, and the rockwork of their garden was composed of masses of lava which had been vomited from the crater overhead. But Mount Eden was now sleeping; the rocks were overgrown with mesembryanthemum, and beds of violets were springing up between them, and though it was a strange place in which to find the most brilliant mathematician that Cambridge has produced for half a century, he and his wife contrived to find life pass pleasantly there. Nay, they looked back on Newcastle, where they had spent their first years after leaving the university, as in comparison a sort of Tartarus, an abode of damned souls. The professor went daily into the town for his duties at the college, and he had pupils, he told me, of real promise, quite as likely to distinguish themselves as any that he had taught at home. Indeed, he spoke very well of the rising generation of colonials. At a university and among students anxious to learn, he was likely to see the most favourable specimens, but I took his testimony as a welcome corrective to the denunciations which I had heard elsewhere, so generally, from their elders. Sons cannot always be the exact copies of their fathers, and their fathers are a little too ready to mistake difference for inferiority.

A practical difficulty in colonial life is to find good servants. Sir George Grey's people were an exception. They were like feudal lieges. But the best emigrants prefer independence; and ladies and gentlemen, after suffering for a year or two under the inflictions of bad domestics, learn to do without and manage for themselves. Professor and Mrs. Aldis had one girl to help them in the house, and a poor creature of a man, fit only for the lightest work, to keep the garden and look after a pony and pony-carriage. So living they described themselves as perfectly happy. Our English universities deserve the gratitude of Victoria and New Zealand. They gave away Martin Irving to one ; they gave Professor Aldis to the other; perhaps, however, without entire consciousness of the worth of what they were parting with. Had Mr. Aldis been a clergyman of the Established Church, he might have risen to an archbishopric. There was no distinction which he might not have claimed, or for which the completeness of his Christian belief would not have qualified him. But in his own judgment, which was probably as excellent on this point as on others, he was better as he was. In his house there was no gossip, political or personal. Of politics he kept prudently clear, as no business of his. But he talked, and talked admirably, on all subjects of enduring interest, with the clearness of scientific knowledge, and the good sense which it is so pleasant to listen to.

On the topics of the day, on the state of the Colony, on the working of responsible government, the relations with the mother-country, &c., I found many persons willing and even eager to give us their opinions. A few things that were said to me are characteristic and worth preserving. I avoid names, as I wish only to give the notions which are floating in the air.

There was considerable unanimity about the existing form of government in New Zealand. No one defended it. Two houses with paid members were allowed to do their work as ill as possible, and to be an expensive instrument for political corruption and jobbery. Those who were in favour of the maintenance of the English connection, and those who were against it, held the same language, though they differed much as to what they would prefer in exchange. One gentleman amused me considerably with his views. He expressed the greatest loyalty to England, which he declared to be the universal feeling of the whole Colony ; but it was a loyalty which implied that we were to continue to do everything for them— protect their coasts, lend them money as long as they wanted it, and allow them to elect a governor who should be entirely independent of us. He repudiated all forms of confederation, would not hear of a political association with the rest of the empire, rejected with scorn Mr. Dalley's notion that the colonies should contribute to the expenses of the navy. A navy, of course, was needed, but we were to bear the whole expense— every part of it. Let us do all this cheerfully and then we should see how attached they would be to us. He did not, indeed, promise that the interest on the money with which we were to provide them would continue to be paid. It was impossible for them, he said, to pay by taxation the interest on the debt as it stood. They would pay as long as they could borrow; and he seemed to think that this ought to be sufficient, and that we could not expect them to do more. It was a maxim of politics that no one was bound by engagements which he could not fulfil. He assured me that at the present time the interest was paid out of the loans, although the Treasury accounts represented it as paid out of revenue. I told him that, if this was so, it was the business of him, and of those who agreed with him, to bring the truth to light and to put a stop to the borrowing. Repudiation would have serious consequences. But he seemed to think that to cease to borrow and to repudiate would go together, nor could I make him see that after all the consequences to *them* would be serious at all. We should lose our money; but they would have paid us if they could. His coolness took my breath away. He did add, at last, that there was one resource between them and bankruptcy. There was the Native Reserve. It was the richest land in the islands, and, if necessary, could be entered upon and sold. The English creditor will scarcely be satisfied with such a return of ways and means.

The conversation of so random a gentleman would not have been worth recording on its own account, but it is true that the rapid increase of New Zealand indebtedness is causing grave anxiety to persons of greater consideration. The debt, they told me, was out of all proportion to so small a community, and though it might appear on the surface that the trade of the Colony was increasing along with it, yet part at least of the seeming prosperity was due to the expenditure of the loans themselves, and to the customs' duties on the goods which the high wages, as long as they last, enabled the workmen to buy. The land, in the North Island at least, was not being developed as it is in Australia. It was falling into the hands of speculators. It was being bought over the heads of the poor by successful men of business, who, when the pressure came, were dreaming of reproducing the old division of a landed aristocracy with tenants and labourers under them. A landed aristocracy growing of itself might be a necessary and useful institution. A landed aristocracy created by legislative manœuvring could be nothing but an evil. So serious appeared the peril to those who had courage to look forward, that there was already an agitation for a land tax. If the debt was not to be repudiated (which, at least for the present, no rational person contemplated), taxation was inevitable sooner or later. It was only postponed by borrowing, and as it was certain that the workmen would not tax themselves or their own favourite commodities, a land tax, and a heavy one, was the form which it was likely to assume.

No one would regret a land tax who is a real friend to New Zealand, but one does and must regret the extravagance which may make it necessary, and may overload for many years the energies of the Colony. I was in an office one day on money business. The member of the firm with whom I was engaged, alluded, when our own affair was disposed of, to the new loan which had just been taken up in the English market, and expressed his surprise that the London capitalists were willing to lend so largely, and on such easy terms, to so small a community. What could they expect? I said that the accounts were published. The money was represented as being spent on railways or on public works sure to be reproductive. This was a sufficient security. He looked at me ambiguously. 'Thirty-two millions,' he said, 'is a large debt for half a million people, and perhaps you do not know that the municipal debts are, at least, as much more as the national debt. No doubt the money goes upon works of some kind, and some of the railways may pay their expenses; but as to reproductiveness, within any reasonable period, in the least corresponding to the cost, there may be some uncertainty.' However, he said, it was our own affair, and as long as we were ready to lend, they would not cease to borrow.

Uncomfortable impressions of this kind do exist among persons on the spot who have means of forming independent opinions. I do not pretend that they are well founded. Sir Julius Vogel, or the agent-general in London, may have a satisfactory reply to all unfavourable criticisms ; but when an alarm is widely felt, and is whispered under breath in so many quarters, it would be well if it could be set at rest by clear statements which cannot be accused of ambiguity. The anxiety may be groundless, but it is not unnatural. A few plain words will quiet the minds of many worthy New Zealanders who are uneasy for the honour of their island.

The South Island was still unvisited, and Lyttelton and Wellington and Christchurch and Dunedin and the Fiords and the Glaciers and the Giant Mountains. But no great variety was likely as yet to have established itself among the colonists. The type of character, the set of opinions, was probably the same, and in the pattern of the cloth you see the texture of the piece. It was better to see a few men deliberately than the outsides of many, and as far as they were concerned I did not feel that a wider acquaintance, however pleasant, would have been of any material advantage to me. Of the country— so varied, so remarkable, the future home, as I believe it to be, of the greatest nation in the Pacific—of that I would gladly have seen more, and would have stayed longer, had other conditions permitted. But the fast-thickening war rumours had established a homeward current for all wandering Englishmen, and we, like the rest, were swept along by the stream. It was not that we could affect the issues of things, or dreamt that we could, but there was not one of us whose domestic life would not be influenced in one way or another by war if it came, and we were too restless to be any longer amused or interested by other things. To me it was all inexplicable. I could understand the eagerness of the army, for they wanted employment. I could understand that the ministers might be driven against their judgment into doing anything which the people clamoured for—ministers, on both sides, having ceased to regard themselves as more than the instruments of the people's wishes. It was true that they were Radicals, and that the Radicals, till their turn of power came, had professed to hate war ; that they had denounced Lord Beaconsfield, and turned him out of office, for the jingoism which they were now adopting. But after we had seen them reddening the sands of Africa with the blood of tens of thousands of poor creatures who had been killed without a scruple to escape an adverse vote in the House of Commons, one could not deny that even they, or at least the politicians among them, might be willing, for the same object, to kill as many more in Asia.

But why were the people themselves so eager ? Not one in a thousand of them could pretend that he had studied the question, and was satisfied that only a war could save our Indian Empire. Danger to the empire might be the excuse ; it could not be the motive. I began to think that Lord —— must have been right when he said to me : 'The reason why the English wish to fight Russia is that they enjoy fighting, and Russia is the only one of the Great Powers with whom they could fight with the slightest hope of a favourable result.' Prudent persons, before they undertake any important enter-prise, balance the result to be gained with the cost of gaining it. A war set going with Russia under the existing conditions would continue either till Russia was exhausted and fell to pieces in revolution ; or, if we were the unsuccessful party— as it was at least possible that we might be—till there was another rebellion in India. Either alternative promised in-calculable misery to millions of the human race ; yet we, who could not manage our own South Africa, who were letting Ireland slip from us, as wanting strength or wanting courage to hold it, were preparing with a light heart to carry fire and sword into the ends of the earth.

Russia, we were told, was extending her conquests in Central Asia. Had *we* made no conquests in Asia ? Russia's Asiatic subjects, counted altogether, do not exceed thirty millions. The Empress of India has two hundred and fifty millions. Russia was attacking the Afghans. Had *we* never attacked the Afghans? Russia was a danger to the Indian Empire. She might encourage disaffection there, and if she could she would. How could we know that she would? and if she did, might she not plead our own example: only seven years ago we had formed a deliberate plan to stir up a revolt in Turkestan? We satisfy ourselves that when we do these things it is for the good of mankind, but that when others do them it is wicked and not to be permitted. Such a plea as this will hardly pass current in the intercourse of nations. For myself, I thought that the war now so clamoured for would be a wicked war, and I clung to my conviction that our better genius would somehow keep us out of it. The greatest fool in the House of Commons, if left to himself and to his own small understanding, would steer the ship of the State better than the galaxy of genius had done which formed Mr. Gladstone's Administration; but even they, I trusted, would still keep us clear of this fresh disaster.

In leaving New Zealand we should be leaving the telegraph. We could hear nothing more till we reached the Sandwich Islands, or probably till we reached San Francisco; and I looked forward with real satisfaction to the month of quiet which lay before us, when we should be no more distracted by the broken patches of news which had been dropping in upon us from hour to hour. E——, who was going home with us, shared none of my feelings. He, a high Scotch Tory, hated the Russians with genuine party vigour. Why the Tories should hate Russia, which alone maintains in Europe the old-fashioned Tory principles, is one of those paradoxes which historians will hereafter puzzle over. As long as the Duke of Wellington lived, the Tories wished well to Russia, and the Whigs detested her; now they have changed places. The two parties seem really to think of little save how to defeat one another. Consistency and principle are valued only as virtues which one's enemies can be accused of being without. They wheel round each other like armies in the field, choosing their ground with a view to the immediate campaign. For decency's sake they cannot avow the true motives of their action, and conceal it, even for themselves, behind a veil of

plausibilities ; but in a few years they may change places
again, and will have excellent reasons for doing it. E——
any way was happy, thinking that we were going in for the
Russians at last ; and so were a number of militia officers who
had been recalled to their regiments, and were in high spirits
at the prospect.

CHAPTER XIX.

Sail for America—The 'Australia'—Heavy weather—A New Zealand colonist
—Ea·ter in the Southern Hemisphere—Occupations on board—Samoa—A
missionary—Parliamentary government in the Pacific Islands—A young
Australian—The Sandwich Islands—Honolulu—American influence—Bay
of San Franci-co.

THE ' Australia ' was a ship of three thousand tons, and smartly
fitted, as these Pacific steamers generally are. The 'City of
Sydney' was American. The 'Australia' was English, with
an English captain and English officers, the crew and attendants being principally Chinese. She was crowded to repletion.
In the saloon we had a hundred and thirty passengers :
colonial tourists going to Europe for the summer ; wealthy
families taking a sea voyage for a holiday ; young married
couples on their honeymoon, &c. All the idle people in
Auckland must have been on the pier to see us off. Deck,
cabins, were thronged with the sisters, aunts, cousins, friends,
who had come on board for a last leave-taking. From the
tears, embraces, and exclamations, it might have seemed we
were taking our departure to the other world. I heard a
young lady who was sitting alone with a single companion
observe, 'Isn't it lovely to have nobody to care about one, and
so escape all that ?'

We were going north, right up to the line. We were
warned that it would be hot, and hot it proved, but under
conditions more intolerable than I had before experienced.
The sky was overcast. We had rain and heavy head-winds.
The seas flew over the deck, the ports were closed, the hatches
shut down. The temperature in the saloon was 85°, and even

U

the windsails were removed, because rain and spray drove
down them, wetted the passages, and gave the stewards
trouble. I protested against this last enormity. I represented
to the captain, who had his own quarters on deck and did not
suffer, that we should all be found smothered some morning,
as in a Black Hole of Calcutta, and that I did not wish to die
of the stench of my fellow-creatures. 'Their *esprit fort*, I
suppose you mean,' said E——. The spirit of wit moved the
captain's heart more than my expostulations. Our windsails
were set up again, and we had a current of air among us,
though damp and tepid as in an orchid house.

When a number of people are shut up together for three
or four weeks, a process is set up of natural selection. We
find out those who suit us, and we have time to become
intimate with them. I was chiefly attracted by a rough,
elderly Scotchman, who had been thirty years in New
Zealand, had made a fortune there, and was now on his way
home, not to remain, but to look about him in the old country
and see how things were going on. He was a shrewd,
original old gentleman, cynical more than enough, but good-
humoured at bottom, and very entertaining. He was rich,
and took the rich man's view of things, but if he had succeeded it had been in fair fight. He had been thrown into
the arena of colonial life with thousands of others. They had
failed, or they were still undistinguished in the general herd.
He had made his way to the front. He was an illustration of
the survival of the strongest, was worth attending to, and was
excellent company. In his youth, when he had nothing, he
had been a Radical. He had become a Tory in his age,
because he had property to lose, and did not wish to lie at the
mercy of those who thought as he had once thought himself.
His political views, however, showed more reading and general
knowledge than I was prepared for. He did not believe in
the permanence of any forms of government. None of them
were good for very much, and they were always corrupting
and requiring change. The English constitution he regarded
as an accidental result of the struggle between the feudal
and popular elements in the British nation. It had been

elevated into a principle, as a final solution of the great
political problem. It had been held up as an example for all
mankind, but its time was nearly out. It had failed everywhere except with us, and with us it would fail too when there
were no longer two parties, and the democracy was completely
supreme.

He was one of those who took an unfavourable view of
the rising generation of colonists. The fathers, he said (just
as if he had been an old Roman in Terence's time), had
worked hard to make their fortune. The children only
thought of spending it. They were idle and extravagant,
living beyond their means, &c., a complaint which has been
heard before and will be heard while the human race continues. He was sceptical about the value of education, or of
what we now understand by that unconsidered word. His
education had been in work. He had been taught to earn his
living with his hands. Lads nowadays, he complained, were
not taught to work at all ; ' education ' was a mere sharpening
of the wits. Suppose a Maori to learn to read and write, to
be sent to college to learn science, mathematics, languages,
and the rest of it ; but suppose him to have lost his courage
and his sense of honour, and to have learnt to cheat, and
to lie, and to gamble, as a good many educated white men
did, had such a Maori gained very much ? In my Scot's
opinion, the only progress worth speaking of was moral progress. The rest was only change, and often a change for the
worse.

He had the national interest in religious questions, and
talked much about such things in a sceptical way. We had
some ritualistic ladies and gentlemen on board, whose tendencies provoked his sarcastic humour. They were indeed
rather provoking. It was Passion week, and one of them
told me that they had arranged for a ' celebration ' in the
cabin on Easter Sunday. It would be so *nice*—didn't I think
so ? I ought to have replied that ' nice ' was a strange word
for such a thing. I let him go on, however, with an unmean-
ing smile, ἀχρεῖον γελάσας, paying homage with the rest of
mankind to the universal genius of cant. But it set mo

thinking how strangely unsuited the Christian festivals were to the seasons of the other hemisphere. We were now in autumn, at the time of the feast of ' ingathering ' of the harvest, and Easter was the feast of the spring at the vernal equinox, when the weather was still cold and a fire was burning on the High Priest's hearth. So with the rest. The Church services were adapted all of them to the occupations of the different periods of the year, beginning with Christmas at the winter solstice, when the sun, which had appeared to be dying, renewed its youth. Our religious traditions, like our poetry, are divorced in the southern hemisphere from their natural associations. They are exotics from another climate, and can only be preserved as exotics.

Time and its tenses are strange things, and at their strangest when one is travelling round the globe. The question is not only what season is it, but what day is it, and what o'clock is it. The captain *makes* it twelve o'clock when he tells us that it is noon ; and it seemed as if a supply of time was among the ship's stores ; for when we reached 180° E. long., he presented us with an extra day, and we had two Thursdays, two eighths of April, in one week. As our course was eastward, we met the sun each morning before it would rise at the point where we had been on the morning before, and the day was, therefore, shorter than the complete period of the globe's revolution. Each degree of longitude represented a loss of four minutes, and the total loss in a complete circuit would be an entire day of twenty-four hours. We had gone through half of it, and the captain owed us twelve hours. He paid us these, and he advanced us twelve more, which we should have spent or paid back to him by the time that we reached Liverpool.

The weather mended with us. The heat continued. The sea water was still at 85°, and the temperature at night could not fall much below it. But the air cleared. The stars shone clear after dark, and we watched for the pointers of the Great Bear, where, at their highest elevation, they stood vertical over the North Star and spoke to us of home. By-and-by the North Star himself showed above the horizon and Canopus

set and the Southern Cross, and we were once more in our
own world. The Pagan gods again ruled in the familiar sky,
and welcomed us back with steadfast, friendly glance. Our
meals were a scramble, the attendance indifferent, the cooking
execrable. Not that cooks or stewards were specially in
fault. There were too many of us, and the vessel's staff was
unequal to the demands upon it. But our windows could
now stand open day and night, and air brought health, and
health appetite. Five minutes after dinner it mattered little
what we had eaten. We played chess, we played whist, we
read books. Every noon there was a sweepstakes for the
number of miles run in the twenty-four hours. The numbers
which promised well were set up for auction, and there was
fresh excitement. The morning bath was another incident.
There were five baths for us gentlemen, at which we were to
take our turn, and every day between seven and eight o'clock
some forty of us were to be seen sitting in rows, in gorgeous
dressing-gowns, in the saloon, expecting our summons, the
modest among us getting pushed aside, as at the Pool of
Bethesda.

On Sundays games were suspended, and we had the Church
of England service, the captain, as usual, officiating. In the
evenings clerical volunteers were allowed to preach. A young
Dissenter of metaphysical tendencies was the chief performer,
and once, being over ambitious, he blundered into the heresy
of the Docetæ. Christ, he told us, was never crucified—never
Christ, but only the body of Christ. We were not our bodies.
We saw a certain figure with special stature, figure, and
organs, and we called it collectively an individual man. But
the man might lose eyes, arms, feet, yet be the same man still.
His members were his, but they were not *he*. The man was
something behind all these. The personality, the *Ich*, was
something which could not be seen, could not be touched, could
not be handled, still less could it be crucified. We were to
reflect on this and find comfort in it. Everyone nowadays
goes in for amateur philosophy or for amateur Catholic ritual-
ism ; but it is curious to see that they are all for toleration,
and seem to think that we all mean the same thing though we
say exactly the opposite.

' Oh for one hour of blind old Dandolo ! ' I sometimes am inclined to cry : Oh for the hard voice of the uncompromising Genevan, who knew, at least, that lies were not truth, and that if taken into the soul they worked like poison there. The Genevans are extinct as the dodo and the moa. Tolerance means at bottom that no one knows anything about the matter, and that one opinion is as good as another. Is there nothing which can be surely known ? Is it true, for instance, that on ' the tracks of all evil deeds there follow avenging hell-hounds from which there is no escape ' ? If such hounds there be, it is dangerous to leave their existence an open question for fools to doubt about. One opinion on that subject is clearly not as good as another, and we may recollect to our advantage how wise men have thought about it in other days.

σοφία γὰρ ἔκ του
κλεινὸν ἔπος πέφανται
τὸ κακὸν δοκεῖν ποτ' ἐσθλὸν
τῷ δ' ἔμμεν ὅτῳ φρένας
θεὸς ἄγει πρὸς ἄταν.

' There was one who wisely spake a famous word, that ill may seem to be good, and that when the gods will bring a man's soul to wreck they make ill to be his good.'

' There is a way that seemeth right unto a man, but the end thereof is death.' That is a fact if anything is a fact ; yet, again, who is to be the judge ? Who is sufficient for these things ? Which is best or which is worst—to tolerate all, to leave one fool to utter his folly and other fools to believe it, or to burn the wrong man at the stake ?

We touched at Samoa, famous lately for the German doings there. It was night. I saw from my berth the gleaming of lights and the large spars and masts of anchored steamers, but we were off again and out of sight of land before morning brought me on deck. A missionary came on board there who had passed his life among these islands. He was over seventy, but was still hale and vigorous. He was going home on business of the society, but intended to return, and seemed as if he had still many years of work in him. His conversation was interesting, for he had new things to tell us, talking expansively about the natives and seeming to like them well. His voice and manners had at first a slight professional twang as if he thought something of that kind was expected of him. He gave me some tracts to read, and it appeared that among his other qualifications he was a polemical divine. There had been a wolf in his fold. A certain Mr. Coxe had been introducing latitudinarianism into Polynesia, had written a pamphlet on Universal Salvation, and had ventured an opinion that wicked men, wicked angels, and even the devil himself, would be eventually converted and received to grace. Mr. Coxe's teaching had been dangerously popular. The missionary had taken the field against him, and had written a pamphlet on Eternal Damnation, which he gave me to peruse, and seemed anxious for my suffrage. Allowing for differences of expression, I was wholly of his way of thinking. If the devil had been capable of redemption, he would have been redeemed before he had been allowed to do so much mischief. But the curious part of the matter was that our new eager friend living in those remote regions had evidently never heard that such an opinion had been avowed before, and imagined that a speculation which had been thrashed out for thousands of years and in half the languages of the world had been uttered for the first time by Mr. Coxe.

He was a very honest man, however. I did not quarrel with his zeal, and he had produced better work than this pamphlet. With the help of his brother missionaries he had translated the Bible into Samoan, and he told us with great satisfaction that the natives had bought thirty thousand copies at two dollars apiece. Actually thirty thousand, handsomely bound, 'with gilt edges.' Fifteen hundred pounds he had been able to remit annually from this source to the parent society, the money and the gilt edges together being a visible evidence of the blessings of Christianity to the heathen.

Doubtless it was an interesting fact, and from those Bibles seeds may have dropped into many a poor unknown soul, to make it better than it had been. But I could not help saying that there were other effects of conversion which would interest me even more if he could tell me of them. The Polynesian had a bad name for idleness and unchastity—was there any improvement in this respect? I admired his candour. The moral effects of religion, he said, were sometimes not very visible even in old-established Christian countries. The Polynesians could read. They had schools and chapels. They had ceased to eat one another, which was one step towards improvement; others might follow. Moral progress was always slow, and I must remember that the intercourse with white traders and sailors was a terrible counteracting influence. This was true and fairly put. I liked the old man much more than I expected to do. Autumn 'gilds ere it withers,' and it is sometimes the same with old age. We had among the passengers a keen Mephistophelic sort of gentleman who believed in nothing—who, like Pistol, had used the world as his oyster and extracted pearls out of it sufficient to make his life flow easily. He had been successful in business; he had done, and would continue to do, effectively and well whatever he undertook; but his theory of existence evidently was that in such a world as this the only wisdom was to get as much enjoyment out of it as could be had. All else was illusion. He was excellent company, intellectually the best that we had—a cleverer man, beyond all comparison, than my poor missionary; but a belief in something—some object outside oneself, for which one can care and exert oneself, brings a grace into the character which is not to be had without it. Simplicity is more attractive than brilliancy, and my missionary had a humour of his own which was often diverting. He told me that in all those groups of islands—Samoa, the Tonga Islands, and the rest—they had now parliamentary government, with ministers responsible to the legislature. The result was ridiculous beyond belief, and even more mischievous than ridiculous. His own brethren had been the means of introducing the system, and in consequence had made their way into office and become considerable people. One of them somewhere had become a democratic despot—a Polycrates without the genius, but with cunning sufficient to keep himself in power. The unfortunate people! Was it not enough that we should give them gun-

powder, and gin, and measles, and smallpox, but that we must
send our political epidemic among them as well ? It will help
at any rate to hasten their end.

We were to halt next at the Sandwich Islands. I had read
Miss Bird's book about these islands, and her glowing description of the burning mountain in Hawaii, the largest active
volcano in the world. Unless we heard on arriving there that
war was actually declared, E—— and three or four others of
our party meant to stop and see it, and they urged me not to
miss the opportunity. Whether I should stop or not depended
on whether I felt curiosity about the inhabitants. I could be
contented to read of lakes of melted lava without wanting to
look at them. A lake of liquid fire is less beautiful to me
than a lake of water. A volcano is only a late relic of the
process by which the earth was prepared for human habitation.
It is now merely an instrument of destruction, and the irrational forces of nature in violent action I feel distressing and
disturbing. I prefer settled districts, where my brother
mortals are rejoicing in the work of their hands. I therefore
postponed my own decision till I had seen at least what Honolulu was like, where we were to stop. Queen Emma was
there, whom we had seen in England. There was a king, and
his parliament, and his constitutional advisers. There was a
separate island—Molokai—given up to lepers, which, if not
pleasant, might be tragical. Leprosy is fatally frequent in the
Sandwich archipelago. They try to stamp it out by separating
the infected from the healthy, and everyone, high or low, who
is seized by the disorder is removed thither to remain till he
dies. This, too, I thought, I could be content to read about ;
but a young Catholic priest was said to be there, a Father
Damiens (let his name be had in honour !), who had spontaneously devoted his life to comforting and helping these poor
creatures in their horrid exile. Such a man as that might be
worth an effort to see, if a burning mountain was insufficient,
or even the working of free political institutions. In 1779,
Captain Cook found a population of three hundred thousand
in these islands. At the last census there were forty-nine
thousand. If parliamentary government 'wishes to work a

miracle,' as the American said when he was falling over a cliff, 'now is the time.' Let it avert, if it can, the swift disappearance of a people who were innocent and happy and prosperous before the white man and his 'notions' came among them.

Meantime I had been studying more at my leisure the human freight of the 'Australia.' There were all sorts among us, and I was sorry to have to agree more than I wished with my rough New Zealand Scot about the younger generation of the colonists. Professor Aldis's pupils had been of the working, industrious sort, and he thought very favourably of them. Those that we had on board, and there were a good many of them, were of the moneyed kind, who had leisure and means and the self-sufficiency which goes along with it. Of these I liked none. They were, as a rule, vain, ignorant, underbred, without dignity, without courtesy, and with a conceit which was unbounded. Middle-class democracy is not favourable to the growth of manners, and, with all my wish to find it otherwise, I had to contrast them, not to their advantage, with two or three English youths among us, who, though belonging to the same social class, might have been another order of beings. They brought back to my mind a gentleman whom I had fallen in with somewhere, who might be taken as a type of the sort to whom my Scot so much objected. He had struck me not so much by his opinions as by the arrogance and insolence with which he expressed them. He belonged, I believe, to a great mercantile house in one of the Australian cities; and if he was the representative in any sense of his contemporaries, the connection with the mother-country will not be of long continuance. Not that he wished to break it immediately. Australia, he told me, had a glorious destiny before it. It was to stand beside the United States as an equal, perhaps as a superior, and they two were to be the greatest countries in the world. Separation from the mother-country was inevitable. The Australian states had too high a destiny to be kept long in leading strings. He and his friends, however, had no wish to cut them prematurely. They would allow us, if we liked it, to continue a little longer to be useful to them, to warn off intruding Germans, to supply them with capital, &c., and to feel ourselves honoured in doing it. The blandness and conviction with which he delivered his sentiments would have been entertaining if it had not been so absurd. He was so satisfied with his country and himself, that if I had told him that we all knew how great the honour was to be the dry nurse to so grand a baby, how delighted we were to be their humble servants, he would never have suspected me of irony. You may venture any liberties, provided you flatter sufficiently. One thing only you must not do. You must not express the shadow of a doubt of their present and future magnificence. An independent Australia, with such persons as my young acquaintance at the head of it, would certainly have a remarkable future before it, though less magnificent than they count upon. Happily in the colonies themselves I had not met with many such specimens. I had been thrown chiefly among their elders. But they do exist and may have some influence, and it is by those who are now growing to manhood, and not by the generation which must soon pass away, that the relation between England and her dependencies will be eventually determined. *Absit omen.*

After the first four days of our voyage the Pacific had justified its name. We had steamed regularly on, with smooth seas, sunny days, and starry nights. The heat, when we crossed the line, ceased to be oppressive. There were complaints that the vessel was slow, but we went along at an average of ten knots, making two hundred and forty miles a day. Life must be lived somewhere, and to spend a few extra hours between the tropics in uninterrupted quiet was not a hardship to be complained of. At daybreak on April 13 we came in sight of Honolulu. We were now in our own hemisphere and had crossed from autumn into spring.

The Sandwich Islands, moistened with continual rains, are never liable to drought, and sun and showers together carpet plain and mountain with exquisite verdure. The substance of them is volcanic rock. The coral insect builds for ever along the shores. The rain washes down from the hills the red dust of the crumbling scoria, which, settling over the coral banks, forms on one side a low, level plain with rich alluvial soil. Here grow the endless trees of the tropics, whose leaf, flower, and fruit renew themselves perpetually as in the gardens of Alcinous. A natural harbour appears to have been formed by floods rushing down through a valley from the mountains, which have hollowed out a large, deep lagoon, have cut a way through the coral reef into the sea, and keep the opening clear with the help of the tidal scour. The depth of water is about six fathoms, and the oval basin is perhaps half a mile in its shortest, a mile in its longest diameter.

The whole Sandwich group is under the protection of the Americans. Guarded by the stars and stripes, a phantom royalty maintains itself at Honolulu. There is a palace, an army (of sixty warriors), a coinage with his majesty's face upon it, a parliament, a prime minister, an attorney-general, a chancellor of the exchequer, a minister for foreign affairs ; how many more secretaries of state I do not know. We steamed in between the two natural coral piers, and brought up in deep water alongside the jetty. The ship was to stay six hours, and we all rushed on shore to feel the land under our feet, and to breakfast at a Yankee hotel, where we were promised all the luxuries which at sea are unattainable. Along the platform were rows of dubious-looking damsels in pink and blue calicoes, soliciting the passengers, with large swimming eyes, to buy coral sprays and tortoiseshell orna- ments. Escaping from these sirens, we made our way into the town, composed of streets of uninteresting wooden houses on the modern American pattern, without local characteristics of any kind. Telephone wires were stretched above the roofs, thick as spider-webs in autumn, for the transaction of the infinite business which these means of swift communication seemed to imply. Men and women were lounging languidly about in loose European costumes, with an evident preference for bright colours. Both sexes were tall, but heavily-limbed, flaccid, and sensual-looking. The Americans have not been idle. They have set up abundant schools, and if the teaching is equal to the professed scheme of instruction, the Sandwich Islanders should be the best educated people to be found anywhere. No great results seem yet to have been arrived at, either intellectual or moral. They have a code of laws equally excellent, but they do not obey them, at least in one most important particular ; for strong drinks are forbidden, yet are freely consumed, the last king dispensing with the law in his own favour, the present king not being a great deal better, and their subjects following the example. So far as I could hear—for my own observation was, of course, worth nothing —there is a varnish over the place of Yankee civilisation, which has destroyed the natural vitality without as yet producing anything better or as good. To the eye of the passing traveller, the human aspect was uninviting ; not quite as much so as the coaling station at the Cape de Verde Islands, but approaching near to it. Miss Bird speaks warmly of the good nature of the people, and, being of Adam's race, they have probably merits of their own which would be appreciated on closer acquaintance ; but I was not encouraged to hope that they would interest me as deserving serious attention.

Outside the streets the original loveliness of a tropical land reasserted itself. Palms towered up, thickly clustered with cocoa-nuts. Bananas waved their long broad leaves. We walked under flowing acacias, palmettos, bread-fruit trees, magnolias, and innumerable shrubs in the glowing bloom of spring. A shower had fallen, and called out the perfume of the blossoms. Hibiscus and pomegranate crimsoned the hedges. Passion-flowers, bougainvillæas, and convolvulus crept up the tree-stems or hung in masses on the walls. Man may be vulgar, but trees and flowers cannot be. Even the wooden boxes in which the poorer natives lived, mean and featureless as they might be, were redeemed from entire ugliness by the foliage in which they were buried, and the bits of garden surrounding them. The strangest thing was the multitude of telephone wires, which followed us everywhere and made a network against the sky. The people looked like the laziest in the world. The wires would indicate the busiest. I was told—I know not how correctly—as an explanation of the mystery, that an American speculator, with a large telephone stock on hand which he wanted to dispose of, induced the government of the Sandwich Islands to relieve him of it, by a promise of the miracles which it would work.

The hotel was half a mile from the landing-place. We flowed on in a stream and came to it at last—a big house of large pretensions, in a grove of trees which kept the sun off. A broad flight of stairs led up into a hall. From the hall we were taken into a vast cool saloon, or coffee-room, and there, under the master eye of a smart Yankee manager, the breakfast which we had come in search of was provided for us, and certainly excellent it was : fresh fish, fresh eggs, fresh butter, cream, rolls, fruit—all the very best which could be provided by nature and art combined. Let admiration be given where it is due. When it was over we dispersed, some to drive in carriages into the mountains, others to examine further into the town. One party went to the palace to wait on the king, but failed to see him. His Majesty had been occupied late the night before and was indisposed. I wandered about the environs, looking at the people and their ways, and wondering at the nature of our Anglo-American character, which was spreading thus into all corners of the globe, and fashioning everything after its own likeness. The original, the natural, the picturesque, goes down before it as under the wand of a magician. In the place of them springs up the commonplace and the materially useful. Those who can adopt its worship and practise its liturgy, it will feed, and house, and lodge on the newest pattern, set them in a way of improving their condition by making money, of gaining useful knowledge, and enjoying themselves in tea-gardens and music-halls ; while those who cannot or will not bend, it sweeps away as with the sword of the destroyer.

The old races of the Pacific islands will soon be utterly obliterated. It is the nigger only who entirely prospers under these new conditions. As a slave he could grow into an Uncle Tom ; as a free citizen he carries his head as high as his late master, and laughs, works, and earns his wages, and enjoys life as becomes a man and a brother. It was predicted of him that he, too, when he was emancipated, would die off like the rest, but he shows no sign of any such intention. The modern system of things, whatever its defects, agrees certainly with the negro constitution.

The slight disposition which I had felt to remain at Honolulu I found to have evaporated. There would be no advantage commensurate with the time which it would cost. I cared nothing about the volcano. Father Damiens I would have gladly seen, but I could be of no use to him, and no personal acquaintance could have increased the respect which I felt for him. It was with real relief that I heard the whistle which called us back on board, and the grinding of the revolving screw.

The rest of our voyage was uneventful. We had lost E——, whose pleasant companionship had brightened so large a part of our expedition. We had lost Mr. Ashbury, who had stayed behind with him, and my entertaining Mephistophelic friend. We made the best of the slight compensation which their departure brought with it. They had 'messed' at our table in the saloon. The Chinese steward, having a smaller number to wait upon, could attend better to such of us as remained. The weather cooled perceptibly when we left the tropics—we met the keen north wind which blows almost all the year down the Western American coast. On April 20, we entered between the Heads into the Bay of San Francisco, and saw the smoke of the Golden City six miles in front of us. The opening is extremely striking—the bay itself is as large as Port Jackson. The hills are higher, the outlines grander. The only inferiority is in the absence of timber. There was grass everywhere, in the freshness of spring, but not a tree that we could see from the water; and we felt the bareness more strongly after New Zealand and Australia. Another difference made itself felt, the effect of which it was impossible to resist. There had been life and energy in Melbourne and Sydney, with crowded docks and growing enterprise; but an American city—and San Francisco especially—is more than they. The very pilot's voice as he came on board had a ring of decision about it. The great liners passing in and out with the stars and stripes flying; the huge ferry-boats rushing along, deck rising above deck, and black with passengers; the lines of houses on the shore, stretching leagues beyond the actual town, all spoke of the pulsations of a great national existence, which were beating to its farthest extremity.

San Francisco, half a century ago, was a sleepy Spanish village. It is now one of the most important cities of the world, destined, if things continue as they are, to expand into dimensions to which the present size of it is nothing, for it is and must be the chief outlet into the Pacific of the trade of the American continent.

CHAPTER XX.

The American Union—The Civil War and the results of it—Effect of the Union on the American character—San Francisco—Palace Hotel—The Market—The clubs—Aspect of the city—Californian temperament—The Pacific Railway—Alternative routes—Start for New York—Sacramento Valley—The Sierra Nevada—Indian territory—Salt Lake—The Mormons—The Rocky Mountains—Cañon of the Rio Grande—The prairies—Chicago—New York and its wonders—The 'Etruria'—Fastest passage on record—Liverpool.

THE problem of how to combine a number of self-governed communities into a single commonwealth, which now lies before Englishmen who desire to see a federation of the empire, has been solved, and solved completely, in the American Union. The bond which, at the Declaration of Independence, was looser than that which now connects Australia and England, became strengthened by time and custom. The attempt to break it was successfully resisted by the sword, and the American republic is, and is to continue, so far as reasonable foresight can anticipate, one and henceforth indissoluble.

Each State is free to manage its own private affairs, to legislate for itself, subject to the fundamental laws of the Union; and to administer its own internal government, with this reservation only—that separation is not to be thought of. The right to separate was settled once for all by a civil war which startled the world by its magnitude, but which, terrible though it might be, was not disproportioned to the greatness of the issues which were involved. Had the South succeeded in winning independence, the cloth once rent would have been rent again. There would not have been one America, but many Americas. The New World would have trodden over again in the tracks of the old. There would have been rival communities, with rival constitutions, democracies passing into military despotisms, standing armies, intrigues and quarrels, and wars on wars. The completeness with which the issue has been accepted shows that the Americans understood the alternative that lay before them. That the wound so easily healed was a proof that they had looked the alternative in the face, and were satisfied with the verdict which had been pronounced.

And well they may be satisfied. The dimensions and value of any single man depend on the body of which he is a member. As an individual, with his horizon bounded by his personal interests, he remains, however high his gifts, but a mean creature. His thoughts are small, his aims narrow ; he has no common concerns or common convictions which bind him to his fellows. He lives, he works, he wins a share—small or great—of the necessaries or luxuries which circumstances throw within his reach, and then he dies and there is an end of him. A man, on the other hand, who is more than himself, who is part of an institution, who has devoted himself to a cause—or is a citizen of an imperial power—expands to the scope and fulness of the larger organism ; and the grander the organisation, the larger and more important the unit that knows that he belongs to it. His thoughts are wider, his interests less selfish, his ambitions ampler and nobler. As a granite block is to the atoms of which it is composed when disintegrated, so are men in organic combination to the same men only aggregated together. Each particle contracts new qualities which are created by the intimacy of union. Individual Jesuits are no more than other mortals. The Jesuits as a society are not mortal at all, and rule the Catholic world. Behind each American citizen America is standing, and he knows it, and is the man that he is because he knows it. The Anglo-Americans

x

divided might have fared no better than the Spanish colonies
The Anglo-Americans united command the respectful fear of
all mankind, and, as Pericles said of the Athenians, each unit
of them acts as if the fortunes of his country depended only on
himself. A great nation makes great men ; a small nation
makes little men.

The Americans, as I said, have settled the matter for them
selves. Can we settle it for ours ? It is *the* question for us,
on the answer to which the complexion of our future depends.
We, if we all please, can unite as they have united, can be
knit together in as firm a bond, and hold the sea sceptre as
lords of Oceana in so firm a grasp that a world combined in
arms would fail to wrest it from us. As the interests of
America forbade division, so do ours forbid it. United, we
shall all be great and strong in the greatness and strength of
our common empire, and the British nation will have a career
before it more glorious than our glorious past. All wise men
know this. Yet it is called impossible, because we have taught
ourselves to believe that there is no other reliable motive for
nations or individuals than a narrow selfishness. With that
conviction, of course it is impossible, and all other great things
are impossible. We are a lost people. Faith in a high course
is the only basis of fine and noble action. ' Believe and ye
shall be saved,' is as true in politics as in religion, and belief
in the superior principle of our corporate life is itself its own
realisation. Let it be understood among us, as it is among
the Americans, that we are one—though the bond be but a
spiritual one—that separation is treason, and the suggestion
of it misprision of treason, and all is done. Divorce between
husband and wife is always a possibility, for divorce is a consequence of sin, and men and women are all liable to sin ; but
a married pair do not contemplate divorce, or speak of it or
make preparation for it, either when they begin their lives
together, or tread through their daily round of duties and enjoyments side by side. Talked of and debated, it is already on
its way to realisation ; and a family would be fit for an asylum
of idiots where the rending of natural ties was a permitted
subject of thought or conversation. Let it be the same in

Oceana. Let separation be dismissed into silence as a horrible thing, 'not to be named among us,' and the union is already made, and the form or forms which it may assume may be left to time and circumstance to shape and reshape. Nature could make no organic thing—not a plant, not a flower, not a man— if she began with the form. She begins with the life in the seed, which she leaves to work; and what the life is in natural objects, the will and determination is in the arrangements of human society.

Feelings of this kind rise in every Englishman when he sets foot on American soil—something of envy, but more of pride, and more still of admiration. The Americans are the English reproduced in a new sphere. What they have done, we can do. The Americans are a generation before us in the growth of democracy, and events have proved that democracy does not mean disunion.

I had already seen the Eastern States, but California was new to me. California with its gold and its cornfields, its conifers and its grizzlies, its diggers and its hidalgos, its 'heathen Chinese' and its Yankee millionaires, was a land of romance the wonders of which passed belief, and it was with a sort of youthful excitement that I found myself landed at 'Frisco.' The prosaic asserted itself there as elsewhere. There were customs officers and a searching of portmanteaus. This over, we had to find our quarters. We were on a long platform, roofed over like a railway station, and within the precincts the public were not admitted. At the far end was a large open door, and outside a mob of human creatures, pushing, scrambling, and howling like the beasts in a menagerie at feeding time. There they were in hundreds waiting to plunge upon us, and (if they did not tear us in pieces in the process) to carry us off to one or other of the rival caravanserais. Never did I hear such a noise, save in an Irish fair; never was I in such a scuffle. We had to fight for our lives, for our luggage, and for our dollars, if the Philistines were not to spoil us utterly. All, however, was at last safely and reasonably accomplished. We were driven away to the Palace

Hotel, where the storm turned to calm, and my acquaintance with California and its ways was practically to commence.

The Palace Hotel at San Francisco is, I believe, the largest in the world—the largest, but by no means the ugliest, as I had expected to find. It is a vast quadrilateral building, seven or eight stories high, but in fair proportions. You enter under a handsome archway, and you find yourself in a central court, as in the hotels at Paris, but completely roofed over with glass. The floor is of polished stone. Tiers of galleries run round it, tier above tier, and two lifts are in constant action, which deposit you on the floor to which you are consigned. There is no gaudiness or tinsel. The taste in California is generally superior to what you see in New York. I expected the prices of New York, or of Auckland or Sydney. Money was reported to flow in rivers there, and other things to be dear in proportion. I was agreeably disappointed. Our apartments—mine and my son's—consisted of a sitting-room *au troisième*, so large that a bed in it was no inconvenience ; a deep alcove with another bed, divided off by glass doors ; a dressing-room and a bath-room, with the other accompaniments. Our meals were in the great dining-room at fixed hours, but with a liberal time allowance. We could order our dinners and breakfasts from the carte, with as large a choice and quality as excellent as one could order in the Palais Royal if one was regardless of expense. Unnumbered niggers attended in full dress—white waistcoat, white neckcloth, with the consequentially deferential manners of a duke's master of the household ; and for all this sumptuosity we were charged three dollars and a half each, or about fifteen shillings. Nowhere in Europe, nowhere else in America, can one be lodged and provided for on such a scale and on such terms—and this was California.

The interviewers fell early upon me, but they were good-natured and not too idly curious, and on this occasion they had a reasonable excuse. A month had gone since our last news from England. War had not yet broken out, but there had been the fight at Penjdeh, and a peaceful settlement was supposed to be all but impossible. They wanted to know

what I thought about it all. I told them that there was no
occasion for a war, that my countrymen were reasonable
people, and that I could not believe that they would go in for
such a thing without stronger justification ; but others, I said,
thought differently and I might easily be mistaken, and I
asked in turn what was the feeling in America. I found that
Americans were taking a practical view of the thing—were
considering how, if war broke out, they could recover the
carrying trade, and how fast an Act could be hurried through
Congress permitting foreign vessels to be sailed under the
American flag. Apart from this, opinion was divided. There
was good-will to the old country, and a hope that she would
come well out of the scrape. There was a recollection also
that Russia was the only European Power which had shown
good-will to the North in the Civil War, and they were still
grateful. The prevailing sentiment was that war ought to be
avoided ; that if it came, both sides would be to blame ; and
there was no enthusiasm for either.

I was myself deluged with advices where I was to go in the
State, and what I was to see. Especially, and with 'damnable
iteration,' I was warned that I must in no case leave it without visiting the big trees and the Yosemite Valley. I had
seen even bigger trees in Victoria. I avoid always, when I
can, going of set purpose to see sights of any kind. I can
admire beautiful objects when they come upon me in the
natural order of things, but I cannot command the proper
emotions when I go deliberately in search of them. This
Yosemite Valley was so battered into my ears that I grew impatient, and said that I would rather go a thousand miles to
talk to one sensible man, than walk to the end of the street
for the finest view in America—a speech which was to cost me
dear, for it appeared in print the next morning, and one
gentleman after another came up and said : 'Sir, encouraged
by words of yours which I have just read,' &c., 'I venture to
introduce myself ;' whether he was the sensible man, or I was
the sensible man, being left uncertain.

But to return to the Golden City. Americans are very
good to strangers, and the Californians are in this respect the

best of Americans. An agreeable and accomplished Mr. G——, who had come from New Zealand with us, lived in San Francisco. He was kind enough to take me in charge, and show me, not trees and rocks, but things and people. The Chinese quarter is to Englishmen the principal object of attraction. They go there at night under a guard of police, for it is lawless and dangerous. Had I known any of the Chinese themselves, who would have shown me the better side of them, I should have been willing to go. But I did not care to go among human beings as if they were wild beasts, and stare at opium orgies and gambling-hells. Parties of us did go, and they said they were delighted. I went with Mr. G—— about the streets. The first place I look for in a new city is the market. One sees the natural produce of all kinds gathered there. One sees what people buy on the spot and ' consume on the premises,' as distinct from what is raised for export. One learns the cost of things, and can form one's own estimate of the manner in which the country people occupy themselves, and how they are able to live. The market-place in San Francisco told its story in a moment. Vegetables and fruits, the finest that I ever saw exposed for sale, were at half the English prices. Meat was at half the English price. I lunched on oysters, plump and delicate as the meal-fattened Colchester natives used to be, at a cent (a halfpenny) apiece. Salmon were lying out on the marble slabs, caught within two hours in the Sacramento River, superb as ever came from Tay or Tweed, for three cents a pound.

From the market we went to the clubs, where the men would be found who were carrying on the business of this late-born but immense emporium—bankers, merchants, politicians. The Eastern question, the Egyptian business, &c., were discussed in the cool incisive American manner, and the opinions expressed were not favourable to our existing methods of administration. How we had come to fall into such a state of distraction seemed to be understood with some distinctness, but less distinctly how we were to get out of it. In the Bohemian Club the tone was lighter and brighter. We do not live for politics alone, nor for business alone. The Bohemian

Club, was founded, I believe, by Bret Harte, and is composed of lawyers, artists, poets, musicians, men of genius, who in the sunshine and exuberant fertility of California, were brighter, quicker, and less bitterly in earnest than their severe fellow-countrymen of the Eastern States. It was the American temperament, but with a difference. Dollars, perhaps, are easily come by in that happy country, and men think less of them, and more of human life, and how it can best be spent and enjoyed. If Horace were brought to life again in the New World, he would look for a farm in California and be a leading Bohemian. The pictures in the drawing-room, painted by one or other of themselves, had all something new and original about them, reminding me of Harte's writings. In the summer weather the club takes to tents, migrates to the forest, and holds high jinks in Dionysic fashion. There was a clever sketch of one of these festivals in the abandonment of intellectual riot. It is likely enough that some original school of American art may start up in California. Their presiding genius at the club is Pallas Athene in the shape of an owl; but, for some reason which they could not, or would not, explain to me, she has one eye shut.

The city generally is like other American cities. It has grown like a mushroom, and there has been no leisure to build anything durable or beautiful. A few years ago the houses were mainly of wood. The footways in the streets are laid with boards still, but are gradually transforming themselves. The sense of beauty will come by-and-by, and they do well not to be in a hurry. The millionaires have constructed palatial residences for themselves on the high grounds above the smoke. The country towards the ocean is taken charge of by the municipality. A fine park has been laid out, with forcing houses, gardens and carriage-drives. Near it is a cemetery, beside which ours at Brompton would look vulgar and hideous. Let me say here, that nowhere in America have I met with vulgarity in its proper sense. Vulgarity lies in manners unsuited to the condition of life to which you belong. A lady is vulgar when she has the manners of a kitchen maid, the kitchen maid is vulgar when she affects the manners of a lady.

Neither is vulgar so long as she is contented to be herself. In America there is no difference of 'station,' and therefore every-one is satisfied with his own and has no occasion to affect any-thing. There is a dislike of makeshifts in the Californians. Greenbacks and shin-plasters have no currency among them. If you go for money to a bank at San Francisco, they give you, instead of dirty paper, massive gold twenty-dollar pieces, large and heavy as medals, and so handsome that one is un-willing to break them. They are never in haste, and there is a composure about them which seems to say that they belong to a great nation and that their position is assured. I observed at San Francisco, and I have observed elsewhere in America, that they have not the sporting taste so universal in England. They shoot their bears, they shoot their deer, in the way of business, as they make their pigs into bacon ; but they can see a strange bird or a strange animal without wishing imme-diately to kill it. Indeed, killing for its own sake, or even killing for purpose of idle ornament, does not seem to give them particular pleasure. The great harbour swarms with seals ; you see them lifting their black faces to stare at the pass-ing steamers, as if they knew that they were in no danger of being molested. There is a rock in the ocean close to the shore, seven miles from the city. The seals lie about it in hundreds, and roll and bark and take life as pleasantly as the crowds who gather on holidays to look at them. No one ever shoots at these harmless creatures. Men and seals can live at peace side by side in California. I doubt if as much could be said of any British possession in the world. Perhaps killing is an aristocratic instinct, which the rest imitate, and democracy may by-and-by make a difference.

In short, California is a pleasant country with good people in it. If one had to live one's life over again, one might do worse than make one's home there. For a poor man it is better than even Victoria and New South Wales, for not the necessaries of life only are cheap there, but the best of its luxuries. The grapes are like the clusters of Eshcol. The wine, already palatable, is on the way to becoming admirable and as accessible to a light purse as it used to be in Spain. I ate there the only really good oranges which I have tasted for many years—good as those which we used to get before the orange-growers went in for average sorts and heavy bearers, and the greatest happiness of the greatest number.

When everything of every sort that one meets with, even down to the nigger waiter at the hotel, is excellent in its kind, one may feel pretty well satisfied that the morality, &c., is in good condition also. All our worst vices nowadays grow out of humbug.

This was the impression which California left on me during my brief passage through it. Had I stayed longer, I should, of course, have found much to add of a less pleasant kind, and something to correct. Life everywhere is like tapestry-work—the outside only is meant to be seen, the loose tags and ends of thread are left hanging on the inner face. I describe it as it looked to me, and I was sorry when the time came for me to be again on the move.

We were to cross the continent by the Pacific Railway—a journey, if one keeps on at it, of seven days and seven nights from San Francisco to New York. One can break it—and one is advised to break it if one wishes to arrive sane in mind and body—at Salt Lake City, at Chicago, or at both.

The original trunk line has thrown out lateral branches, which strike north or south, and sweep through vast ranges of new country, rejoining the principal stem east of the Mississippi. Trains through to New York run on all these divisions. There are rival companies, and the agent of each assures you that his line is the shortest, cheapest, easiest, and most interesting. He produces his maps to prove it to you, where his own line, which may in reality be sinuous as the track of a snake, is represented as if drawn by a ruler, and his adversaries' line, which may be straight as Euclid's definition, is bent into a right angle. Even in San Francisco it appeared that people could lie to some, and indeed to a considerable, extent. I could only hope that these agents were not Californian bred, but an imported article. The trunk line, however, went singly as far as Ogden, on the edge of the Great Salt Lake, and proceeded thence north-east through Omaha to Chicago.

Another line branched off south at Ogden, went through the Mormon city and the territory of Utah, crossed the Rocky Mountains, and descended by the Rio Grande to Denver; thence turning back northward again, it rejoined the main line at the Pacific Junction. Whether this line was, as the agents insisted, the shorter of the two, might or might not be true. But it was reported to be the most picturesque, the engineering in the Rio Grande Cañon to be a triumph of mechanical genius, &c., while it would give us a chance of seeing what the famous Mormons were doing, not on a single spot, but in the wide territory over which they were now spreading. We decided, therefore, for the line of the Rio Grande and the Cañon, and made our preparations accordingly.

The accommodation on all the routes is the same. The carriages are long, high, and spacious, ventilated well from the top, and warmed with stoves in cold weather. Each of them has minor compartments at both ends—at one a washing-room and smoking-room for the men ; at the other, a dressing-room for ladies. The beds stretch along the sides in two tiers. The upper tier folds up in the daytime, and is let down at night. The under tier is formed by an ingenious rearrangement of the ordinary seats. The berths so contrived are nearly three feet wide, and are as comfortable as could in reason be expected, and each pair has a heavy leather curtain hung in front of them. At night, when man and woman has retired to his den and hers, you see only a long narrow passage between leather walls, well lighted by lamps, up and down which the black sentinels of the train slowly parade. When the first sensation of novelty is over, sleep will act like its capricious self, which comes when least expected, and stays as it chooses, irrespective of circumstances. Over part of the line there is a special feeding carriage, where one can break-fast and dine as in an hotel ; over the rest, the trains halt for meals three times a day, with other pauses of ten minutes every fifty or sixty miles ; and thus the 6,000 miles of journey are got over very tolerably by those who are used to it. Those who are not used to it are warned to take a rest at intervals.

The starting-point is some miles distant from San Francisco, on the far side of a wide arm of the bay. We crossed over in a steamer crowded with passengers. Two large trains were to start at the same hour--one east, which was to be ours; another to Lower California and the south, which ought to have been ours had I obeyed orders and gone to the Yosemite Valley.

We found our places, not without difficulty; our tickets were wrongly numbered; we were ejected from our seats, after we had started, by other claimants, and we had to be moved into another carriage; but the change was managed without stopping the train. The American carriages open at each end with a platform outside, and you can walk from one to the other. Everybody is very civil on such occasions, but you have to conform to regulations, though you are in a land of liberty.

All was right at last, and we settled down into our corners and looked about us. There were no empty places, all seats were full, and many of them were occupied by fellow-passengers from the 'Australia.' Boys passed incessantly to and fro in the train, with trays of books, newspapers, fruits, cakes, or sweetmeats, of which the Americans seem inordinately fond. The windows were open, and outside them was a beautiful sunny afternoon, warm as in an English June. The railway followed the course of a broad deep river, crossing and recrossing it, among rich meadows, farms, orchards, and those boundless Californian wheat-fields which are bringing ruin on the English landed interest. The wheat was in the blade, and brilliantly green. The fruit-trees were in blossom, and the vines in full leaf; and the same aspect of luxuriant fertility continued till we had passed Sacramento City, and night fell and the stars came out, and we began slowly to ascend the slope of the mountain barrier which divides California from the rest of the world.

We stood out long on the platform, watching the change of landscape into rock and forest. The air at last grew chilly. We climbed into our roosting-places, and we woke at daybreak eight thousand feet above the sea, on the crest of the Sierra

Nevada. We could see little. For thirty miles we were in an almost continuous gallery of snow-sheds, through the chinks of which gleams of daylight shone like electric sparks. At the rare openings we perceived that we were among mountain ridges black with pines, the stems of which were buried in snow, while the high peaks over our heads were wrapped in a white winding-sheet. The long tunnel ended when we passed the watershed. Thence, skirting magnificent ravines, and following a torrent which ran down out of a lake in the Sierra, we descended about three thousand feet to a solitary station, where we stopped for breakfast. All was desolate. One notable thing only we observed there—trout (which we took for salmon) twenty pounds in weight, bred in the lake and caught all down the river, the fish taken out of it being worth more, I was told, than the produce of the best ranches on its banks.

Leaving this, we struck across the great American desert, Indian territory, a boundless plain stretching for six hundred miles, nothing growing there save a miserable scanty scrub, as if on a soil that was sown with salt. It is left, I suppose, to the Redskins, because no white man could make a living there. We saw some of the descendants of the ancient red warriors when we halted to water the engines. The women brought their papooses in little box-cradles, swathed like Egyptian mummies; the men dangling after them, and all begging. The passengers flung them a few cents. Here, too, the contact with civilisation had done its universal work. These poor wretches, who seemed less human, because less savage, than the African bushmen, were the last representatives of Cooper's Uncas and Chingachgook. All that day we travelled on in wearisome monotony; no sign of life anywhere save a blue rabbit, which sat staring at the train; two or three small creatures slipping behind bushes, which might be prairie dogs; on the wing nothing, except when we passed a long solitary marsh pool, half covered with green reeds, where half a dozen large white birds were sailing slowly over the water; cranes or swans, I know not which, but with the swan's grand regal sweep. The second night closed in, and we were still in the wilderness. Telegraph wires, however, kept us company, and just at dark a newsboy dashed in with sheets fresh from a wayside press, and the morning's message from London. 'Guess you're going to fight,' he said to me, with a mixture of contempt and entertainment.

In the morning we were at Ogden, a rising town at the north end of the Great Salt Lake, forty miles from Brigham Young's City of the Saints. Brigham is now dead. His wives are scattered, his place is filled by a new vicar of the Almighty, but the evangel is believed as vigorously as ever. The lake itself is a great inland sea, salter than the ocean, seventy miles long and five thousand feet above the ocean-level. It is entirely surrounded by mountains, the peaks, though it was the end of April, covered far down with snow, the base of them a rich, deep violet, and the water a greenish-blue. The scene was beautiful, even to us who were fresh from New Zealand. Flights of gulls were hovering about, brought thither by fish of some kind ; but how fish came there which gulls would eat, and what manner of fish they might be, neither guide-book nor American fellow-travellers could tell us.

They were all talking about the Mormons, however ; and the problem of what was to be done with them exercised the American mind much. For the Mormons are prospering ; rising up like a kite in the wind's eye and in the teeth of modern enlightenment. They have spread through the whole territory of Utah, and are flowing over into the adjoining states. The peculiar institution is going along with them, and in greater favour than ever, being fast rooted in the superstition and sanctioned specially by a new revelation, so that all right-minded Americans are as conscious of the scandal as they used to be about slavery. The polygamy is not, as I had supposed, universal. It is a prerogative allowed by the Almighty to a few only of the holiest elders, and the women prefer, it seems, a share in the favours of one sanctified old gentleman to a partnership, however attractive otherwise, with a single husband, because an elder's wives will take precedence of all other ladies in Paradise. A decree has been obtained at last from the Supreme Court of the United States,

declaring a polygamist incapable of holding office, and polygamy itself a criminal offence. My companions assured me
with emphasis that it would be acted on, and that an abomina-
tion as bad as slavery, or worse, would now be put down with
a high hand. But the Mormons have not threatened to secede
from the Union, and as long as the wives are satisfied and
enter the elders' harems of their own free will, it is not easy,
in a country which boasts of the individual freedom which it
allows to everyone, to interfere by force. The Mormons, it is
said, would resist desperately, and another civil war would be
a disgrace, almost as great as the institution itself. Moderate
people would prefer to wait till the Gentiles, of whom many
are now settled on the Salt Lake, obtain a majority, when a
custom out of harmony with the age, they consider, will die of
itself. Joe Smith murdered proved more formidable than a Joe
Smith left alive to get drunk and prophesy would ever have
been, and the lesson has not been forgotten.

The line from Ogden to Denver passed directly through the
sacred city. As we approached, some stranger put in my hands
a book of the latest revelations, modelled by Mormon intellect
on the pattern of the Old Testament : 'I say unto thee, Joseph
Smith Junior, my servant, I am the Lord, stand up and hear
me. Behold, I send thee to my people to say unto them '—
and then follows some new order about the elders' wives.

The idea of the buried gold plates on which Joe Smith the
First declared that he found the first book, was borrowed from
Lucian, whose false Prophet of Galatia pretended to have dug
up plates near Byzantium on which were written the revelations of Apollo. How Joe Smith knew anything about Lucian
is another mystery, but the whole thing is an extraordinary
paradox. Not spiritualism, not table-rapping or planchette-
writing, exceed Mormonism in apparent absurdity. Yet
hundreds of thousands of men and women believe in it as a
new communication sent from heaven, and—as is far more
strange—in worldly wisdom, in practical understanding, in
industry, patience, and all the minor virtues which command
success in life, neither America nor our own colonies can produce superiors to them. The plain of the Salt Lake, when

Brigham Young halted his caravans there after the pilgrimage through the desert, was bare as the shores of the Dead Sea. From the Snow Mountains and from the Sweet Lake of Utah they brought fertilising streams of fresh water and poured it over the soil. They fenced and drained, they ploughed and sowed, they built and planted ; and now literally the wilderness is made to blossom like the rose. Our train ran on among orchards of peach and almond, pink with the early blossoms. The fields, far as one could see, were cleanly and completely cultivated, and green with the promise of abundant harvests. Cattle, sheep, and horses were grazing in hundreds. The houses were neat and well constructed, each with a well-kept garden round it. Place and people formed a perfect model of a thriving industrial settlement, and all this had grown in a single generation from what, to human intelligence, is the wildest absurdity, initiated by deliberate fraud. One can only conclude that man is himself a very absurd creature.

I did not care to observe Mormonism any closer. We remained half an hour at the city station. We saw at a distance the famous tabernacle, like a huge turtle-shell, 'with the finest organ in the world.' We went on leaving the New Jerusalem behind us, but not the proselytes of the faith. For hundreds of miles we saw the fruits of the newest 'religion' in the plantations, in the careful husbandry, in the wholesome and substantial aspect of the farms and dwelling-houses. At Utah, where we dined, I supposed myself to have fallen into actual contact with the peculiar institution itself. The room prepared for us was neat and nice, and the food admirable. Behind a desk sat the master of the establishment, a middle-aged man in spectacles, with serious aspect. We were waited upon by two innocent-looking, extremely pretty girls. I concluded that here was an elder in person, and that these were two of his wives, and I looked at him with repressed indignation. It was an illustration of how unjust we may be with the best intentions. I learnt, on inquiry, that the poor man was a Gentile of exceptionally high character, and that the two young ladies were his daughters.

After Utah the Rocky Mountains were before us, and we began to ascend. Up and up we went, following rivers, through valley and cañon and scenery more magnificent every hour. The snow lay deeper as we rose, till in the drifts the tops of the pines were almost buried. The torrents were in their glory, for the sun was gathering power, and the thaw of the spring had commenced. We zigzagged along the mountain-sides, drawn now by three powerful engines. We crossed ravines at their heads, and doubled back at higher levels, seeing far below us the line over which we had passed. At the highest point we were eleven thousand feet above the sea. There, as a crowning triumph, the rock was tunnelled. The sides of the tunnel, were sheeted with ice, and icicles hung from the roof ; but even at that height they were melting and the temperature was several degrees above freezing-point. We went down as we had come up, through scenery geologically different, but equally wild and picturesque. Finally we entered the famous cañon of the Rio Grande, from which the line takes its name—a deep chasm, at one point not more than ninety feet across, the walls always precipitous and sometimes perpendicular, between which the river rushes along for thirty miles. To have carried a railway down such a place is counted as an engineering achievement. The rock on the left bank has been blown out by dynamite, to form a level on which the rails are laid. At one point a branch of the cañon itself is crossed by a bridge, the iron pillars of which are driven into the cliff on either side.

The journey, in spite of scenery, might have become tedious, but it was enlivened by a few small incidents. A little serves to amuse on such occasions. American ladies and gentlemen came and went at different stages. They came in one day and left us the next, or the day after. Our berths were so closely packed that we heard, in spite of ourselves, what was passing behind our neighbours' curtains. A young husband was reported to me to have said to his young wife as they were dressing (it was at a time when a dining car was attached and breakfasts could be ordered on board), 'My dear, do you feel like eggs this morning?'

Among the friends who had come with us from Auckland was an English gentleman, Colonel ——; high-bred, refined—perhaps' extra-refined—whom the malice of fortune played a trick upon. Happily, with his other good qualities, he had a keen sense of humour, and enjoyed what befell him as much as we did. At some town where we stopped late one night, two ladies had been put into the carriage with us. We were going to bed, and paid no attention to them. The berth under Colonel —— happened to be vacant. To one of these new arrivals, without his being aware of it, this berth was assigned as a sleeping place. The lady gathered herself in, and the same leather curtain fell over them both. In the morning, the Colonel, feeling about for his under garments, dropped his drawers by accident over the side of his bed. From below he saw thrust out a small, dainty, and perfectly white hand, with a diamond ring, and a delicate lace frill round the wrist. It was holding up the article in question, and a brisk, ringing voice said, 'Guess this belongs to you.'

The railway officials are considerate beyond English or European experience. In the train, as they had made it up at Denver, it was found that there was not room for all of us who had sleeping tickets, and they stopped the express at a siding for nearly two hours, while they sent back for another carriage. Beyond Denver we crossed the great prairies, where seven years ago the wild buffalo were feeding in thousands. Now there was not a hoof-mark on the soil. So far as we could see from the line, the land was fenced in on either side. It had been under the plough, and was broken up into farms. I had imagined that a boundless and treeless plain, with infinite capacity for wheat-growing, could never be a home in the old-fashioned sense of the word ; and I had considered mentally what childhood must be in such a country, and what kind of romance boys and girls could find there ; but human souls carry their romance in themselves, and the Wild West at its worst may be a fitter place for a family to grow in than a suburb of London or Birmingham.

Yet dreary the prairies are, and indeed most American scenery is dreary after you have passed the Rocky Mountains. Man has done nothing to give it any human features. He has developed the productiveness of the earth. He has built mushroom towns upon it, and overspread it with a meshwork of railways. But man does not live by bread alone, and there was little grand that I could see in this journey, or indeed have ever seen (with one or two exceptions) anywhere in the United States, except the indomitable energy of the Americans themselves. I found only a lightly undulating country, generally open and untimbered, reclaimed and cultivated, and bearing crops at harvest time ; but crops sown and reaped by machines, and at intervals the contractor-built congregations of streets of brick and corrugated iron, called towns or cities, which have made hideous so much of our own England. Picturesqueness of nature, grace or dignity, in the works of man are alike absent. The forest trees are small and insignificant. I speak of the east of the Rocky Mountains. The rivers ! Yes, the Missouri and the Mississippi are grand rivers, if bigness makes grandeur. The mighty volume of their waters rolls on, carrying with it the rainfall of an enormous continent ; but their turbid and yellow streams, fringed with unwholesome pine-swamps, suggest only to the imagination that they are gigantic drains. It was the end of April, almost May, when I passed through, yet winter had not relaxed its bitter grasp. I had not seen a green leaf, scarcely a green blade of grass, since we left the Salt Lake. It must be with the Eastern and Middle States as they say of Castile, *nueve meses del Invierno y tres del Infierno* (nine months of winter and three of hell). Winter is long and harsh : summer is brief and burning. Perhaps my impressions were coloured by the contrast with the colonies which I had left. California is lovely, as Australia or New Zealand; but omitting California, which never belonged to us, I could not help saying to myself, that although Oceana no longer included the American provinces, she had yet within the circuit of her empire the fairest portion of the late discovered world.

The Northern States of the Union have produced *men*. Finer *men* are to be found nowhere upon the earth. But they work as they do because work alone can make life tolerable on such a soil and in such a climate. The sense of sunny enjoyment is not in them. They feel the dignity of freedom, and the worthiness of moral virtue. But of beauty the sense is latent, if it exists at all. Let the Britisher take heart. The race will vary its type according to the home in which it is planted. The Australian, the New Zealander, the Californian will have as much in them, after all, of the ancient ' Merry England ' as the severely earnest Northern American, who remains a Puritan at the bottom of his heart, though in modern shape.

At Chicago, the last and most triumphant of his achievements, we stayed a night to rest, in a monstrous hotel in a monstrous city—monstrous, for it has no organic frame. It grows by accretions, as coral grows—house upon house, street upon street. Through Chicago passes the trade of the Lakes and the trade of the great West. The more wheat comes out of the soil and the bigger the litters of pigs, the larger grows Chicago—the highest example in the present world of the tendency of modern men to cluster into towns. The site of it is low and flat. The shores of the lake on which it stands are low all round, and we shivered as we were looking at the docks in the nipping wind which blew across from Canada. The city is impressive from its vastness, as the American rivers are impressive ; one street, I was told, was many miles long. The stores are gigantic ; the shops, &c., are large, and as if struggling to be larger, from the amount of business going on in them. If a house is placed inconveniently, they lift it on rollers and move it bodily from one spot to another, while the occupants sleep and eat and go on with their employments as if nothing was happening. I myself saw a mansion travelling in this way without the help of an Aladdin's lamp. To strangers, especially British strangers, the attractive sight in Chicago is the pig-killing. Five thousand pigs in a day, I believe, are despatched, cut up, and made into hams and bacon ready for packing. For myself, I had no curiosity to see pigs killed, nor, indeed, much for Chicago itself, beyond what a walk would satisfy, for towns of this kind are like the articles in which they deal—one part is just like another ; you examine a sample and you multiply this by the dimensions.

From Chicago we went on to Buffalo. I had thought of crossing into Canada, but the cold frightened me, just arrived, as I was, out of the lands of the sun. In Canada there is no spring, and summer was still far off. When I looked at Lake Erie I thought a gale must be blowing over it, from the line of what appeared to be breakers along the southern shore ; but I found the breakers were breakers of ice—huge hills of ice driven in upon the shallows and piled one upon the other. Nor did I think that a visit to the Dominion would help me much in the matter which I had chiefly at heart. There the colonial problem is complicated by the near neighbourhood of our powerful kinsmen, who will expect a voice in any future arrangement, and whom the Canadians will properly consider before any arrangements can be consented to. In no part of the Empire is there a warmer loyalty towards its sovereign, or a warmer value for the connection with Great Britain, than in the Canadian Dominion. There is no thought of annexation with the United States, nor do the Americans desire it. They are content that their neighbours shall remain a self-governed community with institutions analogous to their own. Hitherto, perhaps, they will not have looked favourably on as close a federation of the Canadians with the mother-country as that which binds their own Union. It is possible, it is probable, that as the people become supreme among ourselves, our relations with the Americans will become more and more intimate. The link which holds us together is the community of race and character ; and when the direction of affairs in both countries is in the hands of the same class, differences and jealousies will dissolve of themselves. Any way the Canadas, with their splendid marine, their hardy breed of seamen and fishermen, their territory stretching from the Atlantic to the Pacific, their share in a glorious chapter of English history, will not be the least brilliant of the jewels in the crown of Oceana. The Canadas are part of us as much as Australia and New Zealand, and will not cut themselves adrift while the mother-country continues to deserve their honour and attachment; but their relations with us and with the great power at their side form a separate problem, which need not be considered in a general survey of the Colonial question. They are without adequate naval defences. They depend on us for the protection of their harbours and shipping in time of war, and I have been told, by those who ought to know, that they would agree cheerfully to contribute a subsidy, in common with the other colonies, to the Imperial Navy. It is possible, on the other hand, that they may say that they do not need any naval defence, being sufficiently protected by their neighbours. The Americans have no war-fleet, being safe in the notoriety of their strength. An attack on Canada by a nation at war with Great Britain would, undoubtedly, provoke American interference; and with so formidable a bulwark close to them, the Canadians might decline to give their money for a purpose which they might think unnecessary.

Any way I did not find it essential to go at that time to Canada. If I went at all, it might be at a more convenient season, when colonial federation had become—if it ever is to become—a question of practical politics; when it had been ' read a first time ' by public opinion, and it would be possible to enter into details.

Thus, I decided to go on at once to New York. Buffalo had no attractions; I shiver now at the thought of it. There may be seasons in the year when the ' Buffalo gals ' ' come out at night and dance on the green,' and then it may be pleasant enough; but not at the beginning of an icy May. I did not even turn aside, though it would have cost but three or four hours, to see Niagara. The ' finest waterfall in the world ' becomes uninteresting when the rocks about it are painted in gigantic letters with advertisements of the last quack medicine or the latest literary prodigy. Moreover, much nonsense is talked about the thing itself. I was staying at the house of an American friend at no great distance from it, a few years ago. Someone came in fresh from the spectacle, and poured out his admiring epithets as if he had been studying an English Gradus ad Parnassum. It was 'amazing,' 'astonishing,' 'portentous,' 'wonderful,' to see so vast a body of water falling over such a precipice. 'Why,' asked my host, 'is it wonderful that water should fall? The wonder would be if it didn't fall.'

New York is independent of climate; one goes there to see men and women. It is American, but it is cosmopolitan also; less severe than Boston, and almost as genial as San Francisco. On all subjects you hear as good talk and as sound thought as you hear anywhere; and for myself I had kind friends there, whom I found as warm and as hospitable as Americans know so well how to be. No houses are more pleasant to stay in than those of cultivated people in the metropolis of the western continent. There is splendour there, if you like to look for it; but there is little ostentation, and no vulgarity. Vulgarity is pretence; no American pretends to be what he is not; and ostentation does not answer where the reality below is so quickly detected. There is a manner peculiar to aristocratic circles, which can only be formed within those circles or within the range of their influence: the high breeding, the dignified reserve, the ease and simplicity which, like the free hand of an artist, arises from acquired command of all the functions of life. Of this there is as yet little or nothing in America. It has not been able to grow there. But the ease of good sense and the simplicity of good feeling are as marked in the cultivated society of New York as I had found them in Melbourne and Sydney; while, besides these, there is the intellectual fulness and strength which belongs to their confidence in themselves as citizens of a great nation. Ten years had passed since my last visit. New York had grown as fast as London, and there were new and admirable things to see there: their Metropolitan Railway for one, which does not bore, like ours, through stifling subterranean caverns, but is borne aloft on iron columns down the centres of the busiest streets, the traffic below going on uninterrupted and unmolested. There are two circles, an outer and an inner. There are stations every half-mile, to which you ascend by a staircase. You are carried along in the daylight, and in fresh air. The foot-passengers underneath see the trains fly by, and are neither disturbed nor inconvenienced ; and the structure itself is so light and airy that it scarcely intercepts the light from the windows of the houses. A greater wonder was the Brooklyn Suspension Bridge, spanning the estuary which divides New York from the Eastern Island. When I looked at this I had to qualify my opinion that there was nothing grand in America except its human inhabitants. The inhabitants had erected something at last more admirable to me than their Niagara Falls. It is three-quarters of a mile long, and swings, I believe, nearly three hundred feet above the sea. Two towers have been built out of the water, six hundred yards apart, over which the chains which bear it are carried. The breadth is the miracle. A spacious footway runs down the centre, raised, perhaps, twelve feet above the rest. On either side of it is the railway, and beyond the railway (again on each side) a cart and carriage way. The view from the centre is superb ; New York itself with its spires, and domes, and palaces ; Brooklyn opposite, aspiring to rival it ; the long reaches of the estuary, and the great bay into which it opens, flanked and framed by the New Jersey hills. The crowded shipping, the steamers (smokeless, for they use anthracite) plying to and fro, the yachts, the coasting vessels, the graceful oyster-schooners, swift as steamers in a breeze—I was fascinated at the sight of it all ! The picture, beautiful as it was, became a dissolving view, and there rose through it and behind it the vision of the New York that is to be. As long as civilisation and commerce last, New York and San Francisco are the two outlets, which nature has made and man cannot change, through which the trade of America must issue eastward and westward. Chicago may be burnt again, or sink into a dust-heap ; but these two cities cannot cease to grow till either mankind pass off the globe and come to an end, like the races which have gone before them, or till there rises some new creed or dispensation which may change man's nature ; when,

weary of pursuits which never satisfy, we may cease to run to
and fro, may withdraw each within his own four walls and
garden-hedges, and try again for wisdom and happiness on the
older and more quiet lines. This, too, lies among the possibilities of the future, for man is a creature 'which never con-
tinueth in one stay.' Strange things have come out of him,
which the wise of the day least looked for, and things more
strange may lie behind. To him surely the proverb is always
applicable, that 'nothing is certain but the unforeseen.'

New York stands upon an island ten miles long and a mile
broad. The Central Park was, when I had last seen it, the
greatest ornament of the city. It is still handsome ; but
palaces and vast boarding-houses, let out in flats, have risen
since on either side, encroaching on the pleasure-ground ; and
the full breadth of the island would not have been too much
breathing-space for so vast a population. I walked over it,
regretting the necessity, which I suppose was a real one. In
other ways, I found additions. Near the statues of Shakespeare and Scott—both of which, if not good, are tolerable—
there is a third now erected, of Burns, which I perceived, with
a malicious satisfaction, to be worse than the worst which we
have in London. My friends admitted my criticism ; but they
alleged, as an excuse, that it had been a present from the old
country. There is a new statue also, of Daniel Webster ; this
one American and original. It has neither grandeur nor
beauty, nor attempt at either ; but it has a hard, solid, square
vigour, characteristic, perhaps, of Webster, and a sufficient
likeness.

In sight-seeing and evening hospitalities my time went
pleasantly along. My enjoyments, however, were cut short by
a peculiarly vicious cold, which I had brought from the Rocky
Mountains. In America all things are at high pressure.
Colds assume the general character, and this particular one
seized hold on me with a passionate ferocity. It fastened on
my eyes. It was as if a vulture had driven his talons into my
face and throat, and held them clutched. There was nothing
serious about it, and nothing that was likely to be serious.
But the pain was considerable. I was told that the sea would

take it away ; and finding that a longer stay would only keep me as a useless burden on my kind entertainer's hospitality, we took our passage in the new ' Etruria,' the finest, and as it was believed, and as it proved, the swiftest steamer which was yet upon the Atlantic line. Mr. Charles Butler, to whose active friendship I and other English men of letters owe so long a debt of gratitude, drove me down to the docks in his carriage, supplied us with grapes, with wine, with everything which we could need on our voyage. It was still cold— bitterly cold after the Pacific. The icebergs were about the banks of Newfoundland. We had to take the longer southern course to avoid them, and even so we fell in with a floating archipelago of them, far below the latitudes to which they usually confine their visits. But the sea was smooth. There was no wind save from the swiftness of our own movement. My eyes recovered, and I could walk with a shade over them in a sheltered gallery. The ' Etruria,' outdoing even the ex- pectations which had been formed of her, rushed along four hundred and forty miles a day. We sailed on May 9 ; early on the morning of the 16th—in six days and twelve hours— we slackened speed to drop the mails at Cork. In twelve hours more we had run the remaining two hundred and forty miles to Liverpool. Mr. Cunard was on board, enjoying quietly his ship's success. Off Holyhead, in perfectly smooth water, and in a rollicking exultation over the fastest passage yet made, the engineer quickened the revolutions of the screw, as if to show what she could do ; and the great vessel—eight thousand tons—flew past the land like an express train, and went by the ordinary steamers, which were on the same course as our- selves, as if they were lying at their anchors in the tide-way.

Thus brilliantly ended the voyage which I had undertaken round the globe to see the empire of Oceana. It remains only to sum up briefly the conclusion at which I was able to arrive.

CHAPTER XXI.

The English Empire more easily formed than preserved—Parliamentary party government—Policy of disintegration short-sighted and destructive—Probable effect of separation on the colonies—Rejected by opinion in England —Democracy—Power and tendency of it—The British race—Forces likely to produce union—Natural forces to be trusted—Unnatural to be distrusted —If England is true to herself the colonies will be true to England.

A COMMERCIAL company established our Indian empire ; if India is ever lost to us, there is a common saying that it will bo lost through Parliament. Companies of adventurers founded our North American colonies. Those colonies did not wish to leave us. The Parliament which ruled England in the last century alienated them and drove them into revolt. The English people founded new colonies, richer and more varied than the last. The politicians who succeeded to power when the aristocracy was dethroned by the Reform Bill, discovered that the colonies were of no use to us, and that we should be better off and stronger without them. It would seem as if there was some unfitness in the mode in which our affairs are managed for holding an empire together. Aristotle would explain it by saying that states grow and thrive through ἀρετή, or virtue ; that ἀρετή, like other excellent things, can only be obtained by effort ; and that under popular government virtue is taken too much for granted. It is assumed that where there is liberty virtue will follow, and it is found, as a fact, that it does not always follow. This, though true, is abstract : one may say more particularly that popular government is a government by parties and classes ; that parties consider first their own interests ; and that the interests of no party which has hitherto held power in this country have been involved in the wise administration of our colonial connections. The patricians of England had nothing in common with the colonists in America. Those colonists had sprung from the people. They were plebeians ; they were, many of them, dissenters ; they inherited the principles of the Commonwealth ; they were independent, and chose to have the management of their own affairs. The governing classes at home tried to master them, and did not succeed. Equally little have our present colonies been an object of intelligent concern to the class which has ruled us during the last fifty years. It used to be considered that the first object of human society was the training of character, and the production of a fine race of men. It has been considered for the last half-century that the first object is the production of wealth, and that the value of all things is to be measured by their tendency to make the nation richer, on the assumption that if our nation is enriched collectively, the individuals composing it must be enriched along with it. Accordingly the empire, for which so many sacrifices were made, has been regarded as a burden to the tax-payer. We have been called on to diminish our responsibilities. Great Britain, it has been said, is sufficient for herself within her own borders. Her aim should be to develop her own industries, keep her people at home, that the prices of labour may be low enough to hold at bay foreign competition, and with the national genius for mechanical pursuits, with our natural advantages, &c., we could constitute ourselves the great working firm of the world, and our little England a land of manufacturers, growing, and to grow, without limit. People would increase, wages would increase, to the desirable point and not beyond it. Free trade would bring cheap food, and on a soil blackened with cinders and canopied with smoke, the nation would then enter on a period of unbounded prosperity. The trading class saw prospects of a golden harvest. The landlords were well pleased, for they found their property increase in money value. All went well for a time. Prosperity did seem to come, and to advance with 'leaps and bounds.' As a natural consequence, though we were proud of India and were content to keep India, at least till it could be educated to take care of itself, there grew an indifference to our last acquired colonial possessions. The colonies had no longer any special value as a market for our industries ; the whole world was now open to us, and so long as their inhabitants were well off and could buy our hardware and calicoes, it mattered nothing whether they were independent, or were British subjects, or what they were. They paid nothing to the English exchequer, and our experience in America had taught us that we might not attempt to tax them. If we were at war we should have the burden of defending them. The brood in the nest was already fledged. It was time for them to take wing and find their own livelihood.

Leaving aside the wisdom of this reasoning, it may be doubted whether any country has a right to disown so summarily its responsibilities to its own citizens. The colonists were part of ourselves. They settled in their new homes under the English flag, and were occupied in enlarging the area of English soil. They were British subjects, and between subject and government there are reciprocal obligations, which only violence or injustice on one side or the other can abrogate. They had emigrated in confidence that they were parting with no rights which attached to them at home, and those rights ought not to be taken from them without their own consent.

But there is a graver question : whether the condition to which it was proposed to reduce our own country was really so happy a one as the modern school of statesmen conceived. An England of brick lanes and chimneys ; an England sounding with the roar of engines and the tinkle of the factory-bell, with artificial recreation-grounds, and a rare holiday in what remained of wood and meadow, for those who without it would never see a wild flower blowing, or look on an unpolluted river ; where children could not learn to play save in alley or asphalted court ; where the whole of the life of the immense majority of its inhabitants from infancy to the grave would be a dreary routine of soulless, mechanical labour— such an England as this would not be described by any future poet as

> A precious gem set in the silver sea.

Still less would the race hereafter to grow there maintain either the strength of limb or the energy of heart which raised their fathers to the lofty eminence which they achieved and bequeathed. Horace described the Romans of his day as 'inferior to sires who were in turn inferior to theirs,' and as 'likely to leave an offspring more degraded than themselves.' And it was true that the citizens of the Roman Empire were thus degenerate, and that the progress which we speak of as continuous may be, and sometimes is, a progress downhill. It is simply impossible that the English men and women of the future generations can equal or approach the famous race that has overspread the globe, if they are to be bred in towns such as Birmingham and Glasgow now are, and to rear their families under the conditions which now prevail in those places. Morally and physically they must and will decline. Even the work so much boasted of is degrading on the terms on which it is carried on. What kind of nation will that be which has constituted its entire people into the mechanical drudges of the happier part of mankind, forced by the whip of hunger to be eternally manufacturing shirts and coats which others are to wear, and tools and engines which others are to use? This is no life for beings with human souls in them. You may call such a nation free. It would be a nation of voluntary bondsmen in a service from which hope is shut out. Neither the toilers who submit to such a destiny while a better prospect is open, nor the employers who grow rich upon their labour, can ever rise to greatness, or preserve a greatness which they have inherited. The American colonies were lost by the ill-handling of the patricians. The representatives of the middle classes would have shaken off, if they had been allowed, Australia and New Zealand and the Canadas. The power is now with the democracy, and it remains to be seen whether the democracy is wiser than those whom it has supplanted, and whether it will exert itself to save, for the millions of whom it consists, those splendid territories where there is soil fertile as in the old home, and air and sunshine and the possibilities of human homes for ten times our present numbers. If the opportunity is allowed to pass from us unused, England may renounce for ever her ancient aspirations. The oak tree in park or forest whose branches are left to it will stand for a thousand years; let the branches be lopped away or torn from it by the wind, it rots at the heart and becomes a pollard interesting only from the comparison of what it once was with what fate or violence has made it. So it is with nations. The life of a nation, like the life of a tree, is in its extremities. The leaves are the lungs through which the tree breathes, and the feeders which gather its nutriment out of the atmosphere. A mere manufacturing England, standing stripped and bare in the world's market-place, and caring only to make wares for the world to buy, is already in the pollard stage; the glory of it is gone for ever. The anti-colonial policy was probably but a passing dream from which facts are awakening us. Other nations are supplying their own necessities, and are treading fast upon our heels. There is already a doubt whether we can hold for any long time our ignoble supremacy, and happily the colonies are not yet lost to us. But the holding the empire together is of a moment to us which cannot be measured. Our material interests, rightly judged, are as deeply concerned as our moral interests, and there lies before us, if the union be once placed beyond uncertainty, a career which may eclipse even our past lustre. But, in theological language, it is the saving of our national soul, it is the saving of the souls of millions of Englishmen hereafter to be born, that is really at stake; and once more the old choice is again before us, whether we prefer immediate money advantage, supposing that to be within our reach, by letting the empire slide away, or else our spiritual salvation. We stand at the parting of the ways.

The suggestion of separation originated with us. No one among the colonies indicated a desire to leave us; yet, in the confidence of youth, they believe that, if we desert them, they can still hold their ground alone. They see what America has done, and they think that they can do the same. It may be so, but the example has lessons in it which they may reflect upon. The American plantations were begun in persecution and were cradled in suffering. They were formed into a nation in a stern struggle for existence. They have passed through a convulsion which had nearly wrecked even them, and they have been hammered on the anvil of the Fates, as all peoples are whom the Fates intend to make much of. There is a discipline essential to all high forms of life which cannot be learnt otherwise, yet which must be learnt before a nation can be made. If our colonies survive a Declaration of Independence they will meet with a similar experience. There will be mistakes, there will be quarrels, there will be factions. There will be perils from the rashness of the multitude, perils from the ambition of popular leaders, perils from the imperfect nature of all political constitutions, which from time to time must be changed, and change in the body politic is like disease in the individual system, which takes the shape often of malignant fever. The Spaniards, three centuries ago, were a great people ; as great in arms, as great on sea, as great in arts and literature as their English rivals. Few nobler men have ever lived than the great Gonzalvo, or the generals and admirals who served under Charles the Fifth and Philip the Second. Spain has been compared to the pelican, who feeds her young on her own entrails. She bled herself almost to death to make her colonies strong and vigorous, yet their history since they were launched into independence is not encouraging, and British communities under the same conditions might pass easily into analogous troubles. I do not doubt that in time they would rise out of them. Illustrious men might appear who would make a name in history, and perhaps they might become illustrious nations ; but if they were started now into freedom there would be a long period in which it would be uncertain what would become of them. In these days, when the world has grown so small and the arms of the Great Powers are so long, an independent Victoria, or New South Wales, or New Zealand, would lie at the mercy of any ambitious aggressor who could dispose of fleets and armies.

The colonists, I think, know and feel this. They prize their privilege as British subjects. They are proud of belonging to a nationality on whose flag the sun never sets. They honour and love their sovereign, though they never look upon her presence. Separation, if it comes, will be no work of theirs. Nor shall we part friends, as I have heard expected ; for the dissolution of the bond will be regarded as an injury, to be neither forgiven nor forgotten. If that step is once taken in some fit of impatience or narrow selfishness, it will never be repaired ; for the tie is as the tie of a branch to the parent trunk—not mechanical, not resting on material interests, but organic and vital, and if cut or broken can no more be knotted again than a severed bough can be re-attached to a tree.

Public opinion in England has, for a time, silenced the separation policy as an aim which can be openly avowed. Politicians of all creeds now promise their constituents to maintain the union with the Colonies, knowing that they would forfeit their seats if they hinted at disintegration ; and no practical statesman whatever, with Separatist opinions, can dare to give public expression to them. There is, therefore, no immediate danger ; and the agitation has had its uses, for it has familiarised the public with the bearings of the question, and has put them on their guard against a peril which had crept so close before they knew what was going on. It has also shown the colonists that the coldness of Downing Street and the indifference of politicians is no measure of the feeling with which they are regarded by their general kindred. The union, so much talked of, still exists, though its existence has been threatened.

They *are* a part of us. They have as little thought of leaving us, as an affectionate wife thinks of leaving her husband. The married pair may have their small disagreements, but their partnership is for ' as long as they both shall live.' Our differences with the colonists have been aggravated by the class of persons with whom they have been brought officially into contact. The administration of the Colonial Office has been generally in the hands of men of rank, or of men who aspire to rank ; and, although these high persons are fair representatives of the interests which they have been educated to understand, they are not the fittest to conduct our relations with communities of Englishmen with whom they have imperfect sympathy, in the absence of a well-informed public opinion to guide them. The colonists are socially their inferiors, out of their sphere, and without personal point of contact. Secretaries of State lie yet under the shadow of the old impression that colonies exist only for the benefit of the mother-country. When they found that they could no longer tax the colonies, or lay their trade under restraint, for England's supposed advantage, they utilised them as penal stations. They distributed the colonial patronage, the lucrative places of public employment, to provide for friends or for political supporters. When this, too, ceased to be possible, they acquiesced easily in the theory that the Colonies were no longer of any use to us at all. The alteration of the suffrage may make a difference in the *personnel* of our departments, but it probably will not do so to any great extent. A seat in the House of Commons is an expensive privilege, and the choice is practically limited. Not everyone, however public-spirited he may be, can afford a large sum for the mere honour of serving his country ; and those whose fortune and station in society is already secured, and who have no private interests to serve, are, on the whole, the most to be depended upon. But the people are now sovereign, and officials of all ranks will obey their masters. It is with the people that the colonists feel a real relationship. Let the people give the officials to understand that the bond which holds the empire together is not to be weakened any more, but is to be maintained and strengthened, and they will work as readily for purposes of union as they worked in the other direction when ' the other direction ' was the prevailing one. I am no believer in Democracy as a form of government which can be of long continuance. It proceeds on the hypothesis that every individual citizen is entitled to an equal voice in the management of his country ; and individuals being infinitely unequal—bad and good, wise and unwise—and as rights depend on fitness to make use of them, the assumption is untrue, and no institutions can endure which rest upon illusions. But there are certain things which only Democracy can execute ; and the unity of our empire, all parts of which shall be free and yet inseparable, can only be brought about by the pronounced will of the majority. *Securus judicat orbis.* No monarchy or privileged order could have dared to take the measures necessary to maintain the American Union. They

z

would infallibly have wrecked themselves in the effort. Cæsar preserved the integrity of the Empire of Rome, but Cæsar was the armed soldier of the Democracy. If the Colonies are to remain integral parts of Oceana, it will be through the will of the people. To the question, What value are they? the answer is, that they enable the British people to increase and multiply. The value of the British man lies in his being what he is—another organic unit, out of the aggregate of which the British nation is made; and the British nation is something more than a gathering of producers and consumers and tax-payers : it is a factor, and one of the most powerful, in the development of the whole human race. By its intellect, by its character, by its laws and literature, by its sword and cannon, it has impressed its stamp upon mankind with a print as marked as the Roman. The nation is but the individuals who compose it, and the wider the area over which these individuals are growing, the more there will be of them, the stronger they will be in mind and body, and the deeper the roots which they will strike among the foundation-stones of things. These islands are small, and are full to overflowing In the colonies only we can safely multiply, and the people, I think, are awakening to know it.

It may be otherwise. It may be that the people will say that the days of empires are past, that we are all free now, we are our own masters and must look out for ourselves each in our own way. If this be their voice, there is no remedy. As they decide, so will be the issue. But it was not the voice of America. It need not be the voice of scattered Britain ; and if we and the Colonies alike determine that we wish to be one, the problem is solved. The wish will be its own realisa-tion. Two pieces of cold iron cannot be welded by the most ingenious hammering : at white heat they will combine of themselves. Let the colonists say that they desire to be per-manently united with us ; let the people at home repudiate as emphatically a desire for separation, and the supposed diffi-culties will be like the imaginary lion in the path—formidable only to the fool or the sluggard. No great policy was ever carried through which did not once seem impossible. Of all truly great political achievements the organisation of a United British Empire would probably be found the easiest.

Happily there is no need for haste. The objectors are for the present silent. A war might precipitate a solution; but we are not at war, and there is no prospect of war at present above the horizon. Ingenious schemes brought forward prematurely, perhaps in the interest of some party in the state, can only fail, and are therefore only to be deprecated. Confidence is a plant of slow growth. Past indifference cannot at once be forgotten, and sudden eagerness will be suspected of a selfish object.

All of us are united at present by the invisible bonds of relationship and of affection for our common country, for our common sovereign, and for our joint spiritual inheritance. These links are growing, and if let alone will continue to grow, and the free fibres will of themselves become a rope of steel. A federation contrived by politicians would snap at the first strain. We must wait while the colonies are contented to wait. They are supposed to be the sufferers by the present loose relations. They are exposed to attack, should war break out, while they have no voice in the policy which may have led to the war. It would seem from the example of New South Wales that, whether they have a voice or not, they are eager to stand by us in our trials. So long as they do not complain, we may spare our anxieties on their account and need not anticipate an alienation of which no signs have appeared. If they feel aggrieved they will suggest a remedy. They know, or will know, their own wishes; and when they let us understand what those wishes are we can consider them on their own merits. Meanwhile, and within the limits of the existing constitution, we can accept their overtures, if they make such overtures, for a single undivided fleet. We can give them back the old and glorious flag; we can bestow our public honours (not restricting ourselves to the colonial St. Michael and St. George) on all who deserve them, without respect of birthplace; we can admit their statesmen to the Privy Council, and even invite them in some form to be the direct advisers of their sovereign. We can open the road, for

their young men who are ambitious of distinguishing themselves, into the public service, the army, or the navy ; we can
make special doors for them to enter, by examination boards
in their own cities ; we can abstain from irritating interference, and when they want our help we can give it freely
and without grudging. Above all, we can insist that the word
' separation ' shall be no more heard among us. Man and
wife may be divorced in certain eventualities, but such eventualities are not spoken of among the contingencies of domestic
life. Sons may desert their parents, but sons who had no such
intention would resent the suggestion that they might desert
them if they pleased. Every speech, every article recommending the disintegration of the empire which is applauded
or tolerated at home is received as an insult by the colonists, who do not see why they should be ' disintegrated ' any
more than Cornwall or Devonshire. Were Oceana an accepted
article of faith, received and acknowledged as something not
to be called in question, it would settle into the convictions of
all of us, and the organic union which we desiderate would
pass silently into a fact without effort of political ingenuity.
We laugh at sentiment, but every generous and living relation
between man and man, or between men and their country, is
sentiment and nothing else. If Oceana is to be hereafter
governed by a federal parliament, such a parliament will grow
when the time is ripe for it, or something else will grow—we
cannot tell. The fruit is not yet mature, and we need not
trouble ourselves about it. Agents-general in the House of
Commons without votes ; Agents-general formed into a council ;
colonial life-peers ; these, and all other such expedients which
ingenious persons have invented, may be discussed properly if
they are put forward by the colonists themselves. Till then
they are better let alone. The question is for them more than
for us, and if such councils or methods of representation be
really desirable, they will take effect more readily the less
directly they are pressed forward at home.

After all is said, it is on ourselves that the future depends.
We are passing through a crisis in our national existence, and
the wisest cannot say what lies before us. If the English

character comes out of the trial true to its old traditions—bold in heart and clear in eye, seeking nothing which is not its own, but resolved to maintain its own with its hand upon its sword—the far-off English dependencies will cling to their old home, and will look up to her and be still proud to belong to her, and will seek their own greatness in promoting hers. If, on the contrary (for among the possibilities there is a contrary), the erratic policy is to be continued which for the last few years has been the world's wonder ; if we show that we have no longer any settled principles of action, that we let ourselves drift into idle wars and unprovoked bloodshed ; if we are incapable of keeping order even in our own Ireland, and let it fall away from us or sink into anarchy ; if, in short, we let it be seen that we have changed our nature, and are not the same men with those who once made our country feared and honoured, then, in ceasing to deserve respect, we shall cease to be respected. The colonies will not purposely desert us, but they will look each to itself, knowing that from us, and from their connection with us, there is nothing more to be hoped for. The cord will wear into a thread, and any accident will break it.

And so end my observations and reflections on the dream of Sir James Harrington. So will not end, I hope and believe, Oceana.

PRINTED BY
SPOTTISWOODE AND CO., NEW-STREET SQUARE
LONDON

NOTE.

I have spoken on page 295 of the Samoan mission and of a gentleman connected with it whom I met on the Pacific. What I said requires correction in three points. The Mr. Cox, not ' Coxe,' with whom this gentleman had a controversy was present in Samoa only through a book which he had written, and not in person. The able reply to Mr. Cox was not composed, as I had erroneously thought, under an impression that the subject was a new one.

The 1,500l. transmitted annually by the natives of Samoa to the London Missionary Society does not result from the sale of the translation of the Bible, but from another and separate fund.

Lastly, and what is of most importance, the South Sea missionaries who have connected themselves with politics, and in particular the person to whom I refer in page 296, do not belong to the London Society. I had not said that they did, but my language was not sufficiently clear.

J. A. FROUDE.

Lightning Source UK Ltd.
Milton Keynes UK
UKOW041411280912

199812UK00001B/8/P